THE HOUSE OF COMMONS
SERVICES AND FACILITIES

Another Title in this Series

THE MEMBER OF PARLIAMENT
AND HIS INFORMATION

by Anthony Barker and Michael Rush

THE HOUSE OF COMMONS
SERVICES AND FACILITIES

edited by

MICHAEL RUSH
Lecturer in Politics, University of Exeter

and

MALCOLM SHAW
Senior Lecturer in Politics, University of Exeter

for

POLITICAL AND ECONOMIC PLANNING

and

THE STUDY OF PARLIAMENT GROUP

London
GEORGE ALLEN & UNWIN LTD
RUSKIN HOUSE   MUSEUM STREET

First published in 1974

© George Allen & Unwin Ltd 1974
ISBN 0 04 329020 5

Printed in Great Britain
in 11 on 12pt Times type
by Alden & Mowbray Ltd
at the Alden Press, Oxford

CONTRIBUTORS

MICHAEL LAWRENCE
GEOFFREY LOCK
DAVID MENHENNET
DOUGLAS MILLAR
MICHAEL RUSH
MALCOLM SHAW

PREFACE

This book was conceived by the Study of Parliament Group. The aim is to provide a comprehensive picture of the working environment in which Members of the British House of Commons conduct their business. The Group thought that this was an appropriate subject for investigation because, while the working environment of Members is sometimes a matter of public discussion, no comprehensive description of it exists. Moreover, far-reaching changes in Members' services and facilities have been effected during the last decade, and it was considered desirable to put these changes into perspective.

The Study of Parliament Group (SPG) was formed in 1963 and consists – in nearly equal proportions – of university teachers and Officers of the Houses of Parliament. The Group appointed a small Study Group to carry out the research embodied in this book, and this Study Group, like the SPG itself, combined the resources available to Officers of the House of Commons and to academics. Such collaboration within the SPG has resulted in books and pamphlets, as well as evidence presented to Select Committees on Procedure. The present book has been produced in co-operation with Political and Economic Planning, as was an earlier book (*The Member of Parliament and His Information*, by Anthony Barker and Michael Rush).

The co-editors and the other contributors to the present work all served as members of the Study Group. In the course of their collaboration they were generously assisted by many people inside and outside the Palace of Westminster. The editors are especially grateful to their colleagues in the Study of Parliament Group who read the entire manuscript and made many useful comments on it. They are: David Holland, Librarian of the House of Commons and present Chairman of the Study of

10 PREFACE

Parliament Group; Professor Peter Richards, former Chairman of the Group; and those listed as contributors to the book, all of whom made extensive comments on the manuscript in addition to providing their own parts of it. Dr John Poole of the House of Commons Library gave much valued assistance during the early stages of the work. Thanks are also due to those members of the staff of the House of Commons who assisted the contributors, but who are not named below because they wish to remain anonymous; to those Members of Parliament who replied to the questionnaire on secretarial assistance; to Mrs Helen Liggat, who typed the manuscript; and to Robert Spence, who verified the footnote references.

For their valuable assistance in providing data for particular chapters or sections of the book, the editors would like to thank the following: H. McE. Allen, Head of the Establishments Section of the Administration Department; L. W. Bear, former Editor of the *Official Report* (*Hansard*); W. G. Birch, former Postmaster of the House of Commons; A. Brazier, Postmaster of the House of Commons; Pratap C. Chitnis, Secretary of the Joseph Rowntree Social Service Trust; Richard Dring, Editor of the *Official Report* (*Hansard*); Miss M. Frampton, MBE, Department of the Serjeant at Arms; Mrs S. Hastings, House of Commons Library; Jack Hawke, OBE, former chief parliamentary correspondent of the *Daily Telegraph*; Mrs Jean Winder Hawke, former *Hansard* reporter; A. R. Kennedy, Shorthand Writer to the Houses of Parliament; Major G. V. S. Le Fanu, Deputy Assistant Serjeant at Arms; Dick Leonard, MP; Kenneth Mackenzie, CB, until recently Clerk of Public Bills; Philip Marsden, OBE, Deliverer of the Vote; John Palmer, House of Commons Library; Brigadier N. E. V. Short, MBE, MC, Speaker's Secretary; Mrs M. Stanners, Administrative Secretary, Ashworth & Company; Cdr D. Swanston, DSO, DSC, RN (retd), Assistant Serjeant at Arms; Lt-Col P. F. Thorne, CBE, Deputy Serjeant at Arms; and F. J. Wilkin, OBE, DFM, Accountant, House of Commons. The Study Group of course remain responsible for any errors and for any opinions expressed.

A major difficulty in carrying out a study of this kind is that the type and range of some of the services and facilities involved have changed, and are continuing to change. Although most of the material for the book was gathered in 1972, there has been updating to 1973 in various instances. For example, the matter of the new parliamentary building is of such crucial importance in relation to Members' future accommodation at Westminster that the relevant parts of the text had to be rewritten in terms of the decisive debate in the Commons on 25 June 1973. In many other instances, such as changes in the numbers of staff, footnotes to the text provide updating information. References to Members and their constituencies, however, reflect the position before the general election of February 1974.

One significant development came too late for inclusion in the main body of the text. On 22 October 1973, Mr Speaker made a statement in the House of Commons as follows:

'Following a preliminary inquiry, at the Clerk's request, into his Department by the Management Services Division of the Civil Service Department, I am of the opinion that a review conducted on a wider basis than that of one Department would be of value.

'After consulting the Leaders of the main political parties, the Leader of the House, and others concerned in these matters, I have arranged for a review to be undertaken of the administrative services of the House, with the following terms of reference:

' "To consider and make recommendations (if necessary involving legislation) on the organisation and staffing of the House of Commons, including

' "(i) the structure, organisation and co-ordination of the services now provided by the five Departments, namely, the Departments of the Speaker, Clerk of the House, Serjeant at Arms, the Library and the Administration Department,

' "(ii) recruitment, terms of service, promotion and appointment of all staff, including those in the highest posts."

'I am glad to say that Sir Edmund Compton has accepted my invitation to undertake the review: he will be supported by a team drawn from the Management Services Division of the Civil Service Department. I hope that the recommendations of the review will be available to me by the end of the next Parliamentary Session.

'I propose that the recommendations should then be considered by a small committee of Members before being submitted to the House for decision.'[1]

The results of this review, whatever they may be, will clearly have a major bearing on many of the services described in this book. That is something for the future, however. What follows describes the present situation.

It should be stressed that the account is a factual one. This book does not seek to make recommendations about services and facilities at Westminster. Recommendations can be made only as part of a more far-reaching study of the role of the Member, although it is hoped that the information made available in this book will enhance such a study if and when it is undertaken.

M.R.
M.S.

[1] H.C. Deb., 861, c. 707.

CONTENTS

ILLUSTRATIONS

TABLES

CHAPTER 1

INTRODUCTION

This book seeks to provide a comprehensive account of the official services and facilities available to Members of Parliament. 'Services and facilities' is intended as a generic term to include all means by which Members are assisted in carrying out their parliamentary duties, but has been deliberately limited to those that are in whole or part *officially* provided at the taxpayers' expense. Thus the assistance that Members may receive from their party headquarters, or from their constituency parties, or from business or trade union sources is, for example, excluded from consideration. On the other hand, the secretarial assistance employed by Members is included because official accommodation is provided for a significant proportion of Members' secretaries in the Palace of Westminster, and because, since October 1969, Members have been entitled to draw an official secretarial allowance.

The distinction between 'services' and 'facilities' is not sharply drawn, but in general a demarcation can be made. *Services* are provided by persons, namely the members of the official staff of the House of Commons. They are provided, for example, by Officers and officials who work in the Department of the Clerk of the House and in the Library. *Facilities* consist of various physical and material aids that are officially provided for the convenience and use of Members. The various kinds of accommodation in the Palace of Westminster – the Palace itself for that matter – are examples of facilities for MPs. The various allowances that Members may draw to meet their parliamentary expenses may also be regarded as facilities.

In our view it is of particular importance to know the nature, and extent, of the services and facilities available to MPs in the parliamentary precincts.[1] This is so for three reasons. First, a

---

[1] The precincts consist of the Palace of Westminster, the various courts that are enclosed in the Palace complex, and New Palace Yard.

great deal has been made of the adequacies and inadequacies of the 'environment' in which MPs are required to do their work, but there has been little systematic attempt to examine this setting. We hope that we have done so adequately in this book. Secondly, we believe that one can better understand how an institution works if one understands the conditions under which its work is carried on. Thus we hope to throw a new light on the working of the House of Commons. Thirdly, it is hoped that by putting this information in one place our efforts will provide a useful aid to those who, for various reasons, need to know their way around the Palace of Westminster.

Finally, it should be noted that we have simply examined things as they are and therefore any recommendations for changes are outside our terms of reference.

1.1 CONTEXTUAL FACTORS

The provision of services and facilities for British MPs has always presented two major problems. The first relates to the role of the Member of Parliament; the second, to the fact that Members vary considerably in their work methods. In practice the two matters are closely connected. For example, the extent to which MPs are full-time or part-time is as much a question of the Member's role as it is a matter of work methods.

'Any discussion of the role of the Member of Parliament is complicated by the fact that there is a degree of conflict between theory and practice in that the work of Parliament in general and the House of Commons in particular is carried on in an atmosphere of lip-service to a number of constitutional norms, such as the supremacy of Parliament, individual and collective ministerial responsibility, the official absence of parties and so on, all of which are in practice subordinated to the political realities of Cabinet government whereby the government of the day normally controls the House of Commons rather than the House of Commons controlling the government. Thus the role of the Member is not easy to define, whilst Members themselves are by no means agreed as to what their role is, still less what it ought to be.'[1]

[1] Anthony Barker and Michael Rush, *The Member of Parliament and His Information*, p 21, Allen & Unwin (1970).

Members may be said to have at least three major functions: to sustain or oppose the Government of the day, to scrutinise the activities of the Government, and to represent their constituents and defend their interests.[1] This by no means exhausts the list of possibilities. For example, some Members clearly represent the interests of outside organisations, such as trade unions and business groups, whilst it can be argued that Members have a substantive legislating role. To provide further examples, however, serves only to reinforce the absence of general agreement and the fact that it is more meaningful to speak of a multiplicity of roles, rather than a single role.

Moreover, even in the context of the three major functions mentioned above there is a considerable variety of practice: some Members are far more concerned with sustaining or opposing the Government of the day than they are with scrutinising its activities; some are far more active in the role of scrutiny than others; some devote a great deal of time to constituency matters, others relatively little; and so on. It is also increasingly the case that Members tend to specialise in particular policy areas. These may be related to personal or pecuniary interests, or arise from constituency problems or personal experience. In connection with their specialities, Members may or may not be able to offer professional or occupational expertise, but in each case the fact of specialisation provides yet a further variation in the Member's pursuit of his parliamentary duties.

Clearly, these various roles presuppose different services and facilities. Sustaining or opposing the Government may require little more than a plenary chamber and two division lobbies, whereas scrutinising the Government may require substantial library facilities and information services. At the same time, representing constituents may require some degree of secretarial assistance.

Quite apart from these considerations, however, the working methods of Members also relate to the provision of services and facilities. The survey of MPs conducted by the Boyle Committee found, for example, that 70 per cent of all backbench Members had part-time occupations outside Parliament, although the time spent on these occupations whilst Parliament was sitting

[1] *Ibid.*, pp 21–2.

ranged from the 29 per cent who spent less than five hours per week in outside work to the 5 per cent who spent more than thirty hours per week.[1] An important consequence of Members having outside occupations is that they are able to supplement their parliamentary salaries. However, the range of additional income was found to vary considerably: 11 per cent earned less than £250, whilst 20 per cent earned £5,000 or more per year.[2] Not surprisingly, although the average number of hours per week spent on parliamentary business was sixty-three, the range was from under forty hours (6 per cent) to over ninety hours (5 per cent). Moreover, there was no marked concentration around the average figure of sixty-three hours; half the respondents worked between fifty-one and seventy hours per week.[3]

A similarly varied picture emerges if the expenses claimed by MPs against income tax are examined. In 1969–70 these ranged from £200 to more than £3,600.[4] Most Members have secretarial assistance, but their actual secretarial arrangements vary considerably. Some share secretaries with other Members. Some have part-time secretaries, some full-time. Some secretaries work in or near the Palace of Westminster, others in Members' constituencies.[5] Or again, whilst 87 per cent of backbenchers maintain accommodation of some kind in London, as far as their main place of residence is concerned they divide almost equally into those who live in London (33 per cent), those who live in their constituencies outside London (31 per cent), and those who live elsewhere (36 per cent).[6]

In the context of the foregoing variations, the provision of appropriate services and facilities is a complex matter. Members' duties cannot be adequately performed without them, but the extent to which Members vary in their approach to their parliamentary work makes it difficult to provide services and facilities that adequately meet the needs of all of them. This

---

[1] *Review Body on Top Salaries: Ministers of the Crown and Members of Parliament*, Cmnd 4836, Appendix A, Tables 15 and 16 (December 1971). Hereafter referred to as the *Boyle Report*.

[2] *Boyle Report*, Appendix A, Table 16.

[3] *Boyle Report*, Appendix A, Tables 6 and 7.

[4] *Boyle Report*, Appendix D, Table 3. See also Chapter 6 below.

[5] *Boyle Report*, Appendix A, Table 9; and Chapter 7 below.

[6] *Boyle Report*, Appendix A, Table 4.

becomes clear if the question is examined historically: only once in its history has what may be described as 'purpose-built' accommodation been provided for Parliament. This came after the fire of 1834 which destroyed the greater part of the old Palace of Westminster. Whilst it can therefore be argued that the new accommodation which Parliament occupied in 1852 largely suited the needs of Parliamentarians in the middle of the nineteenth century, it is no longer the case more than a century later.

The mixture of roles that Members perform has changed; state intervention has increased enormously; Parliament has a vastly increased burden of work; the demands upon Members have increased; and the atmosphere of the 'club' has been increasingly superseded by that of the 'workshop'. Parliament itself, as is often suggested, is an evolving institution. Earlier versions were adapted to the exigencies of the time and the philosophy of the day. There have been landmarks, even watersheds, in the history of Parliament, but only during the republican period were there any fundamental attempts to rebuild the whole parliamentary edifice rather than adapt existing arrangements. Thus as the position of Parliament in general, and the roles of Members in particular, have changed, so have attitudes towards, and demands for, services and facilities. But in keeping with parliamentary tradition they have developed in a piecemeal and pragmatic fashion.

The general working environment of Members of Parliament is therefore a Palace that dates from the middle of the nineteenth century and which has been modified and adapted in various ways to meet the needs of twentieth century MPs (see Figure 1.1). It is important to remember that the Palace of Westminster remains a royal palace to this day and that a part of it, albeit a limited part, remains outside the control of either House of Parliament. The Lord Great Chamberlain retains control of the Royal Gallery and the Queen's Robing Room and shares responsibility for Westminster Hall and the Crypt Chapel with the Speaker of the House of Commons and the Lord Chancellor. Furthermore, and of much greater importance, the House of Commons shares the Palace with the House of Lords, responsibility for the areas occupied by the two Houses being vested, respectively, in the Speaker and the Lord Chancellor. Although Members have access to some parts of the

The Houses of Parliament

Plan of the Principal Floor

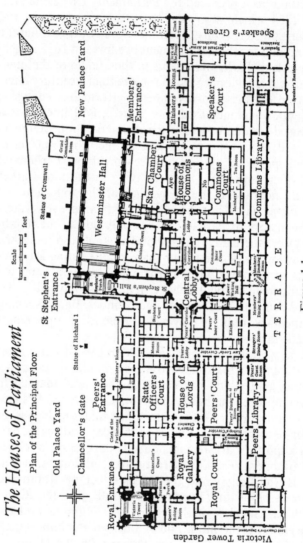

Figure 1.1

Reprinted from *The Houses of Parliament: An Illustrated Guide to the Palace of Westminster* by permission of the author of the 12th edition (1972), Mr. K. R. Mackenzie, CB, and the publisher, Eyre and Spottiswoode Ltd.

Palace occupied by the Lords, such as the Lords Library, such access is limited. Moreover, considerable parts of the Palace are utilised by the staffs of the two Houses, by the Lord Chancellor's Department, and by the residences of the Speaker, the Serjeant at Arms and the Lord Chancellor. Consequently, parts of the Palace that can be considered to be exclusively or mainly the domain of Members of Parliament are relatively limited.

It is perhaps ironic that such limitations should occur in one of the world's largest and most impressive buildings. The Palace of Westminster covers an area of eight acres, and has about 1,200 rooms, 100 staircases, twenty-one passenger lifts and two miles of passages. As the Palace has been modified and adapted to meet modern demands, it has tended to increase in complexity. Various parts of the Palace have been altered to accommodate Members' secretaries, other parts to provide rooms for Members themselves. In buildings near the Palace–in Bridge Street and Abbey Gardens–further such facilities have been provided.

This process of adaptation is perhaps best illustrated by the House of Commons chamber itself. After the destruction of the chamber in May 1941 the opportunity presented itself for constructing a new chamber providing more spacious accommodation, including a seat for every Member. In this situation the House of Commons chose to rebuild its chamber essentially on the model of the old. More accommodation was provided above and below the new chamber, and more seats were provided in the galleries for reporters and visitors. But the chamber itself remained the same: it is the same size as the chamber designed by Sir Charles Barry and it has the same number of seats–346. These seats, together with a further ninety-one in the side galleries, are sufficient for little more than two-thirds of the 635 Members. Because the House wished to retain the close and intimate debating atmosphere of the old chamber, the even greater innovation of desks for Members was hardly considered. Thus whilst the chamber itself was almost unchanged, the opportunity was taken in the process of rebuilding to provide additional ancillary accommodation. It is perhaps significant to note that electric lighting was installed in the chamber of the House of Lords in 1883, in the clock dials of the Clock Tower in 1906, but not in the chamber of the House of Commons until 1912.[1]

1.2 FINANCE OF THE HOUSE OF COMMONS

The House of Commons is financed almost entirely by money voted annually by Parliament out of general taxation, as if it were a government department. In 1973–74 it was estimated that the House would cost the taxpayer some £12·7 million, which, added to the £2·9 million for the House of Lords, made a total of £15·6 million for the legislature. This amount was 0·08 per cent of total expenditure by the central government.[2] Of the expenditure on the Commons, £7·1 million was borne on the Commons' own 'vote' (that is, was included under the

Table 1.1   *The Cost of the House of Commons, 1973–74*

Cost category	£'000s
Members: salaries	2,758
pension contributions, Members' Fund, etc	490
secretarial assistance	630
travelling expenses	746
subsistence payments	441
Staff: salaries and national insurance	1,280
pensions	129
Post Office services	233
Police	130
Maintenance of the building, furniture, fuel, light, etc	3,564
Rates	126
Stationery and printing (mainly publications)	1,906
Refreshment Department – grant in aid	48
Committees: shorthand writers and other expenses	25
specialist advisers	12
expenses of travel abroad	10
Expenses of parliamentary delegations travelling abroad	69
Library – purchase of books and other material	26
Other items net of receipts	101
TOTAL	12,724

Source – Supply Estimates, 1973–74, Class I.

[1] Sir Bryan Fell, *The Houses of Parliament: An Illustrated Guide to the Palace of Westminster*, p 27, revised by K. R. Mackenzie, Eyre and Spottiswoode (twelfth edition, 1972).

[2] Supply Estimates, H.C. 114, 1972–73, Class I: Financial Statement and Budget Report, H.C. 173, 1972–73, p 18. The corresponding percentage for 1938–39 was 0·09 per cent.

heading 'House of Commons' in the Supply Estimates that provide for government expenditure), and £5·6 million was borne on the votes of government departments that incur expenditure on behalf of the House.

One feature of financial arrangements is that the salary of the Speaker is paid out of the Consolidated Fund and is not included in the vote for the House of Commons. Pensions for former Speakers and their widows are similarly treated, as are the salaries of the Leader of the Opposition, the Opposition Chief Whip and two other Opposition Whips. The Speaker's salary is on the same basis as judges' salaries; the arrangement demonstrates his independence of the Government. On the other hand the salaries of the Chairman of Ways and Means and the Deputy Chairmen are included in the ordinary vote; the occupants of these offices usually change with a change of government.

The Estimates for the House of Commons bear a note stating that the remuneration of Officers of the House of Commons is exempt from Treasury control and is controlled instead by the 'House of Commons Offices Commission'. This Commission is set up under the *House of Commons Offices Act 1812* and consists of the Speaker, the Chancellor of the Exchequer, the Secretaries of State and the law officers for England and Wales (provided that they are all Members of the House).[1] In practice the Chancellor is, with the Speaker, one of the two active Commissioners, and Treasury influence can therefore be very effectively wielded via the Chancellor's presence on the Commission. Thus the note in the Estimates does not accurately reflect the actual situation.[2] The gap between the actual system and the theoretical legal framework is even wider than is customary. There are at present thirteen Commissioners, all holding office by virtue of the post they occupy; and some of them would probably be surprised to find out that they were members of the Commission. The Leader of the House of Commons, the Minister actually concerned with House of

[1] The Master of the Rolls was also a member when tenure of this office could be combined with being an MP. In the ten years 1955–65, the Commissioners met as a body only once. See evidence of the Speaker's Secretary to the Select Committee on the Palace of Westminster, 1964–65, H.C. 285, p 56.

[2] On this matter see evidence of the then Clerk of the House to the Select Committee on Science and Technology, Subcommittee on Coastal Pollution, 21 May 1968, H.C. 421–I, p 236.

Commons matters, is *not* a Commissioner; there is no representative of the Opposition; and the Services Committee also has no place in the statutory arrangements. The 1812 Act is drawn up in terms of the two staff Departments existing at that date – the Clerk's and the Serjeant's. A subsequent Act – in 1846 – provides for an Estimate for the Speaker's Department. These acts are still current, but no legislation covers the more recently founded departments. The Select Committee on House of Commons Accommodation (the Stokes Committee) recommended in 1954 that these Acts should be repealed or amended.[1] This view was repeated by the then Minister of Public Building and Works (Charles Pannell, Labour Member for Leeds West) to the Select Committee on the Palace of Westminster of 1965. However they remain in force unchanged.

To complete the above picture, it is right to point out that, in practice, responsibility for the numbers and pay of the permanent staff of the Commons has, since February 1970, been delegated by the Commissioners to the Accounting Officer for the House of Commons Vote, subject to certain broad principles. The Accounting Officer,[2] it should be noted, is also the Clerk of the House of Commons. He acts normally on the recommendations of the Staff Board (see section 1.4) in these matters, and he provides an annual statement of all such recommendations as he approves for the information of the Commissioners.

In 1954 the Stokes Committee recommended that expenditure on the maintenance of the buildings of the House of Commons should be shown separately from the maintenance of other public buildings, as its inclusion in a general total 'does not afford the House sufficient say in the preparation of those . . . draft Estimates which relate to its requirements.'[3] Up to and including 1967–68, this recommendation was followed in that there was a separate Houses of Parliament Buildings Vote. The recommendation is now ignored by the Treasury, which lumps in the Houses of Parliament with public buildings generally.

A series of forecasts of expenditure on 'Parliament and the

[1] The Chairman of the Committee was the late Richard Stokes (then Labour Member for Ipswich).

[2] This is a function performed in government departments by the senior official, usually the Permanent Secretary.

[3] Report of the Select Committee on House of Commons Accommodation, 1953–54, H.C. 184, p xiv.

Privy Council' is contained in the White Paper on public expenditure of December 1972.[1] These estimates envisage no changes in future expenditure in this field. They show figures of £7·5 million (at constant prices) for the two financial years 1973–74 and 1974–75 and £8 million (rounded to the nearest whole million) for 1975–76 and 1976–77.[2] The implementation of the *Boyle Report*, however, has significantly increased expenditure on the House of Commons, not only because of the increase in Members' salaries to £4,500 but also because of the expansion in other services and facilities available to Members.

Members' salaries and those of House of Commons staff are administered by the Fees Office, which also deals with Members' travel expenses, the collection of fees on private bills, the Members' Contributory Pension Fund and the Members' Fund. The Office is headed by the Accountant, who is assisted by a Deputy Accountant, two Assistant Accountants and a Deputy Assistant Accountant. Newly elected Members are seen individually by the staff of the Fees Office, so that financial arrangements can be explained to them, and Members are often in touch with the Office on matters relating to their personal financial affairs.[3]

1.3 CONTROL OF SERVICES AND FACILITIES

On 26 April 1965, control of the use and occupation of the Royal Palace of Westminster passed, with Her Majesty's consent, from the Queen to the two Houses of Parliament. Until that time, supreme control had been vested in the Lord Great Chamberlain who delegated responsibility for the House of Commons' part of the accommodation, when the House was

[1] *Public Expenditure to 1976–77*, Cmnd 5178, p 61.

[2] These figures are considerably narrower in scope than the figure of £12·2 million given above for the annual cost of the legislature. The figures in the White Paper exclude, *inter alia*, the costs of the building and of publications. They therefore do not provide a good indication of the total costs of Parliament, but are included here because they are the only published forecasts.

[3] For details on the Fees Office, see Philip Marsden, *The Officers of the Commons 1363–1965*, pp 181–3, Barrie and Rockliff (1966); Report of the Select Committee on House of Commons Accommodation, 1953–54, H.C. 184, p 148; and Report of the Select Committee on the Palace of Westminster, 1964–65, H.C. 285, pp 50–1.

sitting, to the Serjeant at Arms acting on behalf of the Speaker. At week-ends and during recesses, however, the Lord Great Chamberlain re-assumed his responsibilities for the whole Palace.

The current arrangements date very largely from the Select Committee on the Palace of Westminster which was appointed, on 27 April 1965, to 'make recommendations on the control of the accommodation, powers and services in that part of the Palace of Westminster which is to be vested in Mr Speaker on behalf of this House (of Commons)'.[1] Twelve years earlier, however, the Stokes Committee (Select Committee on House of Commons Accommodation) had been appointed to consider: the arrangements regarding the allocation of accommodation in the House of Commons; the amenities necessary to enable Members to carry out their official duties efficiently; the desirability of setting up a 'sessional committee' which would review and report from time to time on the recommendations that the Stokes Committee might make; and the methods of appointment of the staff of the Commons at all levels. If we are to view the present arrangements in their correct perspective, a short account of the work of the 1953–54 Stokes Committee is desirable.

Before making its first Report to the House in October 1953,[2] the Stokes Committee had time to deal with only the first of the above matters in detail, and its recommendations were consequently in the main confined to specific suggestions for a more efficient allocation of existing accommodation. One more general conclusion was, however, drawn by the Committee: namely, that 'some machinery whereby a unified control of the whole Palace could be exercised' was desirable.[3] This point was re-stated by the Committee in its second Report, made during the following session.[4] The Committee recommended that the powers 'at present exercised by the Commissioners for regulating the offices of the House of Commons by virtue of the *House of Commons Offices Acts, 1812–49*, should be exercised in future by a body from the House of Commons, to be known as the House of Commons Commission'.[5] This new Commission should be

[1] H.C. 285, 1964–65, p ii.
[2] H.C. 309, 1952–53.
[3] *Ibid.*, para. 18, p viii.
[4] H.C. 184, 1953–54.
[5] *Ibid.*, para. 52, pp xiv–xv.

set up at the beginning of each Parliament to serve for the duration of that Parliament, and it should be allowed to delegate its powers to committees. In addition to general financial and staffing responsibilities, the proposed Commission should 'advise Mr Speaker in regard to the Estimates for the House; the allocation of accommodation; the Library; and the facilities and services necessary to enable Members to discharge their duties; and should control the arrangements for the Kitchen and Refreshment Rooms'.[1] The Speaker was to be the Chairman of the Commission which was also to include the Leader of the House, the Leader of the Opposition (or his deputy), the Chancellor of the Exchequer (or other Treasury Minister), the (then) Minister of Works (or his Parliamentary Secretary) and a suitable cross-section of other Members not less than nine in number.[2] It will be clear that these recommendations of the 1953–54 Stokes Committee anticipated the desire of the House of Commons, subsequently expressed in the 1964–65 Select Committee, to have some kind of 'unified control' over its own accommodation and facilities.

The second Report of the Stokes Committee also contained detailed recommendations on the allocation of accommodation and on the methods of appointment of staff. Some of these were implemented. In general, however, comparatively little was changed until April 1965, when control of the use and occupation of the Palace of Westminster passed, as we have seen, from the Queen to the two Houses of Parliament. With effect from that date control of the House of Commons' part of the Palace was vested in Mr Speaker;[3] and the Select Committee on the Palace of Westminster was immediately set up to make recommendations as to how he should be advised in the discharge of these responsibilities. Reporting in July 1965, the Committee recommended that a House of Commons Services Committee should be appointed 'to advise Mr Speaker on the control of the accommodation and services in that part of the Palace of Westminster and its precincts occupied by or on behalf of the House of Commons'.[4] The Report was approved after a debate

---

[1] *Ibid.*, para. 53, p xv.   [2] *Ibid.*, para. 56, p xv.
[3] See the statement by the Prime Minister on 23 March 1965; H.C. Deb., 709, cc. 328–9.
[4] H.C. 285, 1964–65, para. 15, p vii.

in the House in November 1965,[1] and on 7 December the Select Committee on House of Commons (Services) was first set up. It is this important Committee of sixteen Members which today controls, on behalf of the Speaker and of the House generally, the accommodation and official services which are available to Members at Westminster.

When first constituted, the Services Committee set up four subcommittees: the Catering Subcommittee, which took over the duties formerly carried out by the Select Committee on Kitchen and Refreshment Rooms (House of Commons); the Library Subcommittee; the Administration Subcommittee; and the Accommodation and Housekeeping Subcommittee. The duties formerly allotted to the Select Committee on Publications and Debates Reports were passed almost in their entirety to the new Administration Subcommittee. Two of the subcommittees were subsequently merged. There are now three subcommittees: the Catering Subcommittee, the Library Subcommittee, and the Accommodation and Administration Subcommittee. All members of the subcommittees are now also members of the main Services Committee: initially, the subcommittees could and did include up to five 'additional members' who were not necessarily members of the main Select Committee.[2] The Services Committee refers to its subcommittees certain broad areas of responsibility, and also such individual matters arising from time to time which are deemed to be appropriate to a subcommittee's interests. Each subcommittee has power to send for persons, papers and records and to report to the main Committee from time to time. It is the latter, however, that finally adopts or rejects proposals, and which makes periodic reports to the House.

Despite these arrangements, it would be misleading to assume that there is a clear line of authority below the level of the House of Commons itself in the administration of, and responsibility for, services and facilities. No single person is in charge of services and facilities in the Palace of Westminster, and there is in practice a substantial degree of decentralisation to the heads of the five Departments. Although the Speaker does not *directly* administer any of the Departments, including his own, he may

[1] H.C. Deb., 2 November, 1965, 718, cc. 878–957.
[2] H.C. 285, 1964–65, para. 20, p viii.

deal with a variety of matters referred to him by heads of Departments. In practice, however, he is more concerned with some services than others. The role of the Services Committee, moreover, is principally to advise and make recommendations, although it takes executive action with regard to certain restaurant facilities. The Committee may examine all existing services and facilities, but, like the Speaker, it tends to be more concerned with some services and facilities than others, notably those which fall within the ambit of its subcommittees.

1.4 ORGANISATION OF THE STAFF

In February 1972 there were 384 permanent staff directly employed by the House of Commons.[1] Such staff are not civil servants: they serve the legislature as opposed to the executive, and are either 'Officers' or 'officials' of the House of Commons. The former status is accorded to all Heads of Departments and to a number of senior staff, and carries with it privileges such as access to certain parts of the chamber of the House and use of the Members' and Strangers' Dining Rooms. All staff, however, may be accurately described as 'servants of the House of Commons', and all Members are entitled to equal and impartial assistance from them.

Staff are distributed among the five independently administered Departments of the House (see Table 1.2). Inasmuch as separate chapters will be devoted to four of these Departments, only brief mention of them will be made at this point.

The *Department of the Clerk of the House*, with a staff of ninety-five,[2] is responsible for the conduct of the business of the House. Its work is allocated between the Committee Office, the Journal Office, the Overseas Office, the Private Bill Office, the Public Bill Office and the Table Office. These titles are self-explanatory, except perhaps for the last named, which deals with the tabling of Parliamentary Questions and the preparation of the Notice Paper and Order Paper. The Clerk of

---

[1] Since this chapter was written, the overall staff total has increased to 414. The organisation of the permanent staff is described in Erskine May, *Treatise on the Law, Privileges, Proceedings and Usage of Parliament*, pp 234–6, Butterworth (eighteenth edition, 1971).

[2] This figure relates to the situation in February 1972, as do the other figures relating to establishments in this section.

Table 1.2 *Numbers of staff in the Departments of the House of Commons, 1972*

Department	Numbers of staff
Department of the Clerk of the House	
Clerk	1
Clerk Assistant and Second Clerk Assistant	2
Committee Office	20
Journal Office	5
Overseas Office	5
Private Bill Office	3
Public Bill Office	6
Table Office	5
Clerk Administrator	1
Higher Executive Officers	10
Clerical and Secretarial	37
TOTAL	95
Department of the Serjeant at Arms	
Serjeant at Arms	1
Deputy Serjeant at Arms, Assistant Serjeant at Arms and Deputy Assistant Serjeant at Arms	3
Admission Order Office	3
Doorkeepers	41
Office Keepers	6
Attendants	45
Women Cleaners	31
Others	22
TOTAL	152
Department of the Speaker	
Speaker's Private Office	9
Official Report (Hansard)	42
Vote Office and Sale Office	11
TOTAL	62
The Library	
Librarian	1
Deputy Librarian	1
Parliamentary Division (Main Library)	34
Research Division	19
TOTAL	55

Table 1.2—*continued*

Department	Numbers of staff
Administration Department	
Clerk Administrator	1
Personal Secretary	1
Fees Office	14
Establishments Section	4
TOTAL	20
TOTAL	384

Note – The overall total of 384 relates to 1972. The Supply Estimates for 1973–74 (H.C. 114–I, 1972–73) allow for an overall total of 414, an increase of thirty. The 414 are distributed as follows among the Departments: Clerk of the House 96, Speaker's Department 77, Serjeant at Arms 153, Library 63 and Administration 25. These totals relate to the number of full-time staff positions. Certain staff, particularly women cleaners, are employed on a part-time basis, and two part-time staff are normally counted as one full-time staff. Thus the number of individuals employed by the five Departments exceeds the official totals shown in the Table and in the Supply Estimates.

the House of Commons is the senior permanent Officer of the House.

The *Department of the Serjeant at Arms* is currently, with a complement of 152, the largest of the five Departments. The duties of the Serjeant can be divided into two categories: (1) security, order and ceremonial and (2) housekeeping.[1] The former include the maintenance of order in the chamber and its precincts; the control of the police, doorkeepers, Admission Order Office and the galleries of the House; and the issuing of passes. 'Housekeeping' includes the allocation of certain accommodation and of Members' desks and filing cabinets; messenger services; cleaning (in conjunction with the Department of the Environment); and the organisation of amenities for Members, such as television and wireless rooms. The Serjeant is also responsible for seeing that certain rules, such as those relating to smoking, are obeyed.

The various Offices in the *Department of the Speaker* are

[1] Under the *House of Commons Offices Act 1812*, the Serjeant was appointed 'Housekeeper' of the House of Commons.

under the administration of Mr Speaker. They are: the Speaker's Private Office (under the Speaker's Secretary); the Office of the *Official Report* or *Hansard* (under the editor); and the Vote Office and Sale Office (under the Deliverer of the Vote). The Speaker's Counsel and Chaplain are also members of this Department. Of the sixty-two persons who are attached to this Department, about two-thirds belong to the Office of the *Official Report*.

The *Department of the Library*, which has a staff of fifty-five, became a separate Department, under the Librarian, in August 1967. Previously, the Library had been under the supervision of Mr Speaker, and was one of the Offices in his Department. Between 1834 and 1861 a standing committee of Members was appointed 'to assist Mr Speaker in the direction of the Library'; from 1922 until the setting up of the Library Subcommittee in 1965, an unofficial Advisory Committee of Members was appointed each session by Mr Speaker. Today the Librarian directs the Commons' Library in close consultation, as regards policy matters, with the Library Subcommittee.[1]

The *Administration Department*, which has a staff of twenty, was set up in January 1968 (see Figure 1.2). Its Head is appointed by the Speaker and, since its institution, this post has been held by the Clerk Administrator, who is also Clerk to the Services Committee. The Department consists of the Fees Office[2] and an Establishments Section.[3] The Fees Office, under the Accountant, is responsible for the control of expenditure coming under the House of Commons Vote.[4] The Establishments Section assists the five Departments in a variety of important staff matters, including recruitment, salaries and superannuation.

The Head of the Establishments Section also acts as Secretary to the House of Commons *Staff Board*, which consists of the Clerk Assistant as Chairman, the Clerk Administrator and a senior representative from each of the other three Departments.[5]

[1] Erskine May, *op. cit.*, pp 235–6.

[2] Before being transferred to the Administration Department in 1968, the Fees Office was in the Speaker's Department.

[3] Erskine May, *op. cit.*, p 236.

[4] For further information on the Fees Office, see section 1.2.

[5] Erskine May, *op. cit.*, p 236. A history of the Staff Board, and a description of its constitution and functions at the time, were given in a memorandum by its Chairman to the Select Committee on the Palace of Westminster, 1964–65, H.C. 285, pp 73–5.

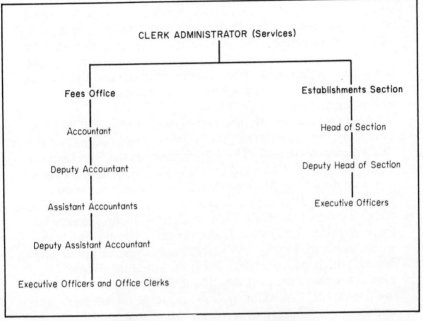

CLERK ADMINISTRATOR (Services)

Fees Office

Accountant

Deputy Accountant

Assistant Accountants

Deputy Assistant Accountant

Executive Officers and Office Clerks

Establishments Section

Head of Section

Deputy Head of Section

Executive Officers

Figure 1.2 ADMINISTRATION DEPARTMENT

The Staff Board considers and co-ordinates establishment proposals from the individual Departments, and also deals with staff matters which the Services Committee refers to it. Similarly, any proposal affecting the remuneration of staff which is put forward by a trade union is normally submitted by the Clerk Administrator to the Staff Board, which deals with it in the same way as with a proposal originating in one of the five Departments. The Staff Board makes recommendations regarding the numbers, grading and pay of the staff of the House of Commons to the Accounting Officer for the House of Commons Vote (this office being held by the Clerk of the House), who received delegated responsibility for these matters in February 1970 from the Commissioners for Regulating the Offices of the House of Commons.[1] The Commissioners make an annual report to the House of Commons. This report is not published, but it may be consulted by Members in the Library.

[1] Erskine May, *op. cit.*, p 234.

A number of booklets or, in the case of the Serjeant's Department, a folder of leaflets, are usually made available to Members
at the beginning of a new Parliament. Such booklets, or folders,
contain information and guidance concerning the various
official services and facilities offered to Members by the
individual Departments. For example, both the Clerk's Department and the Library issued up-to-date booklets to Members
at the beginning of the 1970 Parliament.

Some services for Members are provided by staff *not* employed by the House itself, and in total these outnumber the
directly employed staff. The Department of the Environment
employs a considerable staff for the maintenance of the Palace,
and a contingent of Metropolitan police is stationed within the
building. The Post Office Corporation provides postal and
telephone services, while Members' travel arrangements are
frequently dealt with by the Transport Office (staffed by Thomas
Cook and Son). Finally, the Refreshment Department employs
its staff on its own account. Thus, including the House's own
employees, there are probably about 900 people who work for
the House of Commons in one capacity or another. This
estimate (see Chapter 7) excludes Members' secretaries and
research assistants (now partly paid for out of public funds)
and the staff of whips' and party offices.

1.5 CHANGING SERVICES AND FACILITIES

There is little doubt that there never has been, and it is likely
that there never will be, complete satisfaction with the services
and facilities provided for Members of Parliament because, as
was suggested earlier, Members fulfil a variety of roles and vary
significantly in their methods of work. The provision of services
and facilities is based to a very large extent on compromise: a
compromise between those who are broadly satisfied with whatever services and facilities may exist at a given time and those
who demand more; a compromise between what is possible
within the confines of present parliamentary accommodation
and what would be possible in 'purpose-built' accommodation;
and, above all, a compromise between what may be widely
regarded as desirable and what the Government of the day feels
able to allow from an economic and political point of view.

Thus, although there have been extensive changes over the years in services and facilities, particularly since 1964, these changes have not consisted of a simple process of general expansion: they have been piecemeal, fragmentary and gradual – in a word, *pragmatic*.

It is not therefore surprising to find that the way in which services and facilities have developed has been and continues to be complex. There are, of course, a number of methods open to the individual Member who wishes to complain about, or seek some change in, parliamentary services and facilities. He may informally approach members of the staff of the Department concerned. He may make a formal or informal approach to the Head of a Department. Exceptionally, he could see the Speaker. He may make oral or written representations to the Services Committee or one of its subcommittees, or to any other committee of the House that may from time to time be concerned with particular services and facilities. Alternatively, a Member who has a general interest in services and facilities may seek to be appointed to the Services Committee, whilst a Member who wishes to make more public (though not necessarily more effective) representations may ask a Question in the House. On the last point, the Select Committee on the Palace of Westminster recommended that such Questions should be directed to the Chairman of the Services Committee who, ideally, would also be the Leader of the House. This recommendation has been followed, although the answering of such Questions is often delegated to the chairman of the relevant Services subcommittee. This is particularly true of Questions concerning the catering and refreshment facilities, which are generally answered by the Chairman of the Catering Subcommittee.

Through one or more of these methods a Member may achieve the change he seeks. In many cases, of course, the Member may be seeking a minor redress, such as a different location for his desk or secretary, in which case an informal approach to the relevant official is normally all that is necessary. In other cases the Member may be seeking an important extension of services and facilities and might therefore decide on a more formal approach. There is little doubt that representations made by Members, both individually and collectively, have strongly influenced the provision of services and facilities. Thus most of the backbench Members of the Services Committee may be regarded as unusually interested in these matters, whilst some MPs, such as Arthur Lewis (Labour Member for West Ham North) demonstrate their interest in such matters as Members' salaries and pensions by asking frequent Parliamentary Questions. More recently the collective influence of MPs has found a further outlet through the practice of both the Lawrence[1] and Boyle Committees of sending questionnaires to Members.

It may well be that the views of a particular Member or group of Members are instrumental in actually bringing about important changes in services and facilities, but such views are at least as important in contributing towards the creation of an atmosphere which makes change more likely. There are several ways in which changes are in practice effected. One of the most important instruments is that of a select committee of the House. Committees such as the Select Committee on the Establishment of the House of Commons (1833),[2] on Parliamentary Debates (1907),[3] on the House of Commons Library (1945),[4] on Members' Expenses (1953),[5] on House of Commons Accommodation (1953–54),[6] and the Palace of Westminster (1965)[7] have been landmarks in the development of services and facilities. In addition to these committees, various Select Committees on Procedure have made significant contributions and, since its inception in 1965, the Services Committee has played an important and continuing role.

The use of select committees to examine these matters has a number of advantages: it enables the House of Commons, as opposed to an extra-parliamentary body, to take the initiative in an area of considerable concern to its Members; it provides a means of gauging opinion in the House; and it provides the Government of the day with recommendations on which it may base its decisions, but to which it is not automatically committed and for which it is not responsible. There is one major disadvantage, however, especially in such matters as Members'

[1] *Report of the Committee on the Remuneration of Ministers and Members of Parliament*, November 1964, Cmnd 2516. Hereafter referred to as the *Lawrence Report*.

[2] H.C. 648, 1833.

[3] H.C. 239, 1907.

[4] H.C. 35 and 99–I, 1945–46.

[5] H.C. 309, 1952–53; and H.C. 72, 1953–54.

[6] H.C. 184, 1953–54.

[7] H.C. 285, 1964–65.

salaries, expenses and pensions: the House, through its select committees, may be regarded as a judge in its own cause.

It is probably for this reason that on the last two occasions when Members' remuneration has been examined the inquiry has been conducted by extra-parliamentary bodies. Under present plans, this practice will continue. It is important to note, however, that whereas the Lawrence Committee was concerned entirely with Members' salaries, expenses and pensions, the Boyle Committee ranged more widely over the whole question of Members' services and facilities, because it has become increasingly difficult to deal with remuneration without taking broader factors into account. In dealing with Members' remuneration in particular, extra-parliamentary bodies have the political advantage of relieving Members from the task of making recommendations on their own financial future. At the same time, it is undoubtedly more difficult for a Government to reject totally, or modify substantially, the recommendations of such bodies than those of select committees. Recommendations on remuneration from select committees have in fact been rejected on a number of occasions, as were the major recommendations of the Stokes Committee on the control of the building and staff.

The attitude of the Government of the day is, of course, crucial. Indeed, there have been instances when the Government has taken the initiative in the provision of services and facilities. Thus it was the Government which decided to pay MPs £400 a year in 1911 and it was the Government which took the initiative in raising Members' salaries to £600 in 1937. In many cases the Government, while initiating changes, will be responding to representations from Members. No matter what the source of the initiative, however, the views of the Government remain vital. Even in those cases where free votes have been allowed, the decision to have a free vote has of course been the Government's, and Governments have sometimes rejected the results of such votes.

The matter of the new parliamentary building provides an illustration. After a long and complicated series of proposals and counter-proposals from various sources, including Government spokesmen, the Services Committee recommended (as one of two alternatives) the erection of a new parliamentary building on the Bridge Street site. The House of Commons approved the Bridge Street proposal and then, in July 1970, the Government opened a competition for a design for the new building. In June 1973 the House approved a design and also the principle of constructing the new building. Both of these decisions were made on free votes. Nonetheless, the Chancellor of the Exchequer had already announced that no expenditure on the new building could be incurred until the 1975–76 financial year. Thus the manner in which the Government is brought to the point of decision may vary. At the same time, there is no doubt that in recent years Ministers have become increasingly sensitive to the views of backbenchers on 'parliamentary' matters, including those relating to services and facilities. In the end, however, as in all important matters, the Government, if it chooses to do so, takes the ultimate decision.

CHAPTER 2

THE DEPARTMENT OF THE
CLERK OF THE HOUSE

The Department of the Clerk of the House is the oldest of the
five Departments in the House of Commons, the first known
Clerk having been appointed in 1363, fourteen years earlier than
the first Speaker. As a result of a long process of evolution, the
Clerk – and the other Clerks in his Department – came to owe
their loyalty solely to the House of Commons. Thus the Clerks
are, pre-eminently, the servants of the House. This principle
underlies all the various services provided for Members by the
Clerks and is recognised in every country where parliamentary
government on the British model is practised, though to a
varying degree in the parliaments of the developing countries
both within and outside the Commonwealth. At Westminster
it is undeniable (as is the non-political and impartial role of the
Clerks), yet in theory the Clerk of the House remains to this
day a servant of the Crown, being appointed still by letters
patent as was Robert de Melton, the first known patent holder,
in 1363. The Clerk is appointed by the Crown on the recommendation of the Prime Minister.

2.1 DEVELOPMENT OF THE DEPARTMENT

In 1327 the Commons presented their first common petition, or
public bill in modern jargon, a landmark in their development
as a legislative body. The appearance of a Commons Clerk
thirty-six years later with, no doubt, responsibility for keeping
the records, guiding the proceedings and perhaps steering the
Commons along satisfactory lines in the traditions of the chancery clerks, marked another stage in the development of the
Commons as an organised body. The medieval Clerk was nonetheless very much a royal servant. Thomas Haseley, appointed
Clerk in 1414, was able to continue holding the patent while

pursuing other ventures and performing unparliamentary services to the Crown. The tenure of the Clerkship was also uncertain, and the patent might not be renewed on the accession of a new monarch. This in fact happened when Edward VI did not renew Robert Ormeston's patent and appointed John Seymour, a former Member of Parliament, to succeed him in 1547.

The acquisition by the Commons, in 1547, of their first permanent meeting place – St Stephen's Chapel – coincided not unnaturally with the beginning of a permanent record of the House, the *Journal*.[1] John Seymour, its author, described the first *Journal* as 'a note of Bills, when they were read in the commons house'. Subsequent journals of Seymour's were expanded to include other items such as the committal of bills; divisions; the number of votes cast; the election of a Speaker; the first record of the Speaker's three claims for freedom of speech, freedom from arrest and freedom of access to the sovereign; and the committal to the Tower of an intruder who had assaulted a Member. The *Journal* was carried on in an expanded and neater form by Fulk Onslow, Seymour's successor. Despite the advances that had been made in the standards of the service of the House, Onslow, when absent through sickness, appointed Members of Parliament as his deputies, who apparently combined their two functions without difficulty.

The struggle between Crown and Parliament in the first half of the seventeenth century resulted in the Clerk assuming a more important and active professional role. No longer content to record attendances and proceedings, he became the guardian of procedure and precedents, and Henry Elsynge, appointed to the Clerkship in 1639, edited his father's treatise on parliamentary procedure[2] and conducted the work of the Table with professional efficiency. Increasing work led to the appointment of the first official Clerk Assistant in 1640, at a time when the House was beginning to meet informally as a Committee, not always at Westminster, with a Member other than the Crown-appointed Speaker in the Chair. It has certainly always been a

---

[1] See David Menhennet, *The Journal of the House of Commons: A Bibliographical and Historical Guide*, HMSO (1971).

[2] *The Manner of Holding Parliaments in England*. See the Introduction to the Irish University Press reprint (1972) of the 1768 edition by Thomas Tyrwhitt (himself Clerk from 1760–68).

tradition, maintained to the present day, that the Clerk Assistant attends upon Committees of the whole House. A later Clerk Assistant was appointed as 'not being Clerk to the Clerk but a distinct and proper Clerk of the House, to be appointed by the House as their Clerk Assistant and a check upon the Clerk of the House appointed by the Crown'.

The restoration of 1660 left the Crown in straitened financial circumstances and annual parliamentary sessions lasting about five months became necessary in order to ensure supplies. In such circumstances expansion of the Clerkship was to be expected and it was during Paul Jodrell's forty-three-year tenure of the Office, from 1683 to 1726, that the foundations of the modern Department were laid. Papers and records properly belonging to Parliament, but then in private hands, were delivered up and unauthorised printing of the *Journal* was stopped, both by Order in Council. A Clerk was engaged to arrange and store the records, particularly the *Journal*; this was the genesis of the modern Journal Office. Four junior Clerks were engaged to attend committees on public bills and private bills; this was the origin of the Committee Office. Despite the fact that Jodrell was commended by the Speaker 'for keeping the Journals of the House in a better manner than ever had been done by any of his predecessors', it fell to one of his successors, Nicholas Hardinge, who was Clerk from 1732 to 1748, to organise the printing of the *Journals* from the beginning. A print of 1,000 copies per volume was ordered in 1742.

The later years of the eighteenth century and the beginning of the nineteenth century were distinguished by the Clerkship of the great John Hatsell[1] whose *Precedents of Proceedings in the House of Commons*, first published in 1776,[2] was as authoritative and procedurally informative then as Erskine May is today. Later, in the days of John Ley[3] and John Rickman[4] during the first half of the nineteenth century, reform of the House was not limited to its representative and political aspects but was also actively pursued in the field of procedure, especially by Rickman.

[1] Clerk Assistant 1760–68 and Clerk 1768–1820,
[2] See the Introduction to the Irish University Press reprint (1972) of the definitive edition of 1818.
[3] Clerk Assistant 1814–20 and Clerk 1820–50.
[4] Speaker's Secretary 1802–14, Second Clerk Assistant 1814–20 and Clerk Assistant 1820–40.

The *Votes and Proceedings* were modernised so that they could be available to Members at breakfast next morning; the statutes were indexed; the Library was catalogued; and a new index was provided for Hatsell's *Precedents*. During the later years of this period the Clerk's Department was reorganised. The emoluments of all the Clerks, save the Clerk of the House and the Clerk Assistant, were not at that time fixed and came from many different sources. Such a system resulted in chronically long hours of work, with some Clerks becoming ill as a consequence. Another difficulty was that Clerks were permitted to engage in the promoting and opposing of private bills. Largely as a result of the recommendations of select committees that sat between 1833 and 1848, a system of regular salaries for Clerks was introduced, and the pattern of their working hours was regularised on a basis easily recognisable 120 years later. Clerks were also forbidden to participate in agency for private bills.

The second half of the nineteenth century can only be described as the May period in deference to the great Clerk who as Assistant Librarian, Clerk Assistant and, finally in 1870, Clerk, had been the principal professional witness before various select committees in the cause of procedural reform as well as the author of nine editions, including the first, of the famous *Treatise on the Law, Privileges, Proceedings and Usage of Parliament*. May himself noted that while still Clerk Assistant for fifteen years, he had been generally accepted as the foremost procedural adviser of the House. Not least among his achievements was the creation of grand committees, the precursor of the modern system of standing committees which has played such an important part in parliamentary proceedings since the second world war.[1]

2.2   STRUCTURE OF THE DEPARTMENT

Present-day Clerks, as servants of the House, continue to advise Mr Speaker in particular, and Members of the House in general, on all matters of procedure. The Department of the Clerk is

[1] For an account of the development of the office of Clerk of the House and the Department of the Clerk, see O. C. Williams, *The Clerical Organization of the House of Commons, 1661–1850*, Clarendon Press (1954). For the 'May' period, see House of Commons Library Document No. 9, *Erskine May's Private Journal, 1857–1882*, HMSO (1972). See also Philip Marsden, *The Officers of the Commons 1363–1965*, chapters 1, 2, 5, 6 and 9, Barrie and Rockliff (1966).

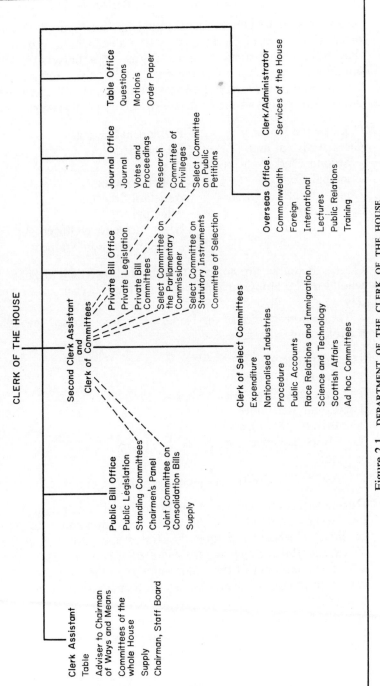

CLERK OF THE HOUSE

Clerk Assistant
Table
Adviser to Chairman of Ways and Means
Committees of the whole House
Supply
Chairman, Staff Board

Public Bill Office
Public Legislation
Standing Committees
Chairmen's Panel
Joint Committee on Consolidation Bills
Supply

Second Clerk Assistant and Clerk of Committees

Private Bill Office
Private Legislation
Private Bill Committees
Select Committee on the Parliamentary Commissioner
Select Committee on Statutory Instruments
Committee of Selection

Journal Office
Journal
Votes and Proceedings
Research
Committee of Privileges
Select Committee on Public Petitions

Table Office
Questions
Motions
Order Paper

Clerk of Select Committees
Expenditure
Nationalised Industries
Procedure
Public Accounts
Race Relations and Immigration
Science and Technology
Scottish Affairs
Ad hoc Committees

Overseas Office
Commonwealth
Foreign
International
Lectures
Public Relations
Training

Clerk/Administrator
Services of the House

Figure 2.1 DEPARTMENT OF THE CLERK OF THE HOUSE

organised into six Offices for this purpose (see Figure 2.1) and the establishment of Clerks is forty-six,[1] all of whom, provided they have obtained an honours degree at a university, are appointed after selection in the open competitive examination for the higher civil service. The various grades of Clerk are linked with grades in the civil service, which in 1973 were:

Clerk of the House	Permanent Secretary
Clerk Assistant and	Deputy Secretary
Second Clerk Assistant	
Principal Clerk	Under Secretary
Deputy Principal Clerk	Assistant Secretary
Senior Clerk	Principal
Assistant Clerk	Higher Executive Officer (A) or
	Administration Trainee

Clerks, of course, are not civil servants but owe their allegiance wholly to the House and do not serve the Government of the day.

The responsibilities of the Department are exercised through the following Offices:

The Table Office
The Public Bill Office
The Journal Office
The Committee Office
The Private Bill Office
The Overseas Office

2.3 THE CLERKS AT THE TABLE

During sittings the service of the House itself is maintained by the Clerks who sit at the Table. They keep the minutes of proceedings, which are subsequently printed and published as the *Votes and Proceedings of the House of Commons*. They also advise the occupant of the Chair – and any other Member who may wish to consult them – on any parliamentary problem that may arise.

[1] This is the establishment as of February 1972. There were in fact forty-eight Clerks then. One of the additional Clerks is serving as specialist adviser to the Expenditure Committee.

The most senior of these is the Clerk of the House of Commons, whose position has been officially recognised for many centuries and who is now the acknowledged expert in the House on parliamentary procedure and precedents. He is also the custodian of records and documents. On taking office the Clerk makes a declaration under the *Promissory Oaths Act 1868* before the Lord Chancellor 'to make true entries, remembrances, and journals of things done and passed in the House of Commons'. He signs the addresses, votes of thanks and orders of the House; endorses bills sent or returned to the Lords; and reads whatever is required to be read in the House. As Accounting Officer, the Clerk is responsible for the House of Commons Vote, including expenditures by other Departments in the House, and may be called to give evidence before the Public Accounts Committee to explain his stewardship. The Clerk also advises the Leader of the House of Commons on procedural and administrative matters falling within his competence.

The Clerk Assistant and Second Clerk Assistant are both appointed by the Crown on the recommendation of the Speaker and can only be removed upon an Address of the House of Commons. The Clerk Assistant is Clerk to Committees of the whole House and although the business of Supply and Ways and Means are no longer taken in Committees of the whole House, the Clerk Assistant retains his traditional role of advising the House on these matters. The Second Clerk Assistant at present holds the appointment of Clerk of Committees and is responsible for co-ordinating the working of standing and select committees, and with the Clerk of the House for advising on the working of the committee system. He rarely sits at the Table – usually only on formal occasions such as the opening of a new Parliament.

The Principal Clerk of the Table Office, however, performs regular duty at the Table in addition to his responsibilities as the Head of his Office. So, also, does the Clerk of the Overseas Office.

2.4   THE TABLE OFFICE

The main office is situated behind the Speaker's Chair and has, in addition to the Principal Clerk, a Deputy Principal Clerk and three Senior Clerks. The main responsibilities of the Table Office are for giving advice on, and for the receipt and printing of, Questions and notices of motions, and for the Order Paper of the House. Questions and motions will be considered in this section, and the Order Paper in a later section.

Although Questions and notices of motions can be handed in to the Clerks at the Table, it is more customary to send them, or take them personally, to the Table Office. A Member may wish to question a Minister on many different matters – on major public policy, or policies affecting the Member's constituency, or the individual case of one of his constituents. Whatever the scope of the Question, it must conform to the rules or order relating to the form and content of Questions. In addition to advising Members on the rules of order relating to Questions the Clerks in the Table Office give general procedural and factual advice to Members on the business of the House.

When a Member takes his Question to the Table Office, he will have a clear idea of its purpose, but there are many restraints of which the Clerks will advise him and with which his Question must comply. The rules that have been built up over many years through rulings from the Speaker are set out in Erskine May.[1] A basic requirement is that a Question may only be asked to seek information or to press for action. In either case it must concern a matter within a Minister's legal powers and within his responsibility. Questions may not cover matters which have been answered previously in a session, and an elaborate index is maintained to complement the memory of the Clerks who read the Questions and answers in *Hansard* each day. Among other rules there are restrictions concerning matters that are *sub judice*; offensive expressions; and reflections on the conduct of the Speaker, judges and peers. The practice has grown up, due to the difficulties involved, of Members using their first Question as a lead into the real subject about which they want to examine a Minister. Supplementary Questions are of course subject to the same rules as Questions of which notice has been given; yet in the spontaneity of the occasion Members are frequently able to circumvent some of the restrictions.[2]

[1] *Treatise on the Law, Privileges, Proceedings and Usage of Parliament*, pp 319–31, Butterworth (eighteenth edition, 1971).

[2] For a detailed discussion of Parliamentary Questions see D. N. Chester and N. Bowring, *Questions in Parliament*, Clarendon Press (1962); and D. N. Chester, 'Questions in Parliament', in A. H. Hanson and Bernard Crick (editors), *The Commons in Transition*, pp 93–113, Fontana (1970).

2.5   THE PUBLIC BILL OFFICE

This Office is situated above the Commons chamber on the Clerk of the House floor and can be reached either by the lift on the right of the Vote Office, off the Member's Lobby, or by the Ministers' lift behind the Speaker's Chair near the Table Office. The Office is concerned with the passage of all public bills through the House of Commons.[1] It is served by two Principal Clerks (the Clerk of Public Bills and the Clerk of Standing Committees), two Deputy Principal Clerks, a Senior Clerk and an Assistant Clerk.

The Office is responsible for examining drafts of Government public bills to ensure that they conform with the rules of the House. This means that matters with which the bills deal must be covered by the title, provisions involving expenditure must be printed in italics, and the explanatory memorandum must be factual and not argumentative. A general supervision is maintained during the passage of bills. During the committee and report stages, the Clerks are responsible for advising the Chair on the selection of amendments and on proceedings on bills. The Office provides standing committees with Clerks who sit on the dais in the committee room on the Chairman's left and whose advice is available not only to the chairman but to all members of the committee. Amendments that can be proposed to a particular bill are limited by the rules of the House, the long title and the relevant money resolution. For this reason, private Members who wish to put down amendments often seek prior advice from the Public Bill Office so that their amendments are not ruled out for technical reasons.

The Clerks also assist Members regarding Private Members' Bills. One of the Deputy Principal Clerks is particularly concerned with such bills and is Clerk to the standing committee that considers them. The Office organises the ballot for Private Members' Bills (and Motions) for a place on a Friday set aside for their consideration.[2] Although not qualified as a parliamentary draftsman, the Clerk may assist a Member in drafting his bill if he has no other source of assistance available. Some

---

[1] Public bills relate to matters of public policy and usually have general application over the entire nation.

[2] Private Members' Motions are also debated on certain Mondays.

bills, such as the *Chronically Sick and Disabled Persons Act 1970*, eventually become law after such a beginning, but are generally heavily amended by the Government in the process. In November 1971 the House agreed to a proposal that each of the Members who secured the first ten places in the ballot for Private Members' Bills could claim payment of not more than £200 towards the cost of drafting assistance for such bills. It is too early as yet to judge the extent to which Members will make use of this allowance.

However a Private Members' Bill may be conceived, the Member in charge can obtain advice from Clerks at every legislative stage but the lack of parliamentary time, which is limited by standing order, is often an obstacle to the passage of such bills through the House. As a result of pressure of time, only about one Private Members' Bill in six becomes law and most of those that are successful are on uncontroversial and minor matters or are bills drafted by the Government which are waiting in the legislative queue. Important social measures such as the Divorce Reform Act and the Abortion Act which started as Private Members' Bills passed into law because the Government gave up some of its time for their consideration.[1]

The Public Bill Office provides some other important legislative services. The Assistant Clerk is Clerk to the Joint Committee on Consolidation &c Bills, which considers consolidation measures proposed by the Law Commissions to codify and simplify the law. One of the Deputy Principal Clerks superintends the compilation of division lists, while the senior Deputy Principal Clerk is responsible, with the Clerk Assistant, for advice to the Speaker on the business of Supply and on Consolidated Fund bills. A Public Bill List is published weekly showing the stage that each bill has reached in its passage through the Commons and the date on which the next stage is due to be taken.

2.6   THE JOURNAL OFFICE

This Office, like the Public Bill Office, is situated above the chamber of the House. It is staffed by a Principal Clerk, two

---

[1] For a more detailed discussion of Private Members' Bills see Peter G. Richards, *Parliament and Conscience*, Allen & Unwin (1970); and P. A. Bromhead, *Private Members' Bills in the British Parliament*, Routledge and Kegan Paul (1956).

Deputy Principal Clerks, a Senior Clerk and two Assistant Clerks. The Office is responsible for the compilation of the daily *Votes and Proceedings* and the *Journal of the House of Commons*, which is published annually. The *Journal* is the official record of the decisions and proceedings of the House and of all papers presented to it. It is not concerned with speeches, which are recorded in the *Official Report* (*Hansard*), the staff of which is in the Department of the Speaker (see Chapter 4). This Office also does research on questions of procedure to provide background material on problems raised or anticipated during sittings of the House. The annual and decennial indices of the *Journal* act as an important part of the corporate memory of the Department.

The Head of the Office, the Clerk of the Journals, has special responsibility for the maintenance of the general rules of the House on which he guides and co-ordinates the work of all other Offices in the Clerk's Department. He also acts as Clerk of the Committee of Privileges, the oldest and constitutionally the most important select committee of the House. One of the Assistant Clerks is Clerk to the Committee on Public Petitions and is responsible for giving advice both to Members and to the public on the drawing up and presentation of public petitions. In order to ensure that its signatures are not invalidated by technical errors, a Member's petition is generally checked by the Journal Office before the collection of signatures has begun. In addition a Member must have a completed petition endorsed, as being in order, by a Clerk in the Journal Office before he may be called by the Speaker to present it.

Perhaps the most frequent contact which Members have with the Journal Office is occasioned by its responsibility for delegated legislation. In addition to recording the laying of parliamentary papers and statutory instruments, the Office will advise Members on the opportunities which they might have to debate or oppose items of delegated legislation. A Member who wishes to challenge the use of such powers by the Government can call upon the Journal Office to identify what he must do to bring the instrument before the House.

Some orders which require an affirmative resolution must come before the House, and motions to approve them will be placed amongst the 'Remaining Orders of the Day' by the

Government. However, other orders can be debated, and perhaps rejected, only if a motion that they be annulled or negatived is proposed within a certain period of time. To assist Members, the Office produces a weekly Statutory Instruments List which includes details of all statutory instruments subject to negative resolution procedure and the number of days which remain for action to be taken against them. The Office also provides briefs for the use of the Speaker and the Table relating to statutory instruments which come before the House for debate.

2.7 THE COMMITTEE OFFICE

This is the largest Office in the Department, occupying rooms at the north end of the committee corridor. It is staffed by two Principal Clerks, seven Deputy Principal Clerks, eight Senior Clerks and three Assistant Clerks. The Office provides Clerks for most of the select committees of the House, among which are the Public Accounts Committee, the Select Committee on Nationalised Industries and the Expenditure Committee. The Expenditure Committee has its own Principal Clerk and specialist adviser and is sub-divided into several subcommittees, each with its own Clerk. The Committee Office also provides the Clerks to the specialist select committees established to examine specific areas of governmental activity, including the policy involved. In addition, whenever the House sets up an *ad hoc* committee, such as the Select Committee on the Civil List in 1970–71, a Clerk usually from the Committee Office is appointed to serve it.

The Clerk to a committee performs many different tasks. In the first place he is responsible for advising the chairman and members on matters of procedure and keeps the minutes of proceedings which are appended to the report of a committee when it has completed its work. Secondly, the Clerk assists his committee in planning their inquiry, arranges the summoning of witnesses, provides briefs for the chairman, and collects and analyses factual information. Thirdly, at the conclusion of the inquiry, the Clerk prepares the heads of report and then a draft report for the chairman based on the deliberations of the committee. He might also draft amendments to the report or alternative reports for members of the committee who were dissatisfied with the chairman's report.

2.8   THE PRIVATE BILL OFFICE

This is situated next to the Committee Office, and is staffed by a Principal Clerk, a Deputy Principal Clerk and two Senior Clerks. The Office is responsible for supervising proceedings on private bills. These are bills that confirm particular powers or benefits on any person or body of persons, including individuals, local authorities, statutory companies and private corporations. Private bills are distinct from Private Members' Bills which are public bills and are dealt with by the Public Bill Office. The practice of the House in regard to private business is largely regulated by a separate series of standing orders, and it is the duty of the Private Bill Office to see that these are complied with by the various parties, including petitioners and parliamentary agents.

This Office provides Clerks for committees on private bills, on special procedure orders and on similar matters, and also for the Committee of Selection, which appoints members of standing committees. The Head of the Office, the Clerk of Private Bills, acts also as Clerk to the Select Committee on the Parliamentary Commissioner for Administration. A Senior Clerk is attached permanently to the Chairman of Ways and Means, who has general oversight of private business in the House, as his official secretary and he assists Members in their relations with the Chairman. This Clerk acts also as Clerk to the Committee on Unopposed (private) Bills and to the Select Committee on Statutory Instruments.

All relevant documents on private bills are available to Members in the Private Bill Office until the rising of the House. Papers on private *acts* are kept in the Victoria Tower and can be made available when the House is sitting and during recesses by making a request to the House of Lords Record Office between 8.45 a.m. and 5.30 p.m.

2.9   THE OVERSEAS OFFICE

This Office, situated above the chamber like the Public Bill and Journal Offices, is staffed by a Principal Clerk, a Deputy Principal Clerk, three Assistant Clerks and a Higher Executive Officer. A main concern of the Office is with the work of

Commonwealth legislatures, assisting them in procedural and administrative matters, for example in the drafting or interpretation of standing orders or the establishment of a parliamentary secretariat. Similar help is given to foreign legislatures when this is requested. This sometimes takes the form of a visit by a Clerk to countries in need of advice. Clerks from overseas legislatures regularly come to Westminster on exchange visits or attachments to study the work of the House at close hand. They spend periods in each of the Offices of the Department and attend debates in the House and meetings of committees.

The Office also gives procedural assistance to European Assemblies and their committees. The House of Commons sends delegations to the European Parliament, to the Assemblies of the Council of Europe and Western European Union, and to the North Atlantic Assembly, as well as sending Members to serve on many committees of these Assemblies. Administrative and procedural guidance is provided by the Office to Members attending such meetings and Members going to international gatherings find the presence of a Clerk of great assistance when faced with procedural complexities of Assemblies whose traditions are very different from those of the British Parliament.

The Overseas Office is also responsible for various public relations and educational duties in Britain. One of these tasks is to arrange for a Clerk, usually from the Overseas Office, to lecture at the Civil Service College on the work of Parliament. The Office is also in close touch with the Central Office of Information to provide advice to Parliamentary visitors coming to Britain and to ensure that information disseminated by the COI concerning Parliament is accurate and up to date.

2.10   CLERK ADMINISTRATOR

The Department also provides a Principal Clerk to be Clerk of the Services Committee and Clerk Administrator. He is assisted by a Higher Executive Officer. The post of Clerk Administrator is normally combined with the headship of the independent Administration Department, the appointment to which is the responsibility of the Speaker (for further details, see section 1.4).

2.11   THE 'VOTE'

The working papers of the House of Commons prepared by the Offices of the Clerk's Department and printed under the direction of the Vote Superintendent are collectively known as 'the Vote'. A bundle of these papers, of varying thickness, is issued each sitting day to Members, Government Departments, Clerks and other officers of the House. It is not a confidential document and can be used, for example, by the Lobby, the press and the general public. It is a complicated collection of technical papers concerned with the business of the House and as such requires explanation. Its main components are:

The Order Paper.
The Remaining Orders of the Day and Notices of Motions.
New Notices relating to private business.
The *Votes and Proceedings*.
New Notices of Questions and Motions.
Division lists.
Lists of amendments to bills to be considered in Committee of the whole House or on report at the day's sitting.
Lists of amendments to bills to be considered during the day in standing committee.
Standing committee proceedings.
Notices of amendments to bills for a future day.

Members may receive the whole bundle of papers (the complete Vote) or the part Vote. The latter consists of only the Order Paper and lists of amendments to bills to be considered in Committee of the whole House or on report at that day's sitting. In addition, Members may obtain the Order Paper, the Notice Paper relating to Questions and motions, and the *Votes and Proceedings* separately on demand from the Vote Office.

2.11.1   *The Order Paper*
Several changes have been made in the format of the Order Paper (see Figure 2.2) in recent years as a result of recommendations of select committees of the House. In 1960, on the advice of the Select Committee on Publications and Debates Reports,[1]

[1] H.C. 420, 1955–56, pp iv–v.

No. 132   **TUESDAY 13TH JUNE 1972**   8095

ORDER PAPER

PRIVATE BUSINESS AFTER PRAYERS

CONSIDERATION OF LORDS AMENDMENTS

BILL WITH AN AMENDMENT*

Mersey Tunnel Bill.

[* *A copy of the Amendment may be seen in the Private Bill Office*]

THIRD READING

Thames Conservancy Bill.

CONSIDERATION OF BILLS ORDERED TO LIE UPON THE TABLE

1 Essex River Authority Bill.

2 Greater London Council (General Powers) Bill.

3 Selnec (Manchester Central Area Railway, etc.) Bill.

THIRD READING

Greater London Council (Money) Bill. (*By Order.*)

Mr Douglas Jay
Mr Nigel Spearing
   On Third Reading of Greater London Council (Money) Bill, to move, That the Bill be read the third time upon this day six months.

CONSIDERATION OF BILLS

1 United Reformed Church Bill [*Lords*]. (*By Order.*)

The Reverend Ian Paisley
   On Consideration of United Reformed Church Bill [*Lords*], as amended, to move, That the Bill be considered upon this day six months.

2 West Sussex County Council Bill. (*By Order.*).

Mr Jerry Wiggin
Mr John Golding
Mr James Wellbeloved
Mr William Hamling
   On Consideration of West Sussex County Council Bill, as amended, to move, That the Bill be considered upon this day six months.

   26 Y

Figure 2.2

8096   **Order Paper: 13th June 1972**   **No. 132**

Mr John Golding
Mr James Wellbeloved
Mr William Hamling
Mr Arthur Davidson

On Consideration of West Sussex County Council Bill, as amended: —

Page 22, line 40, leave out Clause 43.

Page 26, line 14, leave out Clause 44.

QUESTIONS FOR ORAL ANSWER

Questions to the Prime Minister (see pp. 8102-03) will begin at 3.15 p.m.

✱ 1 **Mr David Clark** (Colne Valley) : To ask the Secretary of State for Social Services, what recent representations he has received asking him to raise the age of exemption for the payment of prescription charges from 15 years of age to 16 years, on the raising of the school leaving age.

✱ 2 **Mr Ralph Howell** (North Norfolk) : To ask the Secretary of State for Social Services, if, to help his formation of policy on payment of supplementary benefit to dependants of strikers, he will examine the practice in other countries, and publish his findings.

8102   **Order Paper: 13th June 1972**   **No. 132**

✱ 74 **Mr Bruce Millan** (Glasgow, Craigton) : To ask the Secretary of State for Trade and Industry, if he will publish a table comparing the discounted value to industry as a percentage of the cost of investment, of the new investment incentives set out in the White Paper, Industrial and Regional Development, Command Paper No. 4942, and of the previous two investment incentives systems operating at 26th October 1970 and from 27th October 1970, respectively, distinguishing between assisted and non-assisted areas and assuming that firms do not have sufficient profit to take advantage of tax allowances as early as possible.

Questions to the Prime Minister will begin at 3.15 p.m.

✱Q 1 **Mr Frank Allaun** (Salford, East) : To ask the Prime Minister, what communication he has had with President Nixon about the Vietnam war since the Summit talks in Moscow.

✱Q 2 **Mr Leslie Huckfield** (Nuneaton): To ask the Prime Minister, what discussions he has now held with President Nixon about the mining of Haiphong harbour and the escalation of United States bombing of North Vietnam.

✱Q 3 **Mr Jack Ashley** (Stoke-on-Trent, South) : To ask the Prime Minister, when he next proposes to hold discussions with the Trades Union Congress and the Confederation of British Industry.

✱Q 4 **Mr Norman St. John-Stevas** (Chelmsford) : To ask the Prime Minister, if he is satisfied with the co-ordination between the Ministers concerned in relation to the arrangements being made on the Government's behalf to celebrate British entry into the European Economic Community next year ; and if he will make a statement.

Figure 2.2   *Continued*

62 THE HOUSE OF COMMONS

QUESTIONS FOR ORAL ANSWER—*continued*

∗Q 5 **Mr Peter Blaker** (Blackpool, South): To ask the Prime Minister what autobiographies of former Cabinet Ministers have been acquired for the library of No. 10 Downing Street since 1st January 1972.

∗Q 6 **Mr Dennis Skinner** (Bolsover): To ask the Prime Minister, whether he is satisfied with the co-ordination between the Departments of Trade and Industry and Environment in the preparation of Government evidence for the Stockholm conference on pollution ; and if he will make a statement.

∗Q 7 **Mr Robert Adley** (Bristol, North-East) : To ask the Prime Minister, if he is satisfied with the co-ordination between the Secretaries of State for Trade and Industry, Scotland and Wales on proposals for hotel registration and classification ; and if he will make a statement.

∗Q 8 **Mr W. W. Hamilton** (West Fife): To ask the Prime Minister, if he will take steps to improve the quality and quantity of statistical information supplied by Government departments.

∗Q 9 **Sir Gilbert Longden** (South-West Hertfordshire): To ask the Prime Minister, if he will invite the Leader of the Opposition to attend the next meeting of the National Economic Development Council.

∗Q10 **Mr Phillip Whitehead** (Derby, North): To ask the Prime Minister, what communications he has had since 23rd May with Mr Ian Smith and the illegal régime in Rhodesia.

∗Q11 **Mr Gavin Strang** (Edinburgh, East): To ask the Prime Minister, if he is satisfied with the co-ordination between the Department of Trade and Industry and the Scottish Office regarding the development of Scotland's industrial infrastructure as a consequence of the recent appointment of new Ministers ; and if he will make a statement.

∗Q12 **Mr Dick Douglas** (Clackmannan and East Stirlingshire): To ask the Prime Minister, how the representatives of the Scottish Council (Development and Industry) were informed of the unemployment figures for May at his meeting on 12th May, in advance of their official publication on 18th May.

∗Q13 **Mr Edward M. Taylor** (Glasgow, Cathcart): To ask the Prime Minister, if he is satisfied with the co-ordination of the activities of Government Ministers responsible for Government policy relating to protection of purchasers of all goods and services ; and if he will make a statement.

∗Q14 **Mr John Biggs-Davison** (Chigwell): To ask the Prime Minister, whether he will now invite the Irish Prime Minister to make an official visit to London.

AT THE COMMENCEMENT OF PUBLIC BUSINESS

Notice of Presentation of Bill

Mr Marcus Worsley

PROTECTED TENANCIES (AMENDMENT): Bill to amend section 1 of the Rent Act 1968 to enable dwelling houses of any rateable value to qualify under the provisions of that section relating to protected tenancies.

Figure 2.2   *Continued*

AT TEN O'CLOCK

Notice of Motion

The Prime Minister

BUSINESS OF THE HOUSE: That the Order of the Day relating to House of Commons (Services) and the Motions relating to Parliamentary Expenses may be proceeded with at this day's Sitting, though opposed, until any hour.

To be moved after the interruption of Business at Ten o'clock and to be decided forthwith, pursuant to Standing Order No. 3.

ORDERS OF THE DAY AND NOTICES OF MOTIONS

Those marked thus * are Government Orders of the Day

* **1** EUROPEAN COMMUNITIES BILL [4th allotted Day]:   Committee [*Progress, 8th June*].

       For Amendments, see separate Paper

* **2** HOUSE OF COMMONS (SERVICES): Adjourned Debate on Question [9th June].

       And a Motion being made, and the Question being proposed, That this House doth agree with the Select Committee on House of Commons (Services) in their Fourth Report—(*Mr Robert Carr*):—

3 *PARLIAMENTARY EXPENSES*

Mr Robert Carr

       That, in the opinion of this House, provision should be made as from 1st April 1972 for the reimbursement to any Member, within a maximum of £60, of two-thirds of the cost of a commercial course of study which he has completed in a European Economic Community language.

       As Amendments to Mr Robert Carr's proposed Motion (Parliamentary Expenses):

Mr Arthur Lewis

       Line **2**, after 'any', insert 'businessman, company or taxpayer engaged in work connected with the furtherance of British exports and to any'.

Mr Eric Deakins

       Line **3**, leave out 'commercial'.

Mr Edward Lyons

       Line **3**, leave out 'European Economic Community' and insert 'foreign'.

Mr Eric Deakins

       Line **4**, at end add 'provided that the Member has not studied the said language for four or more years at the secondary level of education'.

Figure 2.2   *Continued*

ORDERS OF THE DAY AND NOTICES OF MOTIONS—*continued*

4 *PARLIAMENTARY EXPENSES*

Mr Robert Carr

That, in the opinion of this House, provision should be made as from 1st April 1972 for the reimbursement of expenses incurred by Members in travelling outside their constituencies, both within the United Kingdom and overseas, for the purpose of informing themselves on subjects of relevance to their Parliamentary work.

As an Amendment to Mr Robert Carr's proposed Motion (Parliamentary Expenses):

Mr Arthur Lewis

Line **4**, at end add ' but such provisions must be operated on a genuinely fair and unbiased basis, whereby all Members will be entitled to be considered for participation in such arrangements and that the past practices of the regular selection of the privileged chosen few, as in the case of the so called " Delegates " to the Council of Europe, Western European Union and other Consultative and representative assemblies and appointments to lecture tours in America and other foreign countries, visits to the forces overseas and to foreign countries, &c., must not be practised with regard to the implementation of this Resolution and towards this end, and full details of the proposed selections and appointments to all such overseas visits must be done by a debatable Motion in the House of Commons '.

On the Motion for the Adjournment of the House under Standing Order No. 1 Mr Robert Adley proposes to raise the subject of shoplifting and supermarkets.

PUBLIC COMMITTEES

1	Standing Committee D (further to consider the National Insurance Bill)	10.30	Room 8
2	Standing Committee G (further to consider the Horserace Totalisator and Betting Levy Boards Bill)	10.30	Room 11
3	Standing Committee H (further to consider the Industry Bill) ...	10.30	Room 14
4	First Scottish Standing Committee (further to consider the National Health Service (Scotland) Bill [*Lords*])	10.30	Room 12
5	Expenditure: Defence and External Affairs Sub-Committee ...	11.15	R.O.F., Leeds
6	Expenditure: Environment and Home Office Sub-Committee ...	4.00	Room 13
7	Nationalised Industries: Sub-Committee A	4.00	Room 8
8	Scottish Affairs: Sub-Committee A	4.15	Room 15
9	Statutory Instruments	4.15	Room 9
10	Science and Technology	4.30	Room 7
11	House of Commons (Services)	4.30	Room 16
12	Expenditure: Public Expenditure (General) Sub-Committee ...	5.00	Room 6
13	Privileges (to consider Chairman's Draft Report)	6.00	Room 13

Figure 2.2   *Continued*

8106   **Order Paper: 13th June 1972**   **No. 132**

COMMITTEE ON A PRIVATE BILL

Anglesey Marine Terminal Bill [Lords]   ...   .   10.30   Room 5

QUESTIONS FOR WRITTEN ANSWER

Questions handed in on Monday 12th June are marked thus ¶

1 **Mr Laurie Pavitt** (Willesden, West): To ask the Secretary of State for Social Services, if he will establish a working party to inquire into the misuse of barbiturate sleeping pills and to recommend action to deal with this problem.

2 **Mr Laurie Pavitt** (Willesden, West): To ask the Secretary of State for Social Services, if he will take steps to ensure that all manufacturers of barbiturate preparations include in all their literature and advertisements warnings in large and distinctive type about porphyria.

3 **Mr Laurie Pavitt** (Willesden, West): To ask the Secretary of State for Social Services, if he will institute a penalty for doctors who pre-sign blank prescription forms.

4 **Mr Michael Barnes** (Brentford and Chiswick): To ask the Secretary of State for Social Services, by how much supplementary benefit rates have risen in real terms since 1960.

5 **Mr Michael Barnes** (Brentford and Chiswick): To ask the Secretary of State for Social Services, on how many occasions the Supplementay Benefits Commission has applied to the High Court for a prorogative order to overrule the determination of a Supplementary Benefits Appeal Tribunal on the grounds that the Tribunal has made its determination in ignorance of or as the result of a mistake regarding some material fact.

6 **Mr Laurie Pavitt** (Willesden, West): To ask the Secretary of State for Social Services, if he will publish in the Official Report the names of drugs which have been approved by the secretariat of the Medicines Commission without undergoing any clinical trial in Great Britain.

No. 132   **Order Paper: 13th June 1972**   **8117**

140 **Mr Ron Lewis** (Carlisle): To ask the Secretary of State for the Home Department, if he will now make a detailed statement on the present position regarding the sale of the Carlisle and District State Management Scheme.   ¶

141 **Mr Ron Lewis** (Carlisle): To ask the Secretary of State for the Home Department, if he will give an indication as to when he now expects to receive the Erroll Report on Licensing ; and if he will make a statement.   ¶

142 **Mr Frank Judd** (Portsmouth, West): To ask the Secretary of State for Foreign and Commonwealth Affairs, what investigations he made, before deciding on Her Majesty's Government's contribution, into the details of the compensation being provided in Rhodesia to wives and families of victims of the Wankie Colliery disaster with special reference to the rates of compensation available to those of different racial groups ; and whether he will publish in the Official Report details of how the British contribution to the special relief fund will be divided between those of different racial groups.   ¶

Figure 2.2 *Continued*

Mr Speaker decided that papers relating to the current sitting and papers relating to future sittings should be distinguished by printing them on different coloured paper. As a result current papers are now printed on white and notice papers on blue paper. A change was also made to insert a black line between effective Orders of the day and non-effective or remaining Orders of the day. A logical development from this was the recommendation of the Services Committee,[1] accepted in 1966, that the remaining Orders be dropped from the Order Paper and printed on a separate sheet. When implemented, this change made the Order Paper correspond more nearly to the agenda of the House. Also in 1966, the insertion in the Order Paper of a list of sessional printed papers delivered on the previous day was discontinued. This was possible because a record of these papers was included in the *Votes and Proceedings* and also on a twice-weekly pink demand form issued to Members for use in ordering papers.

Besides simplification of the contents of the Order Paper, rubrics were added to certain items to make them more informative. For example, where it was intended to take committee and remaining stages of a particular bill on one day, that fact was noted in an italicised rubric beneath the appropriate Order of the Day. A change was also made in regard to the business motion providing for exemption from the Ten O'Clock Rule. It was removed from the section of motions to be moved at the commencement of public business and placed under a separate heading indicating that it was to be moved at 10 p.m. Other minor changes were also made.

The Order Paper shows the date at the top, below which are the words ORDER PAPER, and underneath them a black horizontal line extending across the width of the paper. Below this line on most sitting days is a list of private bills, and sometimes provisional order bills. This list is headed PRIVATE BUSINESS AFTER PRAYERS. The various stages of these items are the first items of business to be taken at the sitting. They can, however, pass only if unopposed, as debate is not allowed and the proceedings must in any case conclude by 2.45 p.m. at the latest, although it is usually much before this time. After the last item on the list there is another long black horizontal line.

The next item, except on Fridays, is QUESTIONS FOR ORAL

[1] 2nd Report, 1966–67, H.C. 94, p 5.

ANSWER. These are grouped by Ministries according to a rota system which enables each Minister to be questioned by turn over a period of weeks. The Prime Minister's place in the rota is on Tuesdays and Thursdays when he answers Questions from 3.15 to 3.30 p.m. There is no limit to the total number of oral questions on any one day, but it is unusual for more than forty to forty-five to be disposed of in the House at one sitting. Individual Members are restricted to two oral questions per day, each to a different Minister, any surplus over this number being placed at the end of the Order Paper among the Questions to be answered by a written reply. There is also an overall limit of eight Questions within ten sitting days.

Questions are followed by the usual black line after which come Notices of Motion, such as motions for Ten-Minute Rule bills or for the suspension of the Ten O'Clock Rule to enable the House to continue its business beyond 10 p.m. This latter motion is not taken in the House until 10 p.m., as explained by an italicised rubric under the motion. Each notice of motion is preceded by the heading AT THE COMMENCEMENT OF PUBLIC BUSINESS or AT TEN O'CLOCK indicating when it will be dealt with by the House. A heavy black line follows.

The next heading is ORDERS OF THE DAY AND NOTICES OF MOTIONS, under which are listed those items of Government business to be taken up at that sitting. These may be a motion to take note of a report; one of the stages of a bill; consideration of an item of delegated legislation; or a mixture of one or more items. Normally all of these items consist of Government business, except on the twenty Fridays which are allotted for Private Members' Bills and motions. The name of the Member who will speak on the motion for the adjournment of the House is printed in italics beneath the last Order of the Day, together with the proposed subject for discussion.

After the next black line one finds a list of PUBLIC COMMITTEES and COMMITTEES ON PRIVATE BILLS, which sit during the day although there may be days, for example a Friday, on which no committee is meeting. The list shows the hour at which the committee will meet and the room allotted to the committee. Finally, and again below a black line, come the QUESTIONS FOR WRITTEN ANSWER. Unlike Questions for oral answer, a Member may ask an unlimited number.

No one day's business is the same as another's, and the foregoing description includes items which are not daily features of the Order Paper, as well as excluding some other items.[1]

2.11.2 *Remaining Orders of the Day*
The second component in the bundle, which is separate from the Order Paper, consists of the REMAINING ORDERS OF THE DAY AND NOTICES OF MOTIONS. These have constituted a separate paper since October 1966, as noted above. They include all items of business formally put down by the Government for consideration (in the case of motions) and all orders of the day, e.g. a stage of a public bill, which are formally before the House. Apart from stages of public bills, the most common items are motions to approve statutory instruments. They are technically 'before the House' in the same way as the Orders of the Day, but will not be reached on the same day because the Government will interpose a motion for adjournment before this can happen. For this reason, and to avoid confusion, they are now printed on separate sheets of paper. Some of these items – mainly those originating with the Government – are dealt with by the House at a later date.

2.11.3 *Private Business*
Whereas the previously mentioned components of the 'Vote' are printed on white paper, the third component – Private Business – is printed on blue paper. The Private Business list is a consolidated list of all NOTICES RELATING TO PRIVATE BUSINESS DEPOSITED ON (date), both in the House and in committee.

2.11.4 *Votes and Proceedings*
Another separate item in the bundle is the VOTES AND PROCEEDINGS OF THE HOUSE OF COMMONS, which is printed on white paper. These are the minutes of the previous day's sitting and constitute a complete record of everything which happened in the House, apart from Question hour which originated as an informal proceeding and therefore was not noted in the *Votes and Proceedings* and *Journal*.

The first few entries relate to the fairly formal proceedings

---

[1] Examples of items not included are: Notices of Presentation of Bills and Notices of Motions for Unopposed Returns.

which take place before Questions. There may be the answer to an Address of the House to the Sovereign, notification by the Speaker of the death of a Member, the moving of a new writ for a by-election, the transaction of private business, or the presentation of a public petition. Following these entries, a formal entry is made drawing attention to the listing of all papers presented to the House in an appendix to the Vote. Reports from committees that have that day completed their tasks – whether in connection with inquiries, bills or other functions – are then recorded, followed by any messages received from the House of Lords. Next may be entered a note of a new Member who has taken the oath or made affirmation on taking his seat. Immediately preceding the main business, the presentation of bills is recorded. The chronological business of the day is then factually recorded, which in the case of the committee stage of a bill may mean several pages. The results of all votes are given and the names of tellers are shown. Finally the adjournment and time of rising is minuted. These are just a few examples of the entries which appear daily in the *Votes and Proceedings*, which, when translated into the *Journal*, constitute the official record of the House. The *Journal* alone is recognised in courts of law as a definitive record.

2.11.5   *Notices of Questions and Motions*

A fifth component, on blue paper, is a list of NOTICES OF QUESTIONS AND MOTIONS GIVEN ON (previous day). This can account for quite a number of pages: an average number of Questions is about 200 which might take up twenty pages. Motions can account for anything from fifteen to thirty pages. It is not only new Questions which are shown, but also those which have been transferred from one Minister to another or which have been deferred by the Member until a later date. Motions are usually those for 'an early day', one of the parliamentary ways open to Members to record expressions of opinion and to indicate the backing behind such views.[1] Motions may be newly put down, or they may be old motions to which Members have added their names. Motions that are put down

[1] For a detailed study of 'early day' motions see S. E. Finer, H. B. Berrington and D. J. Bartholomew, *Backbench Opinion in the House of Commons, 1955–59*, Pergamon (1961).

for a specific date may be Government or official Opposition motions relative to an item of business which is to be taken on that date. Alternatively, they may be backbench Members' motions put down for one of the days allotted to private Members and for which the Member in question has won a place in the ballot.

2.11.6 *Other Items*
Other items in the bundle, varying from day to day, but each one of them separate, could be:

1 *Division lists.* These record divisions held on the previous day, showing the totals of ayes and noes and giving the names of individual Members voting. The question upon which a division was taken is minuted at the head of the list of names.
2 *Amendment sheets* in respect of bills to be considered in Committee of the whole House or on report at that day's sitting. Amendments of which less than one sitting day's notice has been given are starred. This may mean that the amendment has less chance of being selected.
3 *Amendment sheets* in respect of bills to be considered in standing committee during the day. Such a list might also contain starred amendments.
4 *Standing Committee Proceedings.* This is a version of the amendment sheet made up to incorporate the result of the proceedings of a standing committee on each amendment.
5 *Notices of Amendments* tabled in respect of bills to be considered on future days.

2.11.7 *Vote Superintendent*
Finally, mention may be made of the final production of the various components of the 'Vote'. Working outside the Palace of Westminster, but under the supervision of the Principal Clerk of the Table Office, is the Superintendent of Printing of *Votes and Proceedings* (usually known as the Vote Superintendent), a Higher Executive Officer. This official, with his staff, is the representative of the House at St Stephen's Press, where the work of printing all parliamentary papers is discharged by Her Majesty's Stationery Office. The Vote Superintendent edits and

prepares for the printer all copy received from the Offices of the Clerk's Department. He also corrects the proofs, and checks the final arrangement of the Order Paper, the Notice Paper and the *Votes and Proceedings* before they go to press.

2.12   CONCLUSION

It would seem evident from what has been said in this chapter that the Clerk of the House òf Commons is the most important permanent Officer of the House and the Department of the Clerk is the most important of the five Departments. The office of the Clerk as we have seen predates that of Speaker and the Department of the Clerk is one of the two original Departments of the House of Commons. The importance of the Clerk and his Department arises from the pivotal position that they occupy in the work of the House: none of the services and facilities provided by the other Departments of the House is as fundamental as those provided by the Clerks. The organisation of the business of the House and the smooth-running of its procedures are dependent upon the efficiency of the Clerks. Moreover, individual Members are no less dependent upon them for procedural advice and assistance. This is *not* to lessen the importance of the services and facilities provided by other Departments, but merely to stress the central role of the Department of the Clerk, since any failure on the part of the latter serves only to lessen the value of the assistance rendered by other Departments.

CHAPTER 3

THE DEPARTMENT OF
THE SERJEANT AT ARMS

In keeping with the self-imposed limits of the present study, this chapter is concerned primarily with the existing official services and amenities that are available to MPs through the 'housekeeping' side of the Department of the Serjeant at Arms. As in other chapters, a certain amount of historical background is given where it is relevant to an understanding of the current situation, and a discussion of proposals for the future development of the new parliamentary building in Bridge Street is also included. But we have omitted a number of major issues that have occupied Members and outside observers in the last decade or so – for instance, the 'Mods and Goths' architectural controversy which followed a recommendation to build around New Palace Yard in the Gothic style in 1964.[1] Similarly the far-reaching proposals contained in Sir Leslie Martin's *Whitehall: A Plan for the National and Government Centre*[2] have been deemed to fall outside the scope of this study.

The important question of Members' accommodation at Westminster is, of course, ultimately a matter for the House of Commons to decide upon. More specifically, as we have noted earlier (see section 1.3) the House appoints a Services Committee to advise the Speaker on 'the control of the accommodation ... in that part of the Palace of Westminster and its precincts, occupied by or on behalf of the House of Commons, and to report thereon to this House'. Major issues such as the building of a new underground car park for Members at Westminster, or the erection of a new parliamentary building, are considered by the Services Committee, on behalf of the Speaker and the House. Some of the aspects of accommodation dealt with in this chapter therefore transcend the responsibilities

[1] The Commons debated this recommendation on 13 July 1964; H.C. Deb., 698, cc. 849–981. [2] HMSO (1965).

of the Serjeant at Arms' Department, and are matters for the House of Commons to decide upon. However, administrative day-to-day responsibility rests with the Serjeant at Arms on behalf of the Speaker.[1]

The Serjeant at Arms ranks next in seniority, amongst the permanent officers of the House, to the Clerk. His appointment is in the gift of the Crown, under a warrant from the Lord Chamberlain and by patent under the great seal, 'to attend upon Her Majesty's person when there is no Parliament; and at the time of every Parliament, to attend upon the Speaker of the House of Commons'.[2] It is the Serjeant's duty to bring to the Bar of the House persons in custody who are to be reprimanded by the Speaker, or persons who are to be examined as witnesses. He keeps the gangway at and below the Bar clear. He has various ceremonial duties to perform, including that of attending on the Speaker with the mace when the latter enters or leaves the House. He maintains order in the lobby and passages of the House, and the police on duty in the Commons are under his direction. The Serjeant regulates, under the Speaker, the admission of persons to the press gallery and lobby, and has control of arrangements for the admission of all 'strangers', i.e. persons who are neither members nor officers of the Commons. The Serjeant is also, as we have noted earlier, by statute 'housekeeper' of the House of Commons. These 'housekeeping' duties are very wide indeed, and they form the main substance of what follows in the present chapter.

The duties of the three senior supporting Officers in the Serjeant's Department (see Figure 3.1) are summarised in Erskine May:

'The Serjeant is assisted by a Deputy Serjeant at Arms who, in addition to deputising for him, co-ordinates the work of the Department and has special responsibilities for pay, stores, Staff Board and Press Gallery matters; by an Assistant Serjeant

[1] Much of the information in this chapter has been supplied by courtesy of members of the Serjeant's Department.

[2] Erskine May, *Treatise on the Law, Privileges, Proceedings and Usage of Parliament*, p 232, Butterworth (eighteenth edition, 1971). On the question of consultations made before the appointment of a new Serjeant, see the statement by the Prime Minister (Harold Macmillan) on 8 November 1962. H.C. Deb., 666, cc. 1155–7.

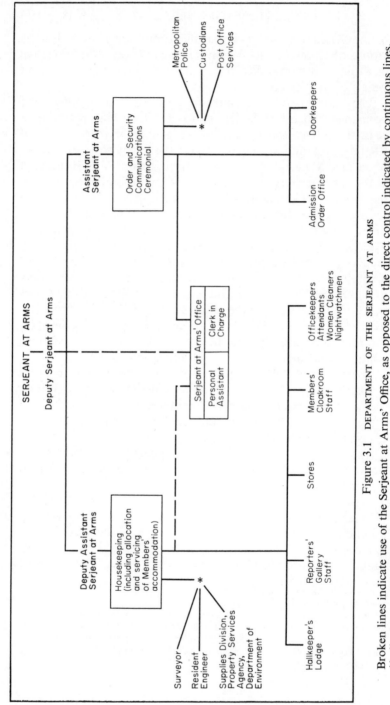

SERJEANT AT ARMS

Deputy Serjeant at Arms

Deputy Assistant Serjeant at Arms

Assistant Serjeant at Arms

Housekeeping (including allocation and servicing of Members' accommodation)

Order and Security
Communications
Ceremonial

*
- Surveyor
- Resident Engineer
- Supplies Division, Property Services Agency, Department of Environment

*
- Metropolitan Police
- Custodians
- Post Office Services

Serjeant at Arms' Office

| Personal Assistant | Clerk in Charge |

Hallkeeper's Lodge

Reporters' Gallery Staff

Stores

Members' Cloakroom Staff

Officekeepers
Attendants
Women Cleaners
Nightwatchmen

Admission Order Office

Doorkeepers

Figure 3.1 DEPARTMENT OF THE SERJEANT AT ARMS

Broken lines indicate use of the Serjeant at Arms' Office, as opposed to the direct control indicated by continuous lines.
*indicates co-ordinating relationship.

who, besides being Executive Officer of the Department and in charge of the office work connected with it, is primarily concerned with the order and ceremonial aspects; and by a Deputy Assistant Serjeant who is concerned with the housekeeping aspects of the Serjeant's duties.'[1]

The supply Estimates for 1972–73 allow for a staff of 152 in the Serjeant's Department. In addition to clerical and secretarial staff, the complement includes two Principal Doorkeepers, thirty-nine Doorkeepers (see section 3.7), six Office Keepers, forty-five attendants, eight nightwatchmen and a large staff of women cleaners.[2]

3.1 ACCOMMODATION FOR INDIVIDUAL MEMBERS

3.1.1 'A Room for Every Member'
On 25 June 1973 the House of Commons approved the construction of 'a new parliamentary building in due course' on a site in Bridge Street, and further resolved that the new building should follow (with certain adjustments where necessary) the architectural design put forward by Robin Spence and Robin Webster.[3] The Leader of the House (James Prior), opening the debate, told Members that at March 1973 prices the overall cost of the new building and all its associated works would be slightly in excess of £33 million, but that the cost of the building itself was estimated at £11 million. The new building – work on which could not begin before the financial year 1975–76 because of restrictions on public expenditure imposed by the Chancellor of the Exchequer – would accommodate 450 Members in single rooms, 450 secretaries and about 300 supporting staff of the House.[4]

The vote at the end of this debate brought to a conclusion a protracted period of discussion (see section 3.11) as to whether a new parliamentary building for Members, secretaries and the staff of the Commons should be built, and as to the design of such a building. For present purposes it will suffice

[1] Erskine May, op. cit., p 235.

[2] The scale of the cleaning job is evident from the following statistic: The amount of waste paper collected annually in the Palace of Westminster amounts to ninety-five tons.

[3] H.C. Deb., 25 June 1973, 858, cc. 1206–76.   [4] Ibid., c. 1210.

to note that, after nine years of public discussion, the House of Commons first approved the construction of a new building on the Bridge Street site in January 1969, and that this decision was followed, in May 1969, by an important report from the Services Committee on *Accommodation in the New Parliamentary Building*.[1] The Committee expressed the hope that the building would provide an area of some 150,000 square feet above ground level, plus 100,000 square feet below ground level.

In the same report it was assumed that 'in due course' every Member would wish to have a room of his own, and that each Member would require adjacent working space for his or her secretary. The report anticipated that 180 Members – including Ministers, Whips, chairmen of committees and the Shadow Cabinet – would continue to be housed in the Palace of Westminster, thus leaving about 450 Members to be provided with a room in the new parliamentary building. An allocation of 180 square feet per Member's room was suggested, and it was stipulated that the rooms should be soundproof. In addition, a minimum area of seventy-five square feet was allowed, in the Committee's report, for each Member's secretary. Thus the Committee envisaged, in May 1969, a total floor-space requirement of 114,750 square feet in the new building.[2]

The Committee were very conscious of the difficulty of planning accommodation which would continue to meet the requirements of Members for many years in the future. Circumstances might well change, and facilities at present unknown might be needed before the end of the century.[3] Nevertheless, the outright statement that every MP should have a room to himself, plus accommodation for a secretary, represented a big step forward. It is certain that the Committee's assumption was based on the growing demand from many Members for increased and better accommodation. Such demands are particularly apparent after general elections when new Members show themselves, for the most part, unwilling to do all their work, while at Westminster, in the busy Commons Library, at writing

---

[1] 3rd Report, Services Committee, 1968–69, H.C. 295.

[2] *Ibid.*, paras. 1–6 and Appendix. In addition, space for House of Commons staff was proposed as follows: about 12,500 sq. ft. for the Clerk's Department; 1,500 sq. ft. for the Serjeant's Department; 3,500 sq. ft. for the Administration Department; 3,500 sq. ft. plus storage space for the Library; and 4,000 sq. ft. of staff sleeping accommodation.   [3] *Ibid.*, para. 51.

places in division lobbies, or in accommodation on interview floors and in writing rooms.

Much argument and discussion was to ensue before the decision in June 1973 to proceed 'in due course' with the new building. In particular, the arguments for and against the proposal for a parliamentary building on the Bridge Street site, and for and against the prize-winning Spence-Webster design, were debated at length in the House of Commons on 9 March 1973.[1] However, the long-term prospects, as regards accommodation, are now clear.

3.1.2 Developments Since 1951

A simplified, chronological summary of post-war developments in relation to Members' accommodation will help to set the current position in perspective.

When the new chamber was opened in 1950, the only desks available to backbench Members – apart from writing places in such locations as the Commons Library and writing rooms – were a few typists' desks in rooms in the Upper Committee Corridor of the Palace. In 1953 the Stokes Committee on House of Commons Accommodation circulated a questionnaire to all MPs, asking them whether they would use a desk if one was made available to them in (presumably) multi-occupied desk rooms. Sixty per cent of Members who replied indicated that they would like to have a desk personally allocated to them, but only ninety-three out of the 489 who completed the questionnaire were prepared to accept a desk outside the precincts of the Palace. After the 1955 general election there were renewed requests from Members of all political parties for better accommodation. Early in 1956 more rooms in the Upper Committee Corridor were converted into desk rooms, thus providing a total of about seventy desks for personal use by backbench Members. In 1960 a further thirty-five desks were made available – this time outside the precincts, in a building opposite the west front of the House of Lords.

In the same year, the Speaker appointed an *ad hoc* Advisory Committee, chaired by a senior Conservative backbencher, Sir James Duncan; and this Committee, in a further questionnaire to all MPs, asked whether the latter would like the use of a

[1] H.C. Deb., 852, cc. 739–844.

single or double room, if this were possible. Two hundred and eighteen respondents indicated that they would welcome this type of accommodation. Improvements came slowly, however. Thirteen single rooms, in premises in Bridge Street formerly occupied by St Stephen's Club, were offered to Members in 1961; and twenty-seven more desks became available within the Palace when the staff of the Fees Office vacated premises in the Westminster Hall Annexe. By 1964 the number of Members' writing places in the Bridge Street premises had risen to sixty-one, including a few more single rooms.

In July 1963 Sir William Holford (now Lord Holford) produced his proposals concerning *Accommodation for the House of Commons*. These suggestions contained a scheme for developing the Bridge Street site[1] for the use of Parliament, Government offices and the police. An *ad hoc* Committee, under Selwyn Lloyd (now Speaker of the House of Commons), subsequently found the Holford scheme unsatisfactory in several respects.[2]

Discussion of the Bridge Street proposals came temporarily to an end with the dissolution of Parliament in the autumn of 1964. Some extra accommodation was, however, subsequently made available over a period of several years. A new extension of the Upper Committee Corridor provided rooms, some of which were allocated to Ministers and members of the Shadow Cabinet, and others to backbench Members for use as desk rooms.[3] In November 1964, forty-seven additional desks, in multi-occupied rooms, were provided in the former Grindlay's Bank premises in 54 Parliament Street. This latter accommodation, though comparatively spacious, was unacceptable to many potential users because of the distance from the chamber; as a result, these Members' desk rooms and the ancillary working space for secretaries were never used to more than about 50 per cent of their capacity. When, in January 1970, this accommodation was 'transferred' to a building more conveniently situated in the Abbey Garden,[4] the use of desks by Members,

[1] The area bounded by Bridge Street, Parliament Street, New Scotland Yard and the Embankment.

[2] Report from the Speaker's Advisory Committee on Accommodation; H.C. Deb., 4 May 1964, 694, cc. 915–8.

[3] A much-needed second lift, connecting the Upper Committee and Committee Corridors with the other floors of the Palace, was installed.

[4] Off Millbank, roughly opposite the Victoria Tower end of the Palace.

although reduced in number from forty-seven to thirty-five, greatly increased. Clearly, the *location* of Members' rooms and desks has been (and remains) a matter of vital significance.

A major development which occurred in 1967 was the completion of the Star Chamber Court building within the Palace. This now provides Ministers' rooms, a suite for the Chairman and Deputy Chairmen of Ways and Means, rooms for members of the Shadow Cabinet, and a few double rooms for backbenchers. Subsequently, the former Members' Waiting Room in the Cloisters of the Palace, together with the Oratory, were converted into desk rooms, offering Members the use of thirty-eight more desks.

Pending the realisation of the scheme for a new parliamentary building in Bridge Street, the Services Committee has considered various interim proposals for further 'in-filling' within the Palace. Proceeding on the principle that such additions should not lead to any major change in the existing amenities of natural light and air and, above all, must not alter the external appearance of the Palace,[1] the Committee recommended in November 1970 that a three-storey building should be erected on top of the Members' Tea Room in Commons Court, and that the extra accommodation so obtained should be devoted wholly to the provision of offices for Members. This three-storey scheme, which also allows for a roof garden, provides forty-nine rooms, offering (mostly in double rooms) accommodation for more than 100 Members. With the completion of this scheme, about 300 MPs (including Ministers) – nearly half the total membership – can be accommodated in single or double rooms inside the precincts. The estimated total cost of the three-storey addition was £184,000.[2] Work on this building has now been completed.[3]

In March 1973 the Services Committee reported to the House their view that 'irrespective . . . of the decision on the proposed new parliamentary building', extra accommodation for Members, secretaries and supporting staff was urgently required. The Committee's view was that the Norman Shaw North building –

[1] 7th Report, Services Committee, 1968–69, H.C. 477, para. 1.

[2] 1st Report, Services Committee, 1970–71, H.C. 152; H.C. Deb., 19 April 1972, 835, cc. 501–2.

[3] In a separate scheme alterations are being made to 3 Dean's Yard to provide desks for forty Members.

on the site of the former New Scotland Yard, close to Bridge Street and the Palace of Westminster – would be suitable for this purpose.[1] This building could accommodate up to 193 Members and 132 secretaries on a sharing basis; alternatively it could provide single rooms for 110 Members and accommodation for 110 secretaries. The time taken to adapt the Norman Shaw North building for these purposes would depend upon which of the two schemes was chosen.[2] Subsequently, when opening the debate on the new parliamentary building in June 1973, the Leader of the House confirmed that the Government were prepared to go ahead as soon as possible with the adaptation of the Norman Shaw North building, if the House so wished.[3]

3.1.3   The Present Position

Over a period of some twenty years, there has been a gradual improvement in the overall position regarding accommodation for individual Members. Perhaps the most significant development has been the growth of informed opinion at Westminster in favour of equipping each Member who wants one with a room of his own. This idea is, of course, far from being realised at present. Table 3.1 shows the situation as it was in November 1971.

The Table shows that seventy single rooms and forty-nine double rooms (for ninety-eight MPs) were available for private Members at that time. Of these, forty-nine single and thirty-nine double rooms were within the precincts of the Palace. The rooms are much sought-after. They are therefore allocated, on behalf of the Services Committee, by the Chief Whips of the Government and Opposition parties, and it is clear that the chances of a new MP obtaining such individual accommodation on his arrival at Westminster are fairly slim. On the other hand, there is a better prospect of a new MP securing – on application to the Serjeant at Arms' Office – a desk in one of the multi-occupied desk rooms. At the end of the 1966–70 Parliament, in fact, there was no waiting list for such desks. Immediately after the 1970 election there was a heavy demand for desks, but all Members willing to accept desks outside the precincts were accommodated by the end of the 1970 summer recess, partly

[1] 1st Report, Services Committee, 1972–73, H.C. 196, p v.
[2] *Ibid.*, p 2.   [3] H.C. Deb., 25 June 1973, 858, c. 1210.

Table 3.1 *Provision of writing spaces for MPs inside and close to the Palace of Westminster, November 1971*

	Single rooms			Double rooms			Desks in desk room			Total writing spaces		
	Inside Palace	Outside Palace	Total	Inside Palace	Outside Palace	Total	Inside Palace	Outside Palace	Total	Inside Palace	Outside Palace	Total
Ministers	55	–	55							55	–	55
Opposition Front Bench	14	–	14	2*	–	2*				16	–	16
Whips†	4	–	4				33	–	33	37	–	37
Speaker, Chairman and Deputy Chairman of Ways and Means	3	–	3							3	–	3
Chairmen of Select Committees	11	4	15							11	4	15
Other Office Holders‡	3	–	3							3	–	3
Private Members	49	21	70	78*	20*	98*	126	137	263	253	178	431
TOTAL	139	25	164	80	20	100	159	137	296	378	182	560

* Figures relate to numbers of MPs, i.e., there are 2 MPs per room.
† Government Chief Whip, Opposition Chief Whip, Deputy Chief Whips, Liberal Whip (single rooms); other Whips (desks in desk rooms).
‡ Leader of the Liberal Party, Chairman of the Parliamentary Labour Party, Second Church Estates Commissioner.

through the provision of additional accommodation in Palace Chambers, Bridge Street.

In a memorandum submitted to the Services Committee in February 1973 the Minister of Housing and Construction reported that at that time there was accommodation within the Palace of Westminster for 500 Members.[1] The accommodation consisted of single rooms for 143 Members, shared rooms (mostly for two persons) for 186 Members and desk-room facilities for 171 Members. The figures included rooms allotted to Ministers and other office-holders. Thus since November 1971 the position in regard to single rooms and desk-room facilities for Members within the Palace has changed very little, whereas the number of Members accommodated in shared rooms has increased considerably, due principally to the completion of the Tea Room scheme.

To complete the picture, one should mention some 200 'unallocated' writing places, available generally to MPs. These are located in the Commons Library, in the writing rooms above the division lobbies and in the division lobbies themselves. Two tables are reserved on the north side of the Cloisters for Members who wish to do their own typing.[2]

3.2   ANCILLARY ACCOMMODATION

3.2.1   *Secretaries' Rooms*

We have seen that working space for 450 Members' secretaries is recommended in the proposals for the new parliamentary building. Meanwhile, a limited number of rooms are available, inside or close to the Palace, where Members' secretaries may work; these rooms are in addition to the accommodation provided for Ashworth's secretarial agency (see Chapter 7). In November 1971 these rooms contained 197 typing desks. By early 1973 the position had slightly improved. At that time

[1] 1st Report, Services Committee, 1973–73, H.C. 196, p 3.

[2] It might be noted that substantial provision is made throughout the Palace for the comfort of non-smokers. For example, smoking is not permitted in the Commons chamber, standing committees, select committees when witnesses are present, division lobbies, the Members' Lobby (when the House is sitting), the Central Lobby, Rooms *C* and *D* of the Library, and the north end of the Members' Reading Room. Some of the telephone kiosks in the Cloisters are reserved for non-smokers.

eighty-three secretaries were accommodated (almost all in desk rooms) within the Palace, and a further 127 had desks in Bridge Street or in other locations close to the Palace. Thus 210 secretaries were accommodated.

A Member wishing to obtain a desk for his secretary must apply to the Serjeant at Arms' Office. He may also apply for a desk for the use of his personal research assistant, but present shortage of accommodation normally makes it impossible for a Member to have more than one desk of this sort; he must choose between his secretary and his research assistant, if he has one.

3.2.2 Filing Cabinets

For many years the policy of the Serjeant at Arms' Department has been to allocate a Member a filing cabinet together with his desk. In addition, about fifty filing cabinets are available for use by Members who have no desk of their own. Suspension cradles and file pockets can be supplied, up to a maximum of eight cradles and 200 file pockets per Member. There are also filing cabinets in the typing rooms used by Members' secretaries.

3.2.3 Interview Floor

Sixteen cubicles and twenty-eight settees are available for use by Members wishing to dictate letters. A Member may also apply to the Serjeant for the use of one of ten interview rooms. These rooms hold up to twenty people, and are particularly suitable for small meetings.

3.2.4 Lockers

A large number of small lockers are situated in the Library Corridor, the Ways and Means Corridor, and a few other convenient locations. Every Member who requires the use of a locker can have one.

3.2.5 Members' Families Room

This room, situated off the Lower Waiting Hall, may be used by the wives and husbands of Members. If space permits, Members' parents, children and other relatives are also permitted to avail themselves of this facility.

3.3 COMMITTEE ROOMS

The twelve committee rooms on the Committee Corridor of the Palace of Westminster are used for select and standing committees and for private bill groups. When not required for committees of the House, they are available to Members for private meetings in connection with parliamentary subjects. The committees of the House have priority, however, over all private meetings, and the latter can be displaced at very short notice if a select or standing committee wishes to sit. Committee rooms are available only when the House is sitting.

No individual MP may reserve a committee room for more than two hours. This rule is designed to prevent one Member booking a room for a conference lasting for a whole day or longer, and to facilitate the use of these rooms by the maximum number of Members. Nor may Members book these rooms for non-parliamentary meetings, such as the annual general meetings of outside bodies.

The lay-out of the committee rooms varies in accordance with their use. When used for standing committees, the arrangement is like the chamber itself. When used for select committees, the rooms have a horseshoe seating plan.[1] Until recently, ten of the twelve committee rooms could be used for one or the other types of committees, but not for both; while the two others could be used for either purpose. When tape recording equipment was installed for the use of the *Hansard* staff (see Chapter 4), new furniture was added, and the situation in terms of flexibility was reversed. Now ten of the rooms can be used by either standing or select committees, while two (Rooms 7 and 13) are usable only for select committee work. Notwithstanding their adaptability, the larger rooms (numbers 9, 10, 11, 12 and 14) are being used exclusively at present by standing committees. The seating capacity of the committee rooms varies from 35 (Room 13) to nearly 200 (Room 14). Some six years ago, loop aerials were fitted to six committee rooms so that simultaneous translation equipment could be fitted into these rooms, if required for some

[1] Standing committees are in effect miniature Committees of the whole House, and their seating arrangements reflect the division of the House into Government and Opposition. Select committees, on the other hand, conduct their business in a less partisan manner and this is reflected in the horseshoe arrangement in which Government and Opposition Members may intermingle.

special meeting. The expense of installing temporary equipment for such meetings is so great, however, that the facility is rarely exploited.[1] Refreshments may not be served in any committee room.

Committee rooms are at their busiest on Tuesdays, Wednesdays and Thursdays. This is partly owing to the party meetings, which mostly take place on these days, partly owing to more Members' private meetings, but due to a very large extent to the greatly increased number of committees of the House sitting on these days. Not only is it possible that a Member may be unable to book a room at the time he wants one, but if he is displaced by a committee it may be impossible to offer him alternative accommodation.

In addition to the above, there is the Grand Committee Room in Westminster Hall, one of the largest committee rooms, which seats 175. It is possible to adapt this room for standing committees and private bill groups, and it may also be used as a cinema. The projection room at the back is fitted with two 35mm projectors and one 16mm projector, and there is a fixed screen; any Member may use this equipment to show a film, provided he supplies the projectionist. The Grand Committee Room is frequently used for large meetings of people who come to lobby Members, as it has easy access from St Stephen's Entrance and Members do not have to take their parties through an already crowded Central Lobby.

The greatly increased demand for committee rooms can be seen from the numbers of meetings held in 1963, 1969 and 1972. In 1963 there were 220 sittings of standing committees, 270 of select committees, and 1,646 private meetings. The comparable figures for 1969 were 280 sittings of standing committees, 625 of select committees and 2,145 private meetings. In 1972 there were 402 sittings of standing committees, 634 of select committees and 2,579 private meetings. The Services Committee, in their Third Report of 1968–69, expressed a hope that six or seven extra committee rooms on the Committee and Upper Committee Corridors might become available when certain offices, at present located there, were moved to the new parliamentary building. Committee rooms in the new building are

[1] The expense must be met by a Member or a private source.

not likely to prove popular with MPs.[1] In the same report the Services Committee recommended that an Assembly Hall, holding at least 250 people and equipped with simultaneous translation facilities, should be located in the new parliamentary building. This hall could be used for large conferences, for instance those organised by the Commonwealth Parliamentary Association and similar bodies.[2]

3.4 RADIO AND TELEVISION ROOMS

The first radio set provided for Members of the House of Commons was installed in 1939; the first television set arrived in 1950. Accommodation for radio and television sets has always been a problem. Initially both were placed in committee rooms, but since then they have been moved several times. These sets and subsequent ones were purchased on the House of Commons Vote, and, up to 1965, were maintained and serviced under a contract with the Post Office. Great difficulties were experienced in obtaining sufficiently good reception in the Palace of Westminster without erecting aerials which would be visible on the skyline of the building, and in 1965 a contract was signed with British Relay for the provision of 'piped' television, eliminating the necessity for aerials. The present television and radio sets are rented from British Relay, who maintain and service them.

As additional television programmes have become available, more television sets have been provided within the Palace, and at present there is one set in each of three Upper Committee Corridor rooms. Colour programmes are obtainable on all of these. BBC-1 is presently available in Room 10, IBA in Room 9, and BBC-2 in Room 8 together with the radio. All three rooms are reserved for Members. The Post Office has waived the necessity for obtaining radio and television licences for these sets. Other owners of television sets in the Palace of Westminster may avail themselves of the 'piped' television provided by British Relay, but must purchase licences in the usual way.

In their Third Report of 1968–69 the Services Committee proposed that two large and two small television studios, as well as sound recording studios, should be provided in the new

[1] H.C. 295, paras. 40–1.   [2] *Ibid.*, para. 43.

parliamentary building. These studios, to be shared by the BBC and IBA, would provide Members with interview facilities, and would also allow for the possible future broadcasting and televising of Parliament.[1]

3.5 CAR PARKING AT WESTMINSTER

Until the end of June 1972, car parking facilities for Members at Westminster were as follows: about 220 spaces in New Palace Yard, twenty-five in Star Court, sixty in Old Palace Yard and fifty under Church House (situated off Great Smith Street). Thus there were a total of 335 spaces in or near the precincts of the Palace. In addition, about twelve cars could be accommodated in Commons Court and in Commons Inner Court and, by permission of the Speaker, thirty-six cars of Ministers and former Ministers could be parked in Speaker's Court.[2] Members shared the parking facilities in New Palace Yard with Officers of the House.

On 1 July 1972 work began on a new underground car park of five floors, to be constructed in New Palace Yard. Work on this major undertaking is expected to continue until the early spring of 1974, during which time severe restrictions have been imposed on the car parking facilities in New Palace Yard. Throughout this period alternative facilities for Members and Officers have been made available in the Broad Sanctuary car park, situated behind the former Middlesex Guildhall close to Westminster Abbey. The other car parking spaces in and near the Palace continue to be available to Members.

In June 1971 the Services Committee approved the plan for the construction of the new car park, which will provide space for 500 vehicles under New Palace Yard. The Committee pointed out in their report:

'The scheme proposed will not only avoid detracting from the architectural merit of the Palace but will improve the setting by creating an attractive landscaped area on the surface of New Palace Yard. It is proposed that the centre should be grassed, with a roadway round it, worked on a one way system in a clock-

[1] Ibid., para. 44.
[2] 4th Report, Services Committee, 1971–72, H.C. 263, p 4.

wise direction, with the entrance and exit to the car park on the south side. This will allow a number of cars to arrive simultaneously and passengers to alight at surface level without causing congestion. Parking on the surface will be banned except perhaps on occasions such as a big division at ten o'clock. Your Committee hope that in addition to the grass the area will be suitably landscaped. Such a scheme will result in a great aesthetic and amenity gain.'[1]

In May 1972 the Services Committee again reported to the House on the underground car park.[2] Despite an increased cost estimate of almost £2 million, the Committee recommended that the work should proceed as originally planned, and the House agreed to the recommendation.[3] By the spring of 1974, therefore, 500 very conveniently situated parking spaces should become available to Members, in addition to those at present available in locations other than New Palace Yard.

3.6   TICKETS FOR THE GALLERIES

3.6.1   *Strangers' Gallery*
'Admission orders' for 140 of the 157 seats in the Strangers' Gallery of the House of Commons are issued to Members, for 2.30 p.m. daily, by an automatic allocation of two orders per Member. Each Member receives an allocation once every nine sitting days (excluding Fridays) without any application being made.[4]

After a general election the Admission Order Office of the Serjeant's Department divides Members' names alphabetically into nine groups, and this grouping is retained until the dissolution of Parliament. A Member coming in at a by-election takes the place of the Member formerly elected for that constituency. As soon as the dates of a recess are announced, the allocation list is made out by the Admission Order Office for the period between the date the House will reassemble and the date on

[1] 6th Report, Services Committee, 1970–71, H.C. 431, p 3.

[2] 4th Report, Services Committee, 1971–72, H.C. 263, p 3.

[3] H.C. Deb., 13 June 1972, 838, cc. 1412–42.

[4] There was a time when the admission of strangers, i.e. visitors, was handled on a rather different basis. A select committee of the Commons found in 1833 that Doorkeepers handling the admission of strangers to the Galleries were making considerable amounts of money in the process. Philip Marsden, *The Officers of the Commons 1363–1965*, pp 214–15, Barrie and Rockliff (1966).

which the House could be expected to rise for the following recess: the next group numerically after the one which has an allocation on the day the House is to rise receives an allocation on the day that the House reassembles. This means that Members know some time in advance when they will receive two orders definitely for 2.30 p.m., and can promise them to anyone who asks, although they will not then, of course, know what the subject for the debate on that day will be. Even on occasions when a very heavy demand may be expected, as on Budget Day, the automatic allocation of orders is followed as usual.

On a Friday a Member may put his name down in advance for two admission orders at 11 a.m. and, since the orders are issued on a 'first come, first served' basis, the first seventy or so Members who apply can be certain of obtaining orders on that day. However, as there is no Question Time on Fridays, and only occasionally are the debates of widespread interest, it is usually reasonably easy for a Member to obtain two orders at quite short notice.

Under an arrangement for educational parties, one party of five bona-fide students is admitted each sitting day at the time the House meets. These educational parties can be booked by a Member, or directly by the school concerned. This is a very popular scheme, and the great demand means that each school has to be limited to one party in each Parliamentary session. The students must come from a 'recognised school or training establishment'; this definition covers a fairly wide field, and includes evening institutes, Services' educational courses and apprentices to trades.

3.6.2 Special Galleries

The seats in these Galleries are intended primarily for those with a direct interest in the debate, and the allocation of admission orders is not made until the business for that day has been announced. Members may put their names down for two orders some time in advance, but they will not know definitely whether or not their application has been successful until much nearer the time of the debate. The orders cease to be valid if they are not presented before 3 p.m. (11.30 a.m. on Fridays).

In the last few years it has become increasingly difficult for a Member to obtain admission orders for the Special Galleries on a Tuesday or Thursday. This is because it is known that the Prime Minister will answer Questions at 3.15 p.m. on these days, whereas formerly there was often an element of doubt as to whether his Questions would be reached.

The Admission Order Office keeps a 'late booking list' to which Members may add their names in advance for orders for the Special Galleries at times *after* the House has met. Four to eight reservations (depending on the time and the likelihood of seats being vacated) may be taken at every half hour from 3 p.m. to 9.30 p.m., but no Member may put his name down for more than two orders at a time, or for a total of more than four orders in any one week. These bookings are accepted on the assumption that the necessary number of visitors already in the Special Galleries will have left by any given time. There is normally little difficulty in fulfilling these bookings, and every effort is made to do so with the minimum delay, even on the busiest days. These orders are time-stamped and must be presented at the Gallery within half-an-hour of the time of issue. After the meeting of the House has begun, all orders for the Special Galleries are issued by the Serjeant at Arms on duty in the Chair in the chamber and Members who have put their names down on the 'late booking list' collect their orders, at the time required from him.

One may illustrate the scale of the work of the Admission Order Office by noting the total number of visitors to the Strangers' and Special Galleries in a year. In 1969 the figure was 175,238. This meant that about one-fourth of the 709,495 visitors to the House of Commons in 1969 watched the House in session. A high proportion of visitors, of course, come on Saturdays and public holidays when the House is not sitting.[1]

3.7 SERVICES PROVIDED BY DOORKEEPERS

The Serjeant at Arms has under his control a permanent staff of thirty-nine Doorkeepers, plus a Principal Doorkeeper and a Second Principal Doorkeeper, who are on duty at all times when the House is sitting. Certain of these Doorkeepers are also required to attend on standing committees which sit in the

[1] H.C. Deb., 24 July 1970, 804, cc. *265–6* written answers.

mornings, and on any select committees which may sit during the recesses.

When on duty the Doorkeepers wear evening dress with black waistcoats, and all except the Principal and Second Principal Doorkeepers wear the silver-gilt badges of Royal Messengers. The Bar Doorkeeper who leads the Speaker's Procession wears knee breeches, silk stockings and white gloves. All the Doorkeeper staff are ex-servicemen who have completed at least twenty-one years in HM Forces and have reached the rank of warrant or chief petty officer.

The Principal and Second Principal Doorkeepers are on duty at the door of the chamber. When a division is called, it is the Principal Doorkeeper who activates the mechanism for ringing the division bells which are located throughout the building. Two Doorkeepers man the Letter Board on the east side of the Members' Lobby and deliver to MPs letters which are handed in for them during the course of the day. Members themselves are limited to sending six items at a time through the letter board system to avoid impeding urgent communications.

Twelve Doorkeepers, in two watches of six, are on duty at the Card Board on the west side of the Members' Lobby. They receive the Green Cards sent in by constituents who come to the Central Lobby and wish to see Members. These Doorkeepers also receive telephone messages from the Members' Telephone Room and telegrams for Members. These are taken round the various 'public' rooms in the House – the Library, the committee rooms, the cafeterias, dining rooms – to see if the Members can be found; or, if a Member has left instructions as to where he is to be contacted, the Doorkeepers get in touch with him (or perhaps his secretary) direct. Since 1964 the 'Card' Doorkeepers have been equipped with a two-way radio-paging system, so that they can be contacted on their rounds when it is necessary to locate a particular Member in a hurry. In a recent article Tom Driberg (Labour Member for Barking) has described the powers of observation and recognition of the Doorkeepers who carry out these messenger services as 'miraculous'.[1]

The remaining Doorkeeper staff carry out attendants' and security duties in the chamber and Galleries. These duties have increased in importance and scope in recent years, and the

[1] *Sunday Times Magazine* (6 June 1971).

difficulties involved, in a public building such as the Palace of Westminster, scarcely need elaboration here. The Political editor of *The Times* noted recently that 'the House of Commons meets today in a Westminster strictly guarded at every entrance as it has never been before'.[1]

In October 1970 a former senior officer of the metropolitan police was appointed Security Co-ordinator at the Palace of Westminster. The Security Co-ordinator advises the Serjeant at Arms in the Commons and Black Rod in the Lords on all matters concerning security in Parliament, other than documentary security. This new post is part of the reorganisation of security arrangements put in hand after the smoke bomb incident in the chamber in July 1970.

3.8 STATIONERY

Stationery, for official use only, is provided free in the Commons Library, writing rooms, the Cloisters, Members' rooms and secretaries' typing rooms, and – except in the Library, where Library staff are responsible – is replenished by the Serjeant at Arms' staff.

Members who wish to take away a quantity of stationery for use outside the Palace of Westminster obtain their supplies from the Serjeant at Arms' stores. In 1955 the Financial Secretary to the Treasury arranged that MPs should get an allowance of up to £8 worth of stationery from the stores per annum – any quantity required above that limit would have to be paid for. This allowance was increased over the years (to £25 per annum in 1969) until in April 1972 Members became entitled to unlimited free stationery (see Chapter 6). The Serjeant at Arms' stores provides paper and envelopes in various types and sizes, with different kinds of House of Commons crest and headings, in accordance with the recommendations of the Services Committee. It does not stock other office requisites such as pens, paper clips and files.

The staff of the Serjeant at Arms' stores deliver, to addresses in the London area, stationery which has been ordered by Members. No charge is made for this delivery service. A charge is made, however, for parcels of stationery sent by post or rail to addresses outside London.

[1] David Wood, 'Put this House in order', *The Times* (21 February 1972).

3.9 photocopying facilities

Rank Xerox copying machines have been installed at various points in the Palace or nearby, for use by MPs and their secretaries. The principal photocopying facilities are available in the Sale Office; there are also several copying machines elsewhere. The Library photocopies material in connection with its work for individual Members, but the two machines possessed by the Library are primarily for use by staff.

The copying machines available to Members are intended for the production of a limited number of copies of documents. Should more than twelve copies of a single sheet be made, there is a charge of 2p for each additional sheet. If a paper is being copied on behalf of a group of Members, the number of free copies may be multiplied by the number of Members in the group; thus a group of twenty Members would be entitled to 240 free copies.

3.10 members' hairdressing facilities

The first appointment of a Barber, or Hairdresser, to the House of Commons was made in 1894, when he came under the control of the Commons Kitchen Committee. In 1895 he was transferred to the jurisdiction of the Serjeant at Arms. The terms under which the first Barber took over were that accommodation, lighting, gowns, brushes and towels were provided by the House, and the laundry of the towels paid for – but he received no salary. The charges were those currently applying in the West End. Against the advantages were to be set the disadvantages of awkward and irregular hours of work and the incidence of recesses and dissolutions when little work could be expected.

When the first incumbent of this post retired, the contract, which stipulated that the hairdressing assistants should be ex-servicemen in receipt of disablement pensions, was offered to several West End firms of hairdressers, but they refused to accept it because (they said) they would not be able to make it pay. Eventually the contract was accepted by Messrs Arding and Hobbs of Clapham Junction, but the stipulation regarding ex-servicemen was deleted. At this time Members could have their hair cut for 1s and their beards trimmed for 6d.

In 1926 Messrs Arding and Hobbs cancelled their contract.

The price of a haircut was raised to 1s 6d in 1925, and in 1927 the then incumbent applied for, and was given, the post of Porter in the Members' dressing room, in addition to his hair-cutting duties. This meant that he came on to the payroll of the Serjeant at Arms' Department.

Apart from one or two modern innovations, the Hairdresser's duties have changed little over the years. The Hairdresser is now in charge of a Sunray lamp, two shower-baths, three bathrooms and the Members' changing room. He has to work long hours, like many other members of the staff. He is permitted to make what profit he can from his hairdressing activities, and from the sale of toothpaste, razor blades and certain other wares including – rather curiously – pencils.

There are no hairdressing facilities for Lady Members.

3.11   PROSPECTS FOR THE FUTURE

Despite the alterations of the last twenty years, it is clear that fundamental improvements to Members' accommodation – and to the working conditions of many of the staff who service the House – are dependent on the construction of the new parliamentary building in Bridge Street. 'Things may be better when the new quarters across Bridge Street are built – How soon? In ten years?' Tom Driberg, who wrote these words,[1] was no doubt expressing a certain sense of frustration shared by many fellow Members in the face of largely inevitable delays.

It is true that the history of this major scheme already stretches back for thirteen years, as the following outline chronology of the proposals shows:[2]

31 March 1960	Possibility mentioned by the then Minister of Works of developing part of the Bridge Street site for parliamentary purposes. (H.C. Deb., 620, cc. 1522–30)
18 April 1962	Committee set up to advise on allocation of the 40,000 sq. ft. to be assigned to the House of Commons in Bridge Street. (H.C. Deb., 658, c. 89 written answers)

[1] *Sunday Times Magazine* (6 June 1971).

[2] Much of the information contained in this chronology was kindly supplied by John Palmer of the House of Commons Library.

8 November 1962	Minister stated that site should be cleared in 1964. (H.C. Deb., 666, cc. *94–6* written answers)
21 November 1962	Committee proposed 50,000 sq. ft. of space instead of 40,000. (H.C. Deb., 667, cc. 1220–7)
July 1963	'Holford Report' on *Accommodation for the House of Commons* published.
1 August 1963	Holford Report debated. The Minister stated: 'We are not likely to be able to begin demolition work before 1965, or to be able to complete the Parliamentary building before 1968'. (H.C. Deb., 682, c. 731)
20 April 1964	Sir Leslie Martin appointed as consultant for the whole area at the bottom of White-hall. (H.C. Deb., 693, c. *119* written answers)
4 May 1964	Advisory Committee reported in favour of an extension to the *existing* Palace of Westminster of 100,000 sq ft. (H.C. Deb., 694, cc. 915–8)
19 July 1965	Publication of reports by Sir Leslie Martin and Colin Buchanan on the Whitehall area. Accepted by the Government as a 'broad framework' for future development of Whitehall and Parliament Square areas. Minister of Public Building and Works (Charles Pannell) stated that the Government accepted in principle the proposal for a new building for parliamentary purposes on the Bridge Street site. (H.C. Deb., 716, cc. 1117–22)
3 November 1965	The Government announced its decision that the new parliamentary building should be the subject of a competition limited to Commonwealth architects. (H.C. Deb., 718, cc. 1037–40)

July 1967	Services Committee reported that the proposed Bridge Street building could be used for staff, but that as Members' accommodation it was 'neither desirable nor practicable'. It proposed an extension to the Palace of Westminster of 80,000 sq ft, with a further 43,000 sq ft to be added later. (H.C. 652, 1966–67)
April 1968	Services Committee now reconciled to the Bridge Street proposal, the building to be of 250–350,000 sq ft, to cost about £5 million, and to take six years to construct between approval and completion. (H.C. 218, 1967–68)
20 January 1969	Assessors announced for the competition for the new parliamentary building. (H.C. Deb., 776, c. 176)
May 1969	Further report from Services Committee. A possible limit on the height of the parliamentary building would restrict accommodation above ground to 150,000 sq ft, but 100,000 sq ft could also be provided below ground. (H.C. 295, 1968–69)
March 1970	Further report from the Services Committee. Hopes had been dashed of a reduction in traffic in Bridge Street; a strip of the site twenty feet wide was required for road widening. The Ministry's proposed timetable: launch competition early spring 1970, completion of building 1977. 'Any delay will almost certainly push the completion date back to 1978.' (H.C. 186, 1969–70)
28 July 1970	Competition launched for design of building. Preliminary designs to be in by 19 April 1971, after which up to a dozen would be chosen for the second stage of the competition. [*The Times* (29 July 1970)]

14 December 1970	Nearly 1,000 applications received for entries in the architectural competition. Of these, some 300 were from overseas. (H.C. Deb., 808, c. *259* written answers)
24 March 1971	Completion of the new parliamentary building is planned for 1978. (H.C. Deb., 814, c. 535).
3 March 1972	Announcement by Minister (Mr Amery) of prize-winning design. Architects are Robin Spence and Robin Webster. Cost ceiling estimated at about £7 million [*The Times* (4 March 1972)]
4 July 1972	Services Committee recommend adoption of the winning design but with modifications. Work to start as soon as possible. Services Committee in the next session should examine details of the accommodation to be provided. (H.C. 342, 1971–72)
25 October 1972	Mr Amery repeats completion target of 1978 'if I receive adequate instructions by the end of this year'. (H.C. Deb., 843, c. *328* written answers)
11 December 1972	Spence and Webster modify design to take account of recommendations of the Services Committee
9 March 1973	Debate on motion that the new building 'be not proceeded with' and that alternative, less costly accommodation be provided instead. Debate adjourned. (H.C. Deb., 852, cc. 739–844)
20 March 1973	Services Committee recommend use of Norman Shaw North building for House of Commons purposes 'irrespective ... of the decision on the proposed new parliamentary building'. (H.C. 196, 1972–73)

21 May 1973   Chancellor of the Exchequer, in a state-
                   ment on public expenditure, announces
                   that no expenditure on the new parlia-
                   mentary building can be incurred until
                   financial year 1975–76. (H.C. Deb., 857,
                   c. 41)

25 June 1973   House of Commons approves the con-
                   struction 'in due course' of a new parlia-
                   mentary building on the Bridge Street
                   site, following the design of Spence and
                   Webster. Leader of the House gives cost
                   estimate for the building and all its
                   associated works as approximately £33
                   million. Cost of building itself would be
                   £11 million. (H.C. Deb., 858, cc. 1206–76)

Thus over the thirteen years since the project was first officially
mooted, it has grown in size from 40,000 to 250,000 square feet
(and has been even larger). Proposed dates for site clearance and
for completion of the building have come and gone while the
existing buildings still occupy the site. On present form it seems
likely that, if all goes well, the building might be completed
more than twenty years after the project was first suggested by
a Minister. If this pace seems leisurely, one may compare it with
the Whitehall Gardens building (now occupied by the Ministry
of Defence), for which the architect – Vincent Harris – was
selected by open competition in 1913, and which was completed, under the same architect, forty-five years later. Alternatively, one could consider the Colonial Office site, opposite
Westminster Abbey, cleared in 1950 and unbuilt-on since.[1] With
these examples in mind, it would not be realistic to think in
terms of a completion date before the early 1980s.

Now that the prize-winning design has been approved by
Parliament, it seems likely that the House of Commons will
eventually achieve the laudable aim of 'a room for every
Member', as well as many other amenities necessary for the
modern legislature. In the design by Spence and Webster:

[1] On both these schemes, see 5th Report, Estimates Committee, 1955–56, H.C.
234.

'The accommodation for MPs is arranged in a rectangular ring of offices, suspended clear of the ground by a giant space grid roof, which is supported by four service towers carrying the weight of the building clear of the Underground below, which runs diagonally across the site. This structural solution coincides with the planning objectives, by providing a unique covered urban space, which will act as a focus and breathing space for tourists and citizens. In the centre of this space, the public can observe the MPs at a distance, in the galleries above or the entrance lobby below, or watch large television screens and newscasters which act as an extension of the public gallery to the House of Commons, and can also link our capital city and parliament with other cities and parliaments in Europe and the world . . .

'The offices for MPs are generous, well-proportioned rooms giving magnificent views to the outside, uninterrupted by balconies or other structures. Carrels for the MPs' secretaries are in wide landscaped galleries, with a view down to the covered urban square, which link the offices to the twelve lifts. These lifts connect the office galleries to the entrance floor, with its large lobby, the suite of recreational facilities, the assembly hall, and the remainder of the supporting accommodation including the library, committee offices, departments, television accommodation and service areas, arranged under the podium. A rapid connecting link to the Debating Chamber during divisions is provided by a travellator which runs from the entrance lobby under New Palace Yard alongside the car park.'[1]

The Leader of the House (James Prior) referred to the controversy over the merits of the Spence-Webster design during the debate in June 1973. 'My personal view', he said, 'is that the winning design meets the needs of the House and I favour it.' He added, however, that before work is begun on the new building some adjustments in its design would be necessary. The Services Committee has also mentioned a need for adjustments in the design.[2]

[1] *New Parliamentary Building: Commonwealth Architectural Competition*, p 6, Department of the Environment (1972).
[2] H.C. 342, 1971–72.

CHAPTER 4

THE DEPARTMENT
OF THE SPEAKER

The Speaker of the House of Commons is in a basically different position from the other officers of the House who head Departments. Unlike the Clerk, the Serjeant at Arms, the Librarian and the Clerk Administrator, the Speaker is not only an officer, but he is also an elected Member of Parliament. Inasmuch as he has a constituency and must stand for election, the Speaker is not designated as a 'permanent' officer, although in practice the Speaker normally remains Speaker until he retires from the House of Commons. When the duties of 'officers' of the House are discussed in Erskine May, a distinction is made between the 'permanent' officers and other officers who are MPs.[1] Included with the Speaker in the latter category are the Chairman of Ways and Means and the Deputy Chairmen of Ways and Means, all of whom take the Chair regularly as Deputy Speaker.

Earlier we characterised the Clerk of the House as the most important permanent officer of the House (see section 2.12). When one takes permanent and non-permanent officers together, the Speaker in his various roles is undoubtedly the pre-eminent officer of the House. As an authority on the Speakership has said: 'The Speaker is the principal officer of the House of Commons'.[2] A former Clerk, Sir Barnett Cocks, has described the office of Speaker as:

'The most significant of those official appointments in the House of Commons whose holders owe a loyal duty to the Sovereign but no special allegiance to the Crown or executive government, and whose particular duty it is to serve the House and its Members without regard to party.'[3]

[1] *Treatise on the Law, Privileges, Proceedings and Usage of Parliament*, pp 223–37, Butterworth (eighteenth edition, 1971).

[2] Philip Laundy, *The Office of Speaker*, p 3, Cassell (1964).

[3] Laundy, *op. cit.*, Foreword, p vii. After the members of the royal family the Speaker ranks sixth in the official order of precedence.

The Speaker fulfils a number of roles. He is the presiding officer of the House of Commons. He is an MP, albeit a non-party one. He has general responsibility for that part of the Palace of Westminster which is utilised by the House of Commons.[1] Finally, he is the head of one of the five departments which provide services to Members. In this chapter we shall be considering the Speaker in the last-mentioned role. More particularly, we shall be examining the working elements of his Department.

Before examining the present-day working of the Department, it will be useful to make some brief comments about its historical development since the first Speaker was appointed in 1377. Before 1700 the office of Speaker was in a far different position from its position today. Not all the early Speakers distinguished themselves, reflecting the fact that 'the House itself was at times venal to a degree unimaginable today. . . . It was natural that the man they selected from their own ranks to preside over their sittings should reflect the spirit of the day.'[2] There was, moreover, less continuity in the Chair than was the case later on. It was not uncommon to have two, or even three, Speakers in the course of a single year. Marsden contrasts the early development of the offices of Clerk and Speaker:

'In the case of the Clerks . . . the development of their office showed a steady and continuous progress from early obscurity, through gradually increasing professional skill and wider acceptance of responsibility, to a position where their authority inside the Commons was . . . universally respected on questions of precedent and procedure . . .

'Speakers, however, have varied tremendously over the centuries, and the great respect which is rightly accorded to the office today is something which is, historically speaking, of fairly recent origin.'[3]

---

[1] 'The Speaker has the control of the accommodation and services in that part of the Palace of Westminster and precincts occupied by or on behalf of the House of Commons. In exercising this control he is advised by the House of Commons (Services) Committee.' Erskine May, op. cit., p 227.

[2] Philip Marsden, The Officers of the Commons, 1363–1965, p 112, Barrie and Rockliff (1966).

[3] Marsden, op. cit., pp 111–12.

After 1725 the situation changed. Individual Speakers began serving through several Parliaments while exercising increasing authority.

In 1833 the House appointed a Select Committee on the Establishment of the House of Commons. According to the Committee's report, 'The Official Establishment of the House of Commons is divided into two extensive Departments, that of the . . . Clerk of the House of Commons . . . and that of the Serjeant at Arms'.[1] The Speaker had no Department in 1833. The only officials working directly for him were his Secretary and Chaplain. After 1833, however, a Speaker's Department began to develop, and the Department is specifically mentioned in the *House of Commons Offices Act 1846*. By the middle of the nineteenth century it was beginning to assume real importance.

By 1965 the Speaker's Department had grown to include the following components: the Speaker's Office or personal staff, the staff of the *Official Report* (*Hansard*), the House of Commons Library, the Fees Office, the Vote Office and the Sale Office. In the course of the major changes in the establishment of the House which took place between 1965 and 1968, two of these units were removed from the Speaker's Department, an important instrument of these changes being a Treasury Organisation and Methods Report in 1967. Following this report, the Library became a separate Department, and the Administration Department was created, with the Fees Office a part of it (see section 1.2). Accordingly, the Speaker's Department at present consists of the Speaker's Office, the *Hansard* staff, the Vote Office and the Sale Office (see Figure 4.1). The staff of the Department numbered sixty-two in 1972 (see Table 1.2).

In practice the Speaker's Department is decentralised. The most recent edition of Erskine May describes the Speaker's Counsel as the administrative head of the Speaker's Department.[2] Other leading Officers in the Department are: the Speaker's Secretary, who works closely with the Speaker on various official matters; the editor of *Hansard*, whose staff is more than twice as large as the rest of the Speaker's Department

[1] Marsden, *op. cit.*, quotation on p 153.
[2] Erskine May, *op. cit.*, p 234.

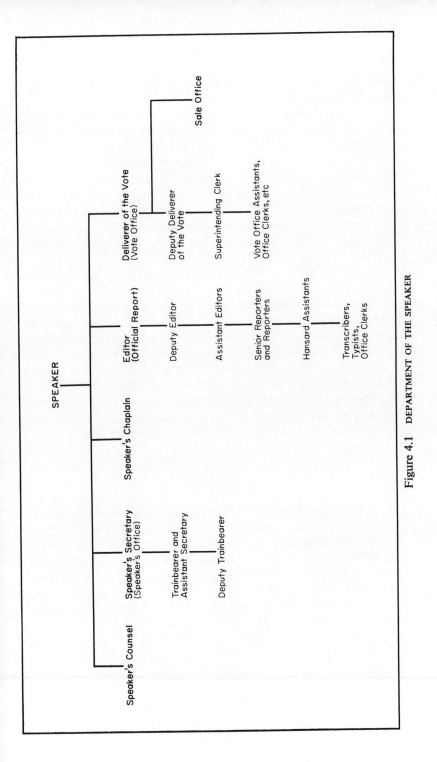

Figure 4.1 DEPARTMENT OF THE SPEAKER

combined; and the Deliverer of the Vote, who is head of the Vote Office and the Sale Office.

The post of Speaker's Counsel, a permanent appointment made by the Speaker, dates from 1838. The holder of the appointment is usually a non-practising QC who was previously a parliamentary draftsman or a member of the legal branch of the civil service. Originally appointed to assist Speakers concerning legal questions, he still provides this service to Speakers and other officers of the House. On the whole, however, his title is somewhat misleading today inasmuch as little legal advice is required by the Speaker, and advice on procedure emanates from the Clerk.

Counsel assists the Chairman of Ways and Means in his examination of private bills, and he similarly assists the Committee on Unopposed Bills. In addition, he attends the Select Committee on Statutory Instruments in rather the same capacity as the Comptroller and Auditor General attends the Committee of Public Accounts. He works closely with the Secretary to the Chairman of Ways and Means who is Clerk to both the Committee on Unopposed Bills and the Statutory Instruments Committee. Counsel also assists the Standing Orders Committee and is a member of the Court of Referees, whose function is to determine whether a petitioner against a private bill has a right to be heard.

4.1 THE SPEAKER'S OFFICE

In general, the Speaker's Office is a channel through which Members may seek advice or assistance from the Speaker on any matter concerning their parliamentary duties. In practice, the Office is responsible for providing Members with the kind of help and guidance that does not require a detailed knowledge of parliamentary rules and procedures. For example, the Speaker's Office receives and consolidates all applications from Members to speak. It receives all requests to ask Private Notice Questions, and is responsible for informing Members of the Speaker's decision and notifying the other authorities concerned. Each week it submits to the Speaker a list of adjournment subjects proposed by Members, and conducts the ballot to select these for days other than Thursday, the subject for

Thursday being selected by Mr Speaker personally. Finally, it deals with subjects proposed by Members for discussion during Consolidated Fund debates, conducting the ballot and notifying the result to all concerned.

In addition, the Speaker's Office is responsible for allotting seats in the Distinguished Strangers' Gallery and the Speaker's Gallery in response to requests from Members. The Office issues tickets for special occasions such as the State Opening of Parliament, Trooping of the Colour or ceremonies in Westminster Hall. It also issues warrants authorising the Clerk of the Crown to make out writs for the election of Members.

The key figure in this field of activity is the Speaker's Secretary. Dating from 1735, the post is a permanent one in the sense that it is customary for a new Speaker to retain the incumbent. Speaker's Secretaries were originally concerned with social arrangements and protocol, which is still the case, but their duties have expanded in a number of directions.

A major task of the Secretary is to deal with the Speaker's heavy correspondence. The Speaker is the focal point for all persons wanting to do business with the House of Commons, and he therefore receives letters from private bodies and persons all over the world, as well as from Ministers, Government departments and backbench MPs. Such correspondents may be concerned with either official or social matters. In the latter connection the Secretary is responsible, for example, for arranging the Speaker's official dinners and receptions.

In addition to helping the Speaker carry out his duties, the Speaker's Secretary has two specific responsibilities of his own. He is a member of the Staff Board and is Secretary to the Commission for Regulating the Offices of the House of Commons (see section 1.3). His desk work is subject to interruption when he must join the Speaker's Procession, be present at the Speaker's social events, and attend the Speaker in the chamber during Question Time and until the House enters upon the business of the day.

The Trainbearer and Assistant Secretary to the Speaker, whose office dates from 1730, has various duties, as his compound title suggests. There are, on the one hand, his formal duties in attendance on the Speaker in the House, at meetings, and on ceremonial and social occasions. In addition, he is the principal assistant to the Speaker's Secretary and has a growing number of administrative responsibilities. He is responsible for seeing that the arm of the Chair is furnished with whatever documents are needed for the day's business.

The holder of the oldest post in the Speaker's Department, other than Speaker, is the Chaplain. The first Chaplain was appointed in 1659. The Chaplain reads the prayers in the House on each sitting day and takes part in the Speaker's Procession. It is usually the Chaplain who officiates at weddings and christenings in the Crypt Chapel, and he gives communion weekly during Lent in the Chapel.

4.2   THE VOTE OFFICE

Publications related to House of Commons proceedings are, in the case of the Vote Office, distributed and, in the case of *Hansard*, produced by separate administrative units within the Speaker's Department.[1] The remainder of this chapter will be devoted to these two units.

The Vote Office is the main channel of supply to MPs of official printed material. It is thought to have been founded about 1682. Until 1835 it was run on 'private enterprise' lines. The fees and gratuities payable by Members formed a lucrative source of income for the head of the Office, called the Deliverer of the Vote,[2] and for the Serjeant at Arms, in whose Department the Office was located until at the time of the reforms of the 1830s it was transferred to the jurisdiction of the Speaker. When the transfer was made, the staff were converted into salaried officials, and Members were no longer charged for official papers.[3]

As we have noted, the 'Vote' consists of a bundle of the working papers for a day's sitting of the House of Commons (see section 2.11). Originally, the Vote Office was concerned with distributing the Vote. First printed in 1681, the Vote in its early

[1] This statement needs to be qualified as it applies to the Vote Office. In addition to documents directly related to Commons proceedings, the Office stocks many items only distantly related, if at all, to Commons proceedings.

[2] The head of the Vote Office began to call himself the Principal of the Vote Office during the early part of this century, but in 1961 he reverted to the title of Deliverer of the Vote.

[3] For further historical details, see Marsden, *op. cit.*, pp 87–90, 161–3, 167–8.

days was basically a copy of the Clerk's *Journal*. From the start the Vote has been so essential to the conduct of the business of the House that it has always been made available to Members on each sitting day. As the Vote was enlarged to include additional information, it was widely circulated outside the House as well as inside, an especially valuable service in the pre-*Hansard* days.

In addition to distributing the Vote, the Office from an early date assumed the responsibility of providing Members with other official printed material. Such material obviously varies in terms of immediacy and relevance. Much of what is needed for a day's sitting – the Order Paper, *Votes and Proceedings*, notices and amendments – is included in the Vote. Other material of vital importance to Members includes public acts, bills, House of Commons papers, Command papers and the *Official Report* (*Hansard*) in its various forms. The foregoing 'parliamentary' publications have been distributed free since 1835 with two exceptions: (a) there are some limitations on the number of copies that Members are entitled to; and (b) Members had to pay for bound volumes of *Hansard* between 1940 and 1945.[1]

In addition to 'parliamentary' papers, Her Majesty's Stationery Office publish an enormous number of titles each year in the category of 'non-parliamentary' publications. Some of these 'non-parliamentary' publications are vitally relevant to MPs; others, arguably, are less vital; still others are marginal or irrelevant, e.g. books on ancient monuments. Policy as to which of them should be provided free to Members through the Vote Office has varied over time. Before 1921 there were few complications about categories because virtually all government publications of any importance were parliamentary papers. Then three things happened: (a) there was an intensive economy drive in government spending, including spending on printing, popularly known as the 'Geddes Axe'; (b) the size of the page used in parliamentary papers was greatly reduced; (c) many series of papers were transferred from the parliamentary to the non-parliamentary category. As a result Members ceased to be entitled to a free copy of many official publications that were

---

[1] Erskine May, *op. cit.*, p 249. The practice has also varied as to how far back Members can obtain papers without payment.

formerly available to them. This policy applied, for example, to statistical papers, which remained in the old page size. If a Member wanted a copy of the report on the population census of his own county, he now had to pay for it.[1]

Under the new arrangement parliamentary papers were meant to include all 'documents relating to matters likely to be the subject of early legislation, or which may be regarded as otherwise essential to Members of Parliament as a whole to enable them to discharge their responsibilities'.[2] But in practice many important government publications were issued as non-parliamentary papers – and indeed still are – and there were soon complaints from Members that free copies were being withheld from them. Some departments got round the new ruling by sending their publications direct to Members known to be interested, but this was unsatisfactory because some Members received free copies and others did not. After two years the full rigour of the economy drive was relaxed, and a new rule was devised:

'. . . that in future any Member shall be able to obtain, on special application to the Controller of the Stationery Office, a copy of any non-parliamentary publication of the current session reasonably required for the discharge of his Parliamentary duties. In any case of difficulty, the Controller will refer the matter to the Treasury.'[3]

At first, Members had to apply to the Controller by letter to obtain non-parliamentary papers, but subsequently forms were provided.

Even after this change, there was some discontent among Members. In 1945 Mr Maxton complained that the filling up of forms for non-parliamentary publications was 'a nuisance and causes delay'.[4] The Treasury's reply was that 'if we opened the door in one direction we should have to open it very widely',

[1] For a list of the series transferred to the non-parliamentary category, see the Select Committee on Publications and Debates Reports, 1923, H.C. 140, pp 65–9.
[2] Treasury letter 38/21.
[3] H.C. Deb., 1 April 1924, 171, c. 1994. For the campaign by the Select Committee on Publications and Debates Reports to secure this relaxation, see H.C. 140, 1923, and H.C. 63, 1924–25.
[4] H.C. Deb., 13 November 1945, 415, c. 1919.

and the policy remained that non-parliamentary publications must be specially applied for. As a result such publications are less widely distributed to Members than parliamentary publications. In one major category – statistical publications – the main papers are now almost all non-parliamentary.[1]

The working of the system may be illustrated by some examples of different categories of papers. Reports of royal commissions, but not usually their evidence, are Command papers; in addition, some reports of departmental committees are Command papers but some are not. Command papers are stocked by the Vote Office. Annual reports of many public bodies are House of Commons papers, as were those of almost all nationalised industries until recently. These categories likewise are stocked by the Vote Office.[2] The following, on the other hand, are examples of non-parliamentary publications: (a) such statistical publications as the Annual Abstract of Statistics and the National Income 'Blue Book'; (b) the Wootton Report on cannabis; (c) the Plowden Report on primary schools; (d) the NEDC Green Books on the growth of the UK economy (the predecessors of the National Plan); (e) most of the Government's 'green papers', which are published for discussion before policies are adopted; (f) the Beeching Report on the future of the railways.[3] None of these would normally be stocked by the Vote Office. In recent years, however, departments have arranged for the Vote Office to stock the most important non-parliamentary papers, thus blurring the distinction between the parliamentary and non-parliamentary categories and undermining the justification, such as it was, for the system. The present practice is that any non-parliamentary papers which a Minister considers likely to be of interest to Members are placed in the Vote Office.

[1] On the supply of statistical publications to Members, see G. F. Lock, 'Statistics for Politicians', *Statistical News*, pp 9–12 (February 1971).

[2] However, there are inexplicable exceptions. Although it used to be one, the annual report of the Bank of England is not now a parliamentary paper. The annual report of the Department of Education and Science has likewise been demoted from the parliamentary to the non-parliamentary category.

[3] Some time after the publication of the Beeching Report, the Ministry hurriedly went through the motions of 'laying' the paper before the House, but without including it in the numbered Command series. The reason was that a debate had been arranged, and the rule is that papers forming the subject of a debate must be laid before the House.

When a Member wants a non-parliamentary publication not stocked by the Vote Office, he fills in a 'green form', and the publication is ordered from the Stationery Office. Thus there is a slight delay in obtaining it. The item is free if the Controller of the Stationery Office regards it as necessary for the Member's parliamentary duties. Grievances can arise in connection with these decisions. For instance, in 1965 Edward Short (Government Chief Whip at the time) complained that he had been granted books on beekeeping and forestry but refused one on Jamaica. When asked about the basis for this type of decision, the Deliverer of the Vote said he had been trying without success to discover the answer to that question for twenty years.[1]

Two further categories of papers may be mentioned, neither of which is stocked or handled by the Vote Office, but which are laid before Parliament. The first consists of printed reports which are published by bodies other than the Stationery Office. Examples are the annual reports of the Port of London Authority, the Scottish Tourist Board and the Trent River Authority. Members wanting their own copies of these have to apply to the bodies that publish them. A copy of each such paper is, however, available in the Library. Secondly, there are papers presented to Parliament in typescript, such as pilotage returns. The Library also has copies of these.

In general, the acquisition by Members of non-parliamentary papers has been facilitated in recent years. The growing tendency of Government departments to arrange for the Vote Office to stock the most important of their non-parliamentary papers has been mentioned. Moreover, the rule limiting the supply of free non-parliamentary papers to those issued during the current session was liberalised in 1956. Since then Members have been able to obtain free copies of such papers for previous sessions as well.[2] A further liberalisation came into effect in February 1972. Since then the number of copies of each of the free non-parliamentary papers allowed to Members has been

[1] Select Committee on the Palace of Westminster, 1964–65, H.C. 285, Q. 370. A further point emerging from the evidence in this report is that Members are entitled to a free copy of bound volumes of the statutes for the period of their membership of the House, but have to pay for volumes for dates before their election. Q. 375.

[2] H.C. Deb., 17 July 1956, 556, c. 1048.

two instead of one.[1] As a further aid to Members, a daily list of available publications is displayed in a window outside the Vote Office. These lists, which have been posted since January 1972, include parliamentary, departmental, HMSO and Common Market publications.

The increased availability of free papers, while generally welcomed by Members, has put new pressures on the resources of the Vote Office. The Office has a distribution point in the Members' Lobby at which Members can collect material, and it has a large reserve store in the basement. But one can well appreciate the storage problems which result from the variability of need and demand, depending on the business that is before the House. The growth in demand is illustrated by figures on the number of items handled by the Office. In 1946 the number was estimated at 850,000; in 1948, at 1,000,000; in 1965, at 1,200,000; in 1969, at 1,750,000; and in 1973, at 2,175,000.[2] As an example of strain on the Office, one recalls the situation on 14 January 1972 when each of the 630 Members became simultaneously entitled to forty-two volumes containing the regulations of the European Economic Community.[3] Documentation from the Common Market has in fact been coming into the Vote Office like a torrent. By September 1973 the number of EEC papers in the Vote Office was twice the number of UK papers!

The Office is required to keep in stock and distribute on demand every parliamentary paper issued in the current session and the two preceding sessions. Because of limitations on shelf space, it is only possible to keep thirty copies of each paper once its initial issue is over. An awkward situation can develop if great numbers of Members ask for a particular paper at once. Should the Office fail to produce a paper which a Member feels he should have in connection with the day's business, the Member can appeal to the Speaker to stop the debate. To avoid such a catastrophe, the Deliverer of the Vote studies future business and tops up relevant stocks appropriately. In addition

[1] H.C. Deb., 10 February 1972, 830, c. *448* written answers.

[2] Select Committee on Accommodation, 1953–54, H.C. 184, pp 148–9; Select Committee on the Palace of Westminster, 1964, H.C. 285, p 53. The 1965, 1969 and 1973 figures were provided by the Deliverer of the Vote.

[3] This was the largest package of documents ever issued to Members. Each set cost the public £143. *The Times* (London), (14 January 1972).

the Department concerned with an item of business places a list of 'older papers' in the Library as a guide to Members. It is the responsibility of Members to order such papers if they want them.

In addition to serving Members in the Palace of Westminster, the Vote Office ensures the delivery of considerable numbers of parliamentary papers to Members' private addresses. These deliveries may be either by post or by hand. Deliveries are by hand if the Member lives within three miles of the Palace of Westminster.[1] Members with no address within this radius may have their papers posted. Deliveries in London provide Members at breakfast-time with such papers as the Vote, bills and papers which Ministers designate for 'full delivery'. In a separate operation, daily *Hansards* are loaded into post office vans at about 4.30 a.m. and delivered by first post to Members in the London area.

4.3 THE SALE OFFICE

The Sale Office, which comes under the control of the Deliverer of the Vote, is a place where Members, parliamentary agents and outside organisations can *buy* government publications. This service is important when Members require more papers than the free issue through the Vote Office allows. Generally, however, the free issue is adequate for most Members. Members are entitled to a free issue of the following: (a) six copies of the daily *Hansard*, (b) six copies of each bill,[2] (c) one copy of all the other parliamentary papers that are issued.[3]

In addition to serving Members, the Sale Office supplies government publications to the staffs of parliamentary agents, who are concerned with proceedings on Private Bills. The Office also provides the main photocopying facilities for Members.

4.4 HANSARD

As was previously noted, the staff which produces the *Official Report* of what is said in the House of Commons is larger than

[1] Deliveries by hand are made by seventeen part-time porters who report for duty each day at 7 a.m.

[2] An MP may obtain up to twenty-five free copies of a bill by special application to the Speaker.

[3] Members are also entitled to have any parliamentary paper mailed to them free of postage.

the rest of the Speaker's Department combined; therefore the service provided by this staff will be examined in some detail. Although we shall be dealing with the *Official Report* of the House of Commons, it should be mentioned that a parallel *Report* is prepared by a similar procedure for the Lords.

The full title of the publication is *House of Commons Official Report: Parliamentary Debates* (*Hansard*), hereafter referred to as *Hansard*. There is a daily *Hansard*; a *Weekly Hansard*, consisting of a week's daily parts; and bound volumes of *Hansard*, each of which includes about two weeks' debates. Each *Weekly Hansard* and bound volume has an index, and there is also a sessional bound index.

4.4.1 *Before 1909*

Records of what is said and done in the House of Commons have been kept in one form or another for a considerable time. Such records can be classified into two categories. First, there are the relatively succinct official minutes of what action has been taken, as recorded in the annual *Journal of the House of Commons* and the daily *Votes and Proceedings*.[1] Secondly, there are the full reports of what has been said in debates, as recorded in *Hansard*. The *Journal* is the oldest of these publications, dating from 1547. Since at least 1623 the *Journal* has been regarded as the official record of the proceedings of the House.

As far as *Hansard* is concerned, there have been two main periods in its life. First, there is the period before 1909 when *Hansard* was an unofficial, private publication that reported the debates of Parliament in summary form. Subsequently, *Hansard* has been an official document, recording speeches on a verbatim basis. Thus, the keeping of a verbatim – not to mention official – record of what is said in the House of Commons (and House of Lords) is a practice little more than sixty years old.[2]

Prior to 1800 MPs were reluctant to have their debates recorded in even summary form. This attitude mainly affected journalists since *Hansard* did not come into existence until 1803,

---

[1] See Chapter 2, *passim*. See also David Menhennet, *The Journal of the House of Commons*, HMSO (1971), (House of Commons Library Document No. 7.)

[2] For a brief account of the history of *Hansard*, see *Official Publications*, pp 4–6, HMSO (1958).

but the issue was one in which journalists and *Hansard* reporters would find common cause. Forbidden from taking notes in the Gallery, journalists had to rely on their memories and hearsay. It was a breach of privilege to report the proceedings of Parliament, and many publishers and printers were brought before the Lords and Commons and cross-examined as to their sources of information. But as the eighteenth century progressed, it became evident that the journalists were winning. With informed opinion against secrecy and with the rivalry between the Commons and the monarchy subsiding, the House became increasingly tolerant of journalists, and the concern of Members turned to the accuracy of journalists' reports.

Coinciding with these changes in parliamentary attitudes, we find the beginnings of *Hansard*. In 1803 William Cobbett began to include a regular report of Parliamentary debates in his *Political Register*.[1] This marked the beginning of what can now be called a continuous record of debates in the two Houses of Parliament during the nineteenth and twentieth centuries. The early reports were summary (not verbatim) in character and were compiled entirely from newspapers, there being no 'Hansard' reporters. However, by combining various press accounts Cobbett was able to produce, at monthly intervals, a reasonably fair and unbiased record.[2] The name Hansard came into the picture in 1812 when Cobbett sold the *Register* to his printer, Thomas Hansard. From 1812 to 1890 the debates were published by the Hansard family, and the publication became indelibly known as *Hansard*. During these years the reports remained summary in content, were compiled mainly from newspapers and were available at about monthly intervals.[3]

As the nineteenth century progressed, journalists and *Hansard* reporters were accorded increasing recognition as essential elements in the life of the House of Commons. In 1803 journal-

[1] See House of Commons Library Document No. 2, *A Bibliography of Parliamentary Debates of Great Britain*, HMSO (1956; reprinted 1967). An early Parliamentary diary kept by Anchitell Grey, MP, and covering the period 1667–94, was first published in 1763 (second edition, 1769).

[2] Cobbett, it should be noted, added very little to the procedures first employed by John Almon whose *Parliamentary Register*, from 1774 to 1803, was published monthly. See *A Bibliography of Parliamentary Debates of Great Britain, op. cit.*, pp 11–12.

[3] For a part of this period (1828–41) Barrow's *Mirror of Parliament* (London, 60 volumes) was a serious rival to *Hansard*.

ists were provided for the first time with seats in the Public Gallery. The back row was given over to them, and they took notes openly. In 1835 the first Press Gallery – above the Speaker's Chair – was incorporated into the temporary Commons chamber. When the new Parliament building opened in 1852, a Press Gallery was again provided in the House. In 1840 the Parliamentary Papers Bill was enacted. It provided that all documents published by order of Parliament were privileged and that their publishers were protected against libel actions. This legislation was deemed necessary after the publishers of *Hansard* were successfully sued for libel for publishing a parliamentary report.[1]

Coinciding with this recognition of the importance of reporting debates came an evaluation by the House of the way in which it was being done. An aspect of this question was the feasibility and economic viability of private control of the *Hansard* operation. In due course the House and the Government became directly involved in what had previously been a private undertaking. The first step in this direction was taken in 1855 when, threatened with bankruptcy, the publishers of *Hansard* were rescued by a Treasury guarantee that it would buy 100 sets of *Hansard*. Three years later the official subscription was increased to 120 sets.

In 1878 a select committee considered the entire question of Parliamentary reporting. As a result of its recommendations *Hansard* was given a Government subsidy on condition that the quality of its report improved. It was at this point that the first *Hansard* reporter was appointed for the purpose of attending debates and supplementing the press reports which up to then had provided the sole source of information for *Hansard*. One problem facing *Hansard* was that newspapers were now devoting full pages to their own Parliamentary reports, making it necessary for *Hansard* to increase its coverage in order to remain viable. MPs meanwhile, were pressing for an even fuller report.

In 1888 another select committee considered the position. Finding the *Hansard* report inadequate, it recommended greater Government control. Accordingly, the Government established a contractual relationship with the publishers, requiring among

[1] *Stockdale* v. *Hansard*, 1837.

other things that a staff of reporters be engaged. Unable to meet the conditions of the contract, the Hansard family sold *Hansard* to another firm. From 1890 to 1909 the contract was held by a series of firms in what one writer has called 'the worst period in the whole story of Hansard'.[1] This period saw an increase in the size of the staff, but the recruits tended to be moonlighting journalists who took little pride in the extra drudgery. By 1907 there were seven reporters on the staff. In an effort to obliterate the designation *Hansard*, the name of the publication was changed to the *Authorized Edition*. (In 1943 *Hansard* was restored to the title page after fifty-one years of non-recognition.[2])

An attempt was made in the pre-1909 period to make the report more comprehensive. The contractors required their reporters to make verbatim reports of frontbench speeches and to report one-third to two-thirds of what backbenchers said. In major debates there was to be a verbatim report of all speeches. The report was published more frequently than before, coming out by 1909 in intervals of a fortnight to a month. Despite such changes, dissatisfaction with the report remained high, and another select committee met in 1907 to consider the situation.

4.4.2   *The New Task*

The 1907 Committee established ground rules for the reporting of Commons debates which have been in effect ever since. The most important outcome was that the *Official Report*, as it was re-designated, was transformed from its existing status halfway between private and public control to full public control. Beginning in 1909, an enlarged official reporting staff was brought under the authority of the Speaker and also under a sessional committee of the House.[3] Thus, although *Hansard* is printed by Government printers and distributed by HM

---

[1] William Law, *Our Hansard*, p 16, Pitman (1950).

[2] Successive editors studiously avoided the word *Hansard* despite its frequent use in the House.

[3] Until 1965 the overseeing committee was the Committee on Publications and Debates Reports. This Committee performed a variety of roles. In addition to the production of *Hansard*, it concerned itself with the form of the Order Paper and the arrangements for Members to obtain official publications. It also acted at times as a supervisory committee for the Stationery Office. Since 1965 the Services Committee has provided oversight in relation to *Hansard*.

Stationery Office, it is the responsibility of the House of Commons.[1]

A further requirement was that coverage would henceforth be on a verbatim basis, thus ending the earlier discrimination between frontbench and backbench speeches. While not literally verbatim, the report would be as verbatim as possible. As the select committee defined the position, the *Official Report* would be one which 'though not strictly verbatim, is substantially the verbatim report, with repetitions and redundancies omitted, and with obvious mistakes corrected, but which, on the other hand, leaves out nothing that adds to the meaning of the speech or illustrates the argument'.[2] Accepting the Committee's recommendations on behalf of the Government, Mr Hobhouse told the House in 1908, when asked what he meant by a 'full' report:

'It means a verbatim report, trimmed of all those excrescences and redundancies with which Members are perhaps in the habit of filling up the matter of their speeches . . . a full report putting into something like literary shape the efforts with which we endeavour to express our thoughts.'[3]

These guidelines are still the rule.

A further change was that the report would henceforth be published more expeditiously. The days of waiting for up to a month to see one's utterances in print were at an end. From now on the report would be published on a daily basis. At first it became available by 4 p.m. on the day following the day of debate. Since 1917 it has been available the following morning. To make this possible, the staff was enlarged to include ten reporters in addition to the Editor. On another matter, the existing practice of Members making wholesale changes in the proofs of their speeches was ended. Members would still be permitted to suggest changes, but none that would alter the sense of what they had said, and the Editor would have the final say.

[1] HMSO took over the responsibility for publishing and printing the Commons and Lords *Hansards* in 1920.

[2] Quoted in J. C. Trewin and E. M. King, *Printer to the House: The Story of Hansard*, pp 261–3, Methuen (1952).

[3] Quoted in Law, *op. cit.*, p 20.

And so in 1909 the daily, verbatim *Hansard* came into being.[1] This meant the beginning of the Fifth Series of bound volumes of *Hansard*, and the first in which Lords and Commons debates were reported separately.[2] Before 1909 the Lords report had always appeared at the beginning of *Hansard*, with the Commons report following it. In 1909 the Lords made arrangements for separate publication, and have since published their own verbatim report.

4.4.3   *Reporters at Work*

There are three separate staffs engaged in reporting the spoken proceedings of Parliament. They are (a) the *Hansard* staff of the House of Commons, which reports proceedings of the House and its standing committees, (b) the *Hansard* staff of the House of Lords, and (c) the staff of the Shorthand Writer to the Houses of Parliament, which reports, among other things, the proceedings of select committees and private bill committees.[3] It is with the first of these staffs that we are concerned.

How does the Commons *Hansard* staff go about its work? By any criterion it is a remarkable editorial operation. As Vincent Hamson, a former Editor of *Hansard* has said: 'Two questions which are always asked whenever *Hansard* is under discussion relate to the extent to which MPs are allowed to correct their speeches, and to the methods by which it is possible to publish the daily report of Parliament so quickly'.[4] What is

[1] Sessions of the Commons have since been reported continuously except for secret sessions in wartime and one peacetime occasion. On 18 November 1958 George Wigg (Labour Member for Dudley) caught his fellow Members unawares when he moved that 'strangers be ordered to withdraw'. In accordance with Standing Order No. 89 the motion was put without discussion and there were no dissents. *Hansard* reporters and journalists were obliged to withdraw for the rest of the day. See Ronald Butt, *The Power of Parliament*, pp 382–3, Constable (1967).

[2] The First Series, consisting of forty-one volumes, covers the period 1803–20. The Second Series, consisting of twenty-five volumes, covers the period 1820–30. The Third Series, consisting of 356 volumes, covers the period 1830–91. The Fourth Series, consisting of 199 volumes, covers the period 1892–1908.

[3] The staff of the Shorthand Writer also reports the proceedings of the judicial sittings of the Lords and trials of election petitions. Although it is not a duty under his official appointment, the Shorthand Writer is also usually asked to report the proceedings of royal commissions. The present holder of the office of Shorthand Writer, which dates from 1813, is A. R. Kennedy. He is associated with W. B. Gurney and Sons, a private shorthand firm.

[4] Vincent Hamson, 'The Production of Hansard', *Parliamentary Affairs*, **8**, p 254 (Spring 1955). Hamson was Editor from 1950 to 1954.

remarkable is that the staff produces a 100-page report, covering proceedings in the House from 2.30 to 10.30 or 11 p.m., and gets it to MPs by breakfast-time the following day. It includes not only everything said in speeches, but also oral questions and answers, written questions and answers, and division lists. Hamson found the achievement duplicated in very few Parliaments in the world:

'While I was editor of the House of Commons *Hansard* I was surprised at the extent to which our help was sought. ... Hardly a week passed without a visit from members or officials from one or another overseas Parliament inquiring into our methods of organisation. ... I was surprised, too, at the primitive and slow-moving methods of many of their official reports and by the fact that daily publication is very rare.'

Hamson suggests why daily publication is rare in other Parliaments: 'In almost every case I have found that the main difficulties are: lack of resources placed at the disposal of the report, and the delay caused by members revising the proofs of their speeches'.[1]

The *Hansard* reporters sit in the centre of the front row of the Press Gallery, which is situated above and behind the Speaker's Chair.[2] Microphones hang from the Commons ceiling, there are loudspeakers in the Press Gallery, and the reporters have ear-phones. Thus everything possible is done to ensure audibility and to assist in the reporting of soft-spoken Members. From all accounts the process is further aided by the strong collaborative spirit which prevails as between *Hansard* reporters and journalists. Even the Doorkeeper, who keeps a list of Members who have spoken, helps out.

The verbatim recording of speeches in the Commons is an arduous and testing task for even the best shorthand writers. This is particularly true during Question time when supplementary Questions and interruptions bordering on tumult may

[1] Hamson, *op. cit.*

[2] The fact that the occupant of the Chair is invisible to *Hansard* reporters can present a problem. Law tells of leaning over the edge of the Gallery, trying to peer around the wings of the Chair, or waiting for the presiding officer to thrust out an identifiable shoe. *Op. cit.*, p 26. In the Lords, *Hansard* reporters sit at floor level opposite the Woolsack at the other end of the chamber.

come without warning from any part of the House.[1] Shorthand speeds of up to 200 words per minute may be required. Fast speakers in oratorical flight reach speeds of 220 words per minute.

The *Hansard* reporter must not only have exemplary short-hand technique. He must also have a good knowledge of Parliamentary procedure and be able to cope with opaque, inaudible and circumlocutious argument. He should also be knowledgeable about current affairs. When a taunting intervention is flung across the floor, it helps comprehension to be *au fait*. His mental processes must be rapid since he will often be obliged to begin his stint in the middle of a complicated legal argument of whose origin he knows nothing. Finally, he must be able to shape a speech in ways which will enhance its coherence without altering its sense.

At present the Commons reporting staff, excluding transcribers, typists and office workers, consists of twenty-six persons. They are the Editor, a Deputy Editor, three assistant editors, eight senior reporters and thirteen reporters. The Deputy Editor, assistant editors and reporters are responsible for the daily part; the senior reporters, for the standing committee *Hansards*. All are officials of the House of Commons, and the Editor and Deputy Editor rank as Officers. The salaries of the reporters and the editorial staff are linked to the Information Officer grades in the civil service.

Reporters work in the 'trench' in short spurts and on a rotation basis. At any time there are three reporters present – a duty reporter who makes the definitive note, a check reporter and a standby reporter. During the first half of the Parliamentary day a stint lasts for ten minutes. Later, when it is necessary to move copy to the printer with a minimum of delay, stints last for only five minutes. While the duty reporter takes his note, the check reporter, who sits beside him, backs him up by taking a check note. During fast speaking or procedural complications, the check reporter may take a full verbatim note, and there is also double note-taking at Question time. At other times the check

---

[1] Question time has been described, from the reporter's point of view, as 'trying to catch inaudible replies to incomprehensible questions, put by unseen Members'. Jean Winder, 'Reporting for Hansard', in Emily D. Smith (editor), *High-Speed Shorthand Round the World*, p 10, Pitman (1961).

reporter may only note interventions or the names of speakers or just listen. At all times he is a second witness if queries should arise, and the standby reporter is a third.

As the duty reporter's turn nears its conclusion, the check reporter, who is about to take over, is by now taking a full note and watching the clock. The check reporter whispers 'right' to his colleague and becomes the duty reporter.[1] The retiring reporter completes his sentence and departs to transcribe his take. The standby slips into the seat beside the new duty reporter and another reporter enters the gallery to replace him as the standby.

With the words he has recorded fresh in his mind, the reporter with a completed take immediately dictates his notes to a typist.[2] As he dictates, he begins the tidying up process. He must correct grammatical errors, complete unfinished sentences and shorten overlong sentences so as to make the speech readable, while retaining as nearly as possible the speaker's own style. One gathers that a side benefit of being a *Hansard* reporter is that it provides an opportunity, while dictating to typists, to re-create the Member's speech, affecting his or some other speaking style, such as a clergyman's. Law recalls these occasions as pleasant experiences which ideally should be free from such distractions as a noisy typewriter. As for the typists, they ask only that the reporter speaks clearly and does not smoke a pipe, especially when grappling with such passages as: 'We believe the Clause to be restrictive, ossifying, petrifying, atrophying, lapidifying, corrupting, stiff-necked, inflexible – a cretinous Clause in a bunkum-filled Bill'.[3]

After a transcript is typed, the reporter takes it to the *Hansard* reporters' room and reads it through. The transcript is carefully scrutinised at this stage, and further editing normally takes place. The reporter verifies names, figures and quotations he has

---

[1] One reporter frequently said 'right' in a voice loud enough to be heard on the floor. Law tells of a Budget debate when a Member said: 'I am sure that many people would be grateful to the Chancellor if their cup of tea could be just a little cheaper'. 'Right', said the reporter, and the Member nodded his thanks for this unexpected support. Law, *op. cit.*, p 30.

[2] Until he has dictated its contents, a reporter's notebook is a precious document. Stories are told of one reporter who dropped his notebook into the Thames from the Members' Terrace and another who, having taken a late-night transcription home, dictated the contents from his bed in his dying breaths. Law, *op. cit.*, p 33.   [3] Law, *op. cit.*, pp 35–6.

noted, and he may ask the Member for *his* notes as a means of facilitating the process, especially if the speech contains a lot of factual detail. Members are usually very co-operative in this. The reporter endeavours not only to ensure that he got the Member's version right, but also – up to a point – that the Member himself got it right, particularly where parliamentary procedure is concerned. If a Member is merely 'honourable', he must not be called 'gallant'. Quotations are checked with sources – the most frequent being the Bible, Shakespeare and earlier *Hansards*. The speech must also be made coherent and shorn of repetitions and bad English. In the whole revision process the bias must always of course be strongly in favour of leaving the speech as the Member made it.

The next step for the reporter is to take his transcript to an office where the Deputy Editor and three assistant editors are at work. This is where all transcripts come to rest after reporters have completed their revisions. Hamson has described this office as 'the busiest room in the whole building while the House is sitting'.[1] The final revision of transcripts is made at this stage. These revisions must be made rapidly in order to cope with the steady flow of incoming copy and to ensure that the flow continues beyond the editors to the printer. The continuity becomes particularly important as the parliamentary day nears its end and pressures build up at the printing plant.

In the course of their scrutiny the editors bring a broader perspective to the day's proceedings than any reporter is able to do. Whereas a duty reporter will normally have heard only a part of one Member's speech, the editors read all that is said in the House throughout the day. This broader perspective – in regard to speeches and whole debates – enables editors to consider factors of sequence and overall coherence.[2] The editors make further alterations relating to coherence, grammar and facts.

As reporters' 'takes' come into the editors' office, so do other

---

[1] Hamson, *op. cit.*, p 256.

[2] Hamson tells of a reporter who was a master of condensation. This reporter did not hesitate to abridge a speech if he considered a Member too verbose, a judgement which was often made judging from his short takes. One can appreciate the difficulties of an editor dealing with an abridged section of a Member's speech sandwiched between full takes of the same speech. 'Such is the kindly tolerance of Members', said Hamson, 'that though I daily shuddered at the possible consequences, I did not once hear of a complaint'. Members christened the reporter the 'short cutter'. Hamson, *op. cit.*, pp 257–8.

bits and pieces. The Department of the Clerk supplies division lists. Oral and written Questions are taken from the Order Paper. Answers to Questions are provided by Government Departments. The only things not said in the House that are included in *Hansard* are oral and written Questions and answers to written Questions. Parts of oral answers may also be unuttered. When there are long statistical passages, it is usual for a Minister to say, 'I will, with permission, circulate it in the *Official Report*'.

Editors perform an exacting task when they clear all this material for printing, not least because they will not see the proofs. All proof-reading is done at the printer's. Every half-hour a batch of copy is picked up by a messenger and taken to the printing plant. At the same time messengers are picking up copy from the House of Lords and from standing committees.

In order to meet printing requirements the report is normally 'closed' by the Deputy Editor at about 10.30 p.m. If the House sits beyond that hour, the remainder of the debate is included in the next day's *Hansard*. Sometimes, however, debates are reported beyond 10.30 and up to 11 p.m. This will occur if, for example, there is a convenient break during that period or a Minister is speaking or there is a division. In any event, the final 'takes' of the day must be moved rapidly and may be dispatched to the printer as soon as forty-five minutes after a speech has been made.

At the printer's, meanwhile, Linotype operators are setting-up type and providing proofs to proof-readers. Corrections are made, and the daily part is printed, wrapped and addressed. All MPs in the London area can expect to get their daily parts in the first post. Thus it is not unknown for a Member to deliver a speech at 10 p.m. and read it in printed form at 8 a.m. the following morning.

When the daily parts are printed, extra sheets are laid aside for making up every Friday into the *Weekly Hansard*. Thus the *Weekly Hansard* is literally a putting together of daily sheets. This explains something that MPs often fail to understand, namely why corrections cannot be made for the *Weekly Hansard*.[1] The bound volumes, on the other hand, incorporate corrections inserted after the daily and weekly parts have been

[1] The Commons *Weekly Hansard* was first published in 1946; the Lords', in 1947.

published. The Editor reads each daily part after it is published and makes final revisions for the bound volumes. MPs, too, may submit corrections for the bound volumes within a week of giving their speeches, but such corrections must be approved by the Editor.[1] Corrections for the bound volumes are important because these volumes constitute the definitive record of what is said in the House.

4.4.4 Members' Corrections

While Members may submit corrections for the bound volumes, the more usual time to do this is during the pre-publication editing of the daily part. In this process there may be some contact between the duty reporter and the MP, but it is more usual for MPs to intervene after transcripts have reached the editors' office.

Members have no right to see transcripts of their speeches, and most do not ask to do so. But in practice any Member may see his transcript in the editors' office, although this must normally take place within an hour of the delivery of his speech. From an editing point of view, this practice has its beneficial side in that mistakes may be caught. Indeed, an editor may himself initiate an unofficial contact with a Member if in doubt about a point.

We have already discussed the kinds of editorial alterations that can be made in what is said on the floor. Within these boundaries Members may make their own suggestions, and in such discretionary areas as style, coherence and grammar their suggestions are often accepted. But the Editor has the final say. If a Member should desire to take a matter beyond the Editor, the Speaker is the final arbiter, but in practice very few disputes of this kind are brought to the Speaker.[2]

On two occasions – in 1914 and 1944 – Speakers have laid down guidelines for Members' corrections. They based their rulings on the practices of editors and made it clear that the grounds for alteration are narrow. Speaker Lowther said in 1914:

'I have consulted the Editor . . . he said that the chief principle

---

[1] Members make corrections for the bound volumes on proofs obtained from the Vote Office. In the case of Ministers and Privy Counsellors, proofs of their speeches are automatically provided to them.

[2] Trewin and King, *op. cit.*, p 263.

which guided him was to obtain an absolutely correct report of what was said. .... He is very careful not to allow any corrections which would in any way alter the general sense of the speech made, but that he does accept corrections, for instance, of faults of grammar, split infinitives, redundancies or incorrect dates.'[1]

In his 1944 ruling Speaker Clifton-Brown referred to Members' 'who are rather in the habit, I almost might say, of rewriting their speeches', adding that 'some hon. Members do not know what may or may not go into *Hansard*'. Speaker Clifton-Brown recalled a correction that had been submitted to him; a Member wanted the following words inserted: 'Loud cheers by hon. Members'.[2]

Problems arise when a Member wants to strike out a passage which he regrets having uttered or desires to insert an afterthought. New Members in particular will request substantive alterations of this kind. They are not allowed. Even Ministers are required to conform. As Hamson has said:

'Ministers' speeches are usually revised by their departmental private secretaries, who are inclined to be a little perturbed if a minister departs from his official brief ... I have frequently had to resist attempts, usually made by new secretaries, to alter a speech to conform to the brief. We are, and must be, adamant in refusing to allow this.'

The remedy for a Minister wanting to make a correction is to do so in a subsequent statement in the House, as is often done.[3]

However, the situation is not completely inflexible. Sir Henry Morris-Jones has revealed an occasion during World War II when the sense of one of his speeches was modified. As he tells it in his book, after the landing of Rudolf Hess in Scotland in 1941, Sir Henry spoke 'somewhat impetuously, and perhaps unwisely' in the House. Afterwards, he was taken by the Speaker to the latter's room to modify the sense of his speech for *Hansard*. There was concern that what he had said would be read by

---

[1] Quoted in Law, *op. cit.*, p 45.   [2] Law, *op. cit.*, p 47.
[3] Hamson, *op. cit.*, p 259. Answers to supplementary Questions are closely noted by Ministers' private secretaries who always check with editors on their wording.

the enemy.[1] Jack Hawke, a former *Hansard* reporter and journalist, recalls an instance in the 'thirties when Speaker Fitzroy expunged 'The Prime Minister is a swine' from the daily part. This remark had been directed at Ramsay MacDonald by a Labour backbencher.[2]

According to Hamson, Members make few corrections and often comment that their speeches have come out better in print than they thought they would. Disputes between the Editor and Members over what was said appear to be relatively infrequent. When, in cases of dispute, the reporter is in doubt whether he heard the Member correctly, the Member's version is accepted. But not all Members have been complaisant. A few have told editors that they objected to their speeches being 'improved', preferring them to be reported exactly as spoken. One Member wanted hesitations in his speeches indicated, as well as false starts to sentences. When he had been emphatic, another Member said, the words should be italicised. All such suggestions for literal reporting have been rejected. As Hawke says, 'If you started putting in people's mistakes, very soon the report would be unreadable.'[3]

Finally, although Members may read transcripts of their own speeches, they may not read those of other Members. Such requests are often made by Members, but they are invariably turned down. The following reason has been given: 'Apart from the confusion and delay that would be caused in the Hansard office by permitting this, it would spoil the whole spirit of debate if Members were able to absent themselves from the House and come in and reply to something they had not troubled to listen to'.[4]

4.4.5 *Interventions and Verbal Oddities*

In the course of reporting debates various recurring problems arise. One such problem is what to do about things that are said and done in the House which do not constitute parts of speeches. As readers of the parliamentary reports in the press are aware, proceedings are frequently enlivened by interventions, 'prolonged' applause and 'ironical' cheers. The general rule, as far as

[1] Sir Henry Morris-Jones, *Doctor in the Whips' Room*, p 158, Hale (1955). Quoted in Peter G. Richards, *Honourable Members*, pp 79–80, Faber (second edition, 1964).
[2] Interview with Jack Hawke (27 July 1970).　　　　[3] *Ibid.*
[4] Hamson, *op. cit.*, p 258.

Hansard is concerned, is to omit bracketed descriptive comment unless the debate does not make sense without it. It is felt that a fuller inclusion of such descriptions would give unfair prominence to some speeches.

Nevertheless, 'laughter' will appear in brackets when a Member remarks, for example, 'It is all very well for Members opposite to laugh'. Moreover, a major break in a speech is covered by the all-purpose 'Interruption'; but as one reporter has said, 'as this is needed to convey the nearest thing to a brawl which ever takes place in the House, it has to be used sparingly'.[1] A case in point arose in July 1970 when a visitor threw two canisters of CS gas from the Gallery to the floor of the House, resulting in complete and prolonged confusion. While the incident was given extensive front-page coverage in the press, it was disposed of in *Hansard* with: [Interruption].[2] Similarly, when Bernadette Devlin (Independent Unity Member for Mid-Ulster) struck Mr Maudling (the Home Secretary) after launching herself across the House with a cry of 'that murdering hypocrite', the fracas was recorded in *Hansard* by: [Interruption].[3]

One of the most famous interventions in the history of the Commons occurred on 2 September 1939. As Churchill recalled the occasion:

'... when Parliament met in the evening a short but very fierce debate occurred, in which the Prime Minister's temporising statement was ill-received by the House. When Mr Greenwood rose to speak on behalf of the Labour Opposition, Mr Amery from the Conservative benches cried out to him, "Speak for England". This was received with loud cheers. There was no doubt that the temper of the House was for war.'[4]

Amery's intervention was not included in *Hansard*.

Various problems which chronically bedevil reporters may be classified under the headings mis-hearings, mis-typings, non-hearings, repetitions and mixed metaphors. Law has assembled

[1] Winder, *op. cit.*, p 17.   [2] H.C. Deb., 23 July 1970, 804, c. 785.
[3] *The Times* (London), (1 February 1972). H.C. Deb., 31 January 1972, 830, c. 41.
[4] *The Second World War: The Gathering Storm*, p 318, Cassell (1948).

an amusing collection of mis-hearings and mis-typings. They include (the correct word is in brackets): God's [Dod's] Parliamentary Companion. A full-bottomed Whig [wig]. Half a chair [Hertfordshire]. Some call him a strong man, but I say he is potty [putty]. Miss Noma [misnomer]. The Government are mopping the floors [dropping the Clause].[1] One might also mention the occasion when R. A. Butler, then Chancellor of the Exchequer, gave out a string of figures in dollars. *Hansard* and the *Times* reported the figures as pounds, giving the impression that the drain on gold and dollar reserves had been three times as great as it actually was.[2]

As for unheard utterances, there was the occasion when one of Churchill's words, carefully chosen as ever, was heard in three different versions by three members of the reporters' Gallery sitting side by side. Repetitious speeches present another problem. One Minister had two pet phrases – 'up and down the country' and 'so far as ... is concerned'; and he sometimes succeeded in using these expressions several times in one sentence. The rule is to let these superfluities go in once in a speech and to excise them thereafter. Mixed metaphors, contradictory idioms and illogical antecedents are recalled by reporters with some relish. 'My first duty must be to congratulate the hon. Member who has just sat down on his maiden speech', one Member said. Other examples: 'We have prodded these people in the places where they needed prodding, and our actions are now beginning to bear fruit'. 'The Treasury is not proposing to carry the whole baby, but the greater part of it.' 'The future of this island depends on increased productivity, on us all knitting together.' One Member envisaged road haulage contractors springing up like mushrooms; another, 'the final swinging uppercut that brings the crowd to its feet'. In many cases the risible elements are evident in print, but not during the speech. In general, semantic awkwardnesses are eliminated during editing.

4.4.6   *Standing Committees*

So far we have been concerned with the reporting of proceedings on the floor of the Commons. We now turn to the other main

[1] Law, *op. cit.*, pp 60–2.
[2] Winder, *op. cit.*, p 15.

task carried out by the *Hansard* staff – the reporting of proceedings in the standing committees.[1]

Many of the points made apply to the committee room as well as the Commons chamber. Nevertheless, there are important ways in which the task of reporting committee debate presents the reporter with a different situation. This was so before 1964 when all reporting on the floor and in committee was done by shorthand reporters, and the difference became even more marked after 1964 when a fundamental change in reporting technique was introduced.

In 1964 the tape recorder was first used in official reporting in Parliament, and a standing committee was the setting for this innovation. Since 1964 tape recorders have increasingly been used to record committee debates until by now they have replaced shorthand reporters, so far as it is possible to do so, in a substantial proportion of committee work. About two-thirds of the standing committees are now serviced by tape recorders; the others, by shorthand reporters.

As in the House, there is verbatim reporting of standing committees, a service which has been available to Members and the public since 1924. There are daily parts and bound volumes for each committee, the daily parts normally being available to Members the morning following debates.[2] It should be noted that in compiling verbatim reports of all standing committees, the *Hansard* staff is providing an uncommon service. While verbatim reports of plenary meetings of legislative bodies are available in a number of the world's legislatures, it is very rare to find verbatim committee reports.

The setting for committee reporting is very different from that in the House. Proceedings in committee are more intimate and informal, and there is no amplification of speeches. When recording by shorthand alone, a senior reporter sits at a table in the gangway between the two front benches. This proximity

[1] In the 1971–72 session there were eighteen standing committees to report, including the Scottish and Welsh grand committees, two Scottish standing committees and six Second Reading Committees. These committees held a total of 427 sittings.

[2] However, pressure of work at the printers can delay production. Generally speaking, daily parts of committee proceedings are available the following morning provided the number of standing committees on a given day does not exceed seven and provided neither the Commons nor the Lords sits very late into the night.

to Members has its advantages, but there are disadvantages, too. It is sometimes easier for the reporter to hear private conversations on the front benches than to hear the speech at the other end of the room that he is trying to record. Occupants of the two front benches may disconcertingly talk across the reporter in private conversations. A further hazard results from the tendency of some Members to assume that taking shorthand is a simple, mechanical process requiring little mental concentration; these Members will engage the reporter in conversation, expecting him to take notes simultaneously.

Turning to taping procedures, it might first be mentioned that recorders were introduced in 1964 because a practical problem existed. The *Hansard* staff could not cope with the increased committee work which resulted from the heavy legislative programme of the new Labour Government. As a consequence, all committee rooms were set up for taping. At about the same time the House itself was wired for taping when the prospect of morning sittings produced further manning problems. Although morning sittings were held for a short time, no sittings of the House have as yet been officially recorded on tape, although there have been some experimental tapings.

When a committee sitting is recorded on tape, the tape recorders and operator are not physically in the committee room, but two senior reporters are. These reporters are not shorthand writers; they are sub-editors who will put transcriptions from tape into final form. During the committee meeting three recorders are used. One records continuously during the meeting as insurance against mechanical failure. The others record in alternation, ten minutes at a time. Each ten-minute tape is sent to a transcriber. Meanwhile, one of the senior reporters, aided by a standby reporter, is writing the 'log'. The log is a record of names of speakers, the first words of speeches, interventions, and instructions to transcribers clarifying what is on the tape. The log is sent to the transcriber at ten-minute intervals along with the tape. MPs who have spoken may supplement the tape and log by supplying notes of their speeches.

The transcribers produce typed versions of literal speeches from the tapes. In the case of floor reporting, as has been noted, some editing is done when the reporter dictates from his shorthand notes. But committee transcripts provide a word-for-word record, warts and all. The senior reporters who get these transcripts into final shape can do so during the afternoon since committee meetings are normally held in the morning. When the final versions are ready, they go to the printer where committee parts are produced and distributed in the usual way.

Although the machine has not replaced the man in the committee room, it has meant that less shorthand writing is needed, a vital consideration. Also, *fewer* reporters are required. When verbatim shorthand notes are taken in a committee, there must be five reporters on rotation in addition to the reporter on duty. The less arduous task of keeping a log means there is less need for back-up personnel. On the other hand, the need for thirty transcribers, as well as taping equipment, makes taping more expensive than shorthand taking, according to L. W. Bear, a former Editor of *Hansard*.[1] But the problem of recruiting shorthand writers is an overriding consideration.

It is expected that the gradual substitution of machine for man will continue in the committees and possibly also in the House itself. The present Editor of *Hansard* – Richard Dring – has said: 'Since it is easier to recruit temporary transcriber staff than shorthand writers the number of committees tape-recorded is bound to increase'.[2] Bear, Dring's predecessor, said in 1970 that he believes that in the near future the tape recorder will have supplanted the shorthand reporter not only in the rest of the committees but in the House as well.[3] Dring does not go this far, stressing the advantages of the shorthand writer:

'Whether or not we have to switch over to tape-recording depends entirely on the supply of good shorthand writers with experience in this type of work. Ideally the machine is no substitute for a skilled reporter who performs a whole series of functions which have to be separately provided in the case of tape-recording. He is highly mobile since all he (or she) requires is a pen and notebook to perform his duties and he is not subject to mechanical breakdowns. The shorthand writing system of reporting is both cheaper and so far speedier in production of the finished transcript.'

[1] *The Times* (London), (8 February 1972).
[2] Letter to the editors (8 October 1972).
[3] Interview with Bear (22 July 1970). Bear was Editor from 1954 to 1972.

But Dring concludes: 'Unfortunately the profession [of short-hand writers] is a small and diminishing one'.[1] That the problem is not a new one is clear from a statement made by Thomas O'Donoghue at the time of his editorship (1947–50); 'There is a shortage of fully competent verbatim reporters. . . . It is an art in itself, and the number of its practitioners seems to be diminishing'.[2]

Despite the disadvantages of taping, in at least one important respect it has an advantage over even the best reporter. If taping is employed and a Member queries a transcript, the tape can be replayed. In the absence of taping, no such option exists.[3]

4.4.7   Members' Use of Hansard

Since we are examining *Hansard* as a 'service', it may be useful to indicate how much use Members make of it.[4] A recent survey of Members provides us with data on this point.[5] The survey produced the findings shown in Table 4.1.[6]

These figures suggest a somewhat modest readership of *Hansard* on the part of MPs. Only 8 per cent of those interviewed claimed to read the Commons *Hansard* regularly. At the other end of the scale, 21 per cent said they seldom or never look at it. The remaining 71 per cent either skim through *Hansard* regularly, read particular debates, or skim particular debates. The most prevalent uses to which *Hansard* appears to be put by MPs are for reading particular debates, on the one hand, and for supplying relevant extracts to constituency interests, on the other. Few MPs appear to follow Disraeli's advice to a young

[1] Letter to the editors (8 October 1972). Whether salary is an incentive or disincentive for *Hansard* shorthand reporters depends on one's view of the salary range, which at present is £3,144 to £3,653 per year, with overtime earnings in excess of £500.

[2] Quoted in Law, *op. cit.*, p 68.

[3] T. F. Lindsay, *Parliament From the Press Gallery*, pp 126–7, Macmillan (1967).

[4] Members are entitled to free copies of all versions of *Hansard*, i.e. the daily, weekly, bound and committee versions.

[5] The survey was conducted in 1967 by Anthony Barker and Michael Rush for *The Member of Parliament and his Information*, Allen & Unwin (1970). The respondents were a sample drawn from backbenchers and Opposition front-benchers. The response rate was 62·7 per cent.

[6] Barker and Rush, *op. cit.*, pp 135, 407. The question Members were asked was: 'When you're not able to listen to much of a debate in the House for your-self, about how often do you read or look at the *Hansard* report of it?'

Table 4.1 *Respondents' use of House of Commons 'Hansard'*

Response	Conservative MPs, %	Labour MPs, %	Total MPs, %
Read regularly	9·1	8·1	8·4
Skim regularly	23·6	18·4	21·5
Only read particular debates	34·5	44·9	39·2
Only skim particular debates	7·3	14·3	10·3
Seldom or never look at it	25·5	14·3	20·6
TOTAL	100·0	100·0	100·0

Member: 'When the House is sitting, be always in your place. When it is not sitting, read *Hansard*.'[1]

It is interesting to examine party differences in regard to readership of *Hansard*. Labour MPs appear to make more use of it than Conservative MPs. Nearly twice as many Conservative respondents said they seldom or never look at *Hansard*. On the other hand, somewhat more Conservatives – 33 per cent – said they read or skimmed the whole *Report* regularly, while only 26 per cent of Labour MPs claimed to. A further finding concerns newer entrants to the Commons compared with longer-serving Members. The 1964 and 1966 entrants tend to be more selective in their reading of *Hansard*. More than half of them said they read only particular debates, which may reflect a more specialist approach to their work. At the same time, a much smaller proportion of the 1964–66 entrants than of longer-serving Members said that they seldom or never read *Hansard*.[2]

Whatever the readership and whatever the method of recording the debates, the importance of making the record cannot be denied. This is particularly so in Britain where, by convention, Ministers are required in the first instance to make all important announcements to the House of Commons. Moreover, the arguments behind the announcements and policies must be put forward and defended in the House. Thus *Hansard* is a rich source of facts and opinions for Members and the broader public, and a major official service at Westminster.

[1] Quoted in Trewin and King, *op. cit.*, p 245.
[2] Barker and Rush, *op. cit.*, p 136. The Conservative and Labour respondents are not strictly comparable because the Conservative respondents included front-bench spokesmen; but their inclusion did not significantly affect the results.

CHAPTER 5

THE HOUSE OF COMMONS LIBRARY

5.1 INTRODUCTION[1]

Shortly after the setting up of the House of Commons Library in 1818, Thomas Vardon, a loyal and accomplished servant of Parliament who was to guide the Library through many years of difficult and significant development, described his duties to a select committee as follows:

'My duties, as attending the parliamentary department of the Library, I consider to embrace the attendance on Members generally, or select committees specially, and upon the House during the progress of public business. The attendance on Members generally is rather indefinite, but it amounts in fact to this, that to the extent of time which I can give, which is day and night during the sitting of the House, the practice is, that there is no subject connected with parliamentary business, on finance, or the forms of the House, or the progress of Bills, or the contents of Acts, on which I am not called upon to afford instant information. In respect to select committees, the notes continually sent me from the Chairmen or members of Committees do not specify "I want such and such a volume of such a work", but their notes contain generally queries whether there

[1] Much useful information on the organisation, work and prospects of the House of Commons Library may be found in Anthony Barker and Michael Rush, *The Member of Parliament and his Information*, Chapter VI, Allen & Unwin (1970). See also: G. F. Lock, 'The Role of the Library', in A. H. Hanson and Bernard Crick (editors), *The Commons in Transition*, pp 130–51, Fontana (1970); David Menhennet, 'The Library of the House of Commons', *Political Quarterly*, **36** (3), pp 323–32 (July–September 1965), David Menhennet, 'The House of Commons Library: Research and Information Services', *Information Scientist*, pp 75–83 (September 1967); David Menhennet and J. B. Poole, 'Information Services of the Commons Library', *New Scientist*, **35**, pp 499–502 (7 September 1967); a series of four articles by John Palmer, David Holland and David Menhennet on 'Parliamentary Libraries' in *The Parliamentarian* (1968–69).

be law upon such and such a subject; if there be, where it can be found; in what Acts: or regarding parliamentary papers, whether such information can be given, and whether, without troubling the Members with long papers, I can state briefly the information desired in their queries, which of course involves a great deal of indefinite labour during the whole of the day. Then, to the House at night, every Member must be aware of the sort of applications which are made to the Librarians, by the minute, I may almost say, for the debates, or the divisions which have taken place on particular occasions; for information concerning Finance Papers, Trade or Acts of Parliament relating to the subject under discussion.'[1]

Many features of today's services are anticipated in the above statement, notably in the emphasis on the provision of precise and instant information.

However, it could not in all fairness be claimed that the Commons Library of the 1970s represents the natural flowering of the seeds sown by Thomas Vardon and his promising young assistant, Erskine May. It would be truer to say that the germination of those seeds was for long deceptive and uncertain. There were numerous distractions and difficulties to be coped with, as the age of Empire and Industrial Revolution wound its way through Parliament. Perhaps the greatest of all these concerned the consequences of the fire of 1834 which destroyed not only the Library's existing accommodation overlooking what was then Cotton Garden to the river, but also almost the whole of a priceless collection of parliamentary manuscripts and archives and about half the holdings of printed books.

The original intention had been to have a good library of 'historical and constitutional information'. When it came to restocking the Library, the essential condition of building up a comprehensive collection of parliamentary papers and other official documents was, fortunately, scrupulously observed. However, a great deal of general literature, more suited to a country gentleman's private library, was also acquired during the nineteenth and early twentieth centuries. Even today the Commons Library – despite having disposed of much of this

[1] H.C. 104, 21 March 1835, Evidence, p 11.

material – remains surprisingly rich in older works of travel, topography, natural history, French literature and similar luxuries.

Despite Vardon's brave words, there was for a long time little attempt made to provide a proper information service for MPs. Whatever social and other reasons there may have been for this policy – and for Members' general acquiescence in it – there was no doubt in the minds of a select committee of 1945–46 as to what the most urgent requirement was:

'Your Committee think that the essential purpose of the House of Commons Library is to supply Members with information rapidly on any of the multifarious matters which come before the House or to which their attentions are drawn by their parliamentary duties. . . . Your Committee feel that the Library of the House of Commons can, and should, be made into a unique organisation. It should be far more than a repository of books and parliamentary papers. *It should aim at providing Members rapidly with precise and detailed information on subjects connected with their duties.*'[1]

The first important step, namely a careful reappraisal of policy and of Members' requirements, had been taken. The post-war expansion and reorganisation of the Library, including the setting up of its Research Division, followed from the principal recommendations of the 1945–46 Committee. Progress was gradual and not without its setbacks. Nevertheless, the basic modern function of the Library as a legislative reference service may fairly be said to date from those early post-war years. The *Library Handbook*, which was issued to all Members at the beginning of the 1970 Parliament, refers to the recommendations of the above Committee, and continues:

'The approved policy, since then, has been to develop the reference and research functions of the Library in the service of the House, its Committees and Members individually. The

[1] 1st and 2nd Reports, Select Committee on Library (House of Commons), H.C. 35 and 99–I; 1st Report, para. 5, and 2nd Report, para. 8. Author's italics.

principal aim of the Library service is . . . to provide for Members whatever books, documents, oral or written information they may require in connection with their parliamentary duties.'[1]

The *Library Handbook* adds that, 'in the general interest', the service is limited by the following provisos: (a) only those inquiries can be entertained which are directly connected with the work of Members in their official capacity as Members of Parliament; (b) work performed for Members is prepared in a factual, politically impartial form.[2]

Before turning to a more detailed consideration of the present-day organisation and services of the House of Commons Library, we should refer in passing to the existence, since 1826, of a separate House of Lords Library. The fact that two libraries exist surprises many outside observers; but the two Houses of Parliament are historically and constitutionally separate, and so are their respective libraries. The House of Lords Library has fine legal and parliamentary collections; its staff, however, is a very small one, and consequently does not offer the range of services which its counterpart in the Commons provides. There is much informal co-operation between the two parliamentary libraries and Peers are allowed to use the facilities of the Commons Library as a matter of courtesy.[3] The Commons *Library Handbook* points out that this co-operation is mutually advantageous:

'By a reciprocal arrangement which is extremely valuable to this Library, the House of Lords kindly permits Members and Officers of the House of Commons to use its Library for purposes of reference, preferably in the mornings when the House of Lords is not sitting. A copy of the House of Lords Library Catalogue is in the Oriel Room of the Commons Library, and more recent acquisitions appear in the Lords Library card catalogues. Books may be borrowed only through the staff of

---

[1] *The Library of the House of Commons: Handbook*, p 1 (1970). Hereafter referred to as the *Library Handbook*.

[2] *Library Handbook*.

[3] For brief accounts of the two libraries see Christopher Dobson, 'The Library of the House of Lords' and Strathearn Gordon, 'The Library of the House of Commons', in R. Irwin and R. Stavely (editors), *The Libraries of London*, pp 90–98, Library Association (second edition, 1961).

the House of Commons Library and must on no account go outside the Palace of Westminster.'[1]

Finally, there are the holdings and services of the House of Lords Record Office, which is located in the Victoria Tower:

'The Clerk of the Records of the House of Lords has charge of a most important collection of documents including all the original Acts, both public and private, from 1497, the Papers laid on the Table of the House of Lords, from 1509, and most of the extant manuscript records of the House of Commons including the famous manuscript Journals dating from 1547. The documents are stored in the Victoria Tower. A short handbook entitled 'The Records of Parliament' is available free to Members on application to the Clerk of the Records, who has kindly placed himself at the service of Members to produce any documents they may wish to consult, and to offer any advice they may require in connection with them.'[2]

5.2 GENERAL ORGANISATION

The Supply Estimates provided for a total Library budget of £178,000 in 1972–73, compared with £175,000 in 1971–72. Of the former sum, salaries, national insurance contributions, and related expenses accounted for £155,000 (£153,000 in 1971–72) and allowed for a staff of fifty-five (fifty-four in 1971–72).[3] Book, newspaper and journal purchases, subscriptions, binding and various miscellaneous expenses accounted for £23,000 (£22,000 in 1971–72). Lest these latter amounts should seem unusually small, it should be remembered that Parliament's own publications, and the publications of the Government and many international bodies, form no charge upon the Vote. They are received free by the Library.

The staff of the Library, in common with all other permanent staff of the House, are not civil servants (see Fig. 5.1 for details

---

[1] *Library Handbook*, p 18.

[2] *Library Handbook*. See also M. F. Bond, *Guide to the Records of Parliament*, pp 26ff, HMSO (1971).

[3] Since this chapter was written, the numbers of Library staff have risen from fifty-five to sixty-three, and the Supply Estimates for 1973–74 provide for a total budget of £210,000. H.C. 114, 1972–73.

of the staff structure). However, they have certain things in common with civil servants, including salary comparability with a particular group of classes in the service. Twenty of the staff,[1] all of them in the Library Clerk or more senior grades, rank as Officers of the House, and their 'linkages' with civil service grades are at present as follows:

Librarian (1)	Under Secretary
Deputy Librarian (1)	Assistant Secretary
Assistant Librarians (2)	Keepers (Museums)
Deputy Assistant Librarians (5)	Deputy Keepers
Senior or Assistant Library	
Clerks (11)	Assistant Keepers I or II

Candidates for Library clerkships are recruited through the Civil Service Commission, as nearly as possible in accordance with the rules governing the recruitment of Assistant Keepers of the British Museum, but with modifications to meet the specialised needs of the House of Commons.[2] All Library Clerks are required to hold a good honours degree; special qualifications are called for in regard to some posts, whilst for other posts graduates in any subject may apply. Eleven other members of the staff belong to the professional and executive grades. The remainder are in the clerical, secretarial and other supporting grades.[3]

Since August 1967 the Library has been one of the five Departments of the House of Commons. Administratively, it is controlled by the Librarian, who is appointed by the Speaker. All other staff are appointed by the Librarian. Together with the Deputy Librarian, the Librarian has general responsibility for the organisation and smooth running of his Department. As regards policy matters, but not staff matters, he works in consultation with the Library Subcommittee of the Services Committee. At the beginning of each session the House normally orders 'That any Subcommittee which may be appointed to

[1] Increased in 1973 to twenty-two.
[2] Erskine May, *Treatise on the Law, Privileges, Proceedings and Usage of Parliament*, p 235 Butterworth (eighteenth edition, 1971).
[3] For further details on staffing see G. F. Lock in A. H. Hanson and Bernard Crick (editors), *The Commons in Transition, op. cit.*

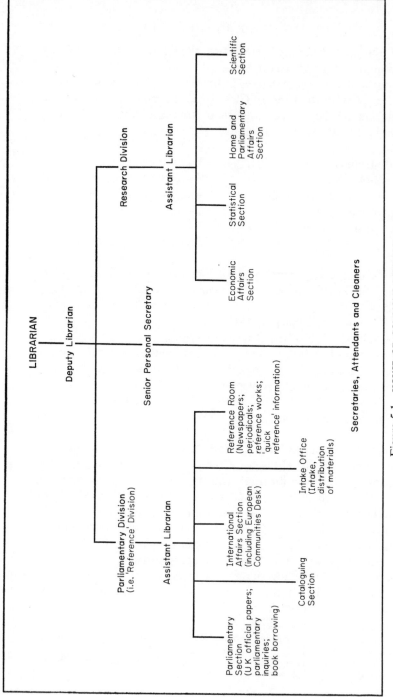

Figure 5.1 HOUSE OF COMMONS LIBRARY

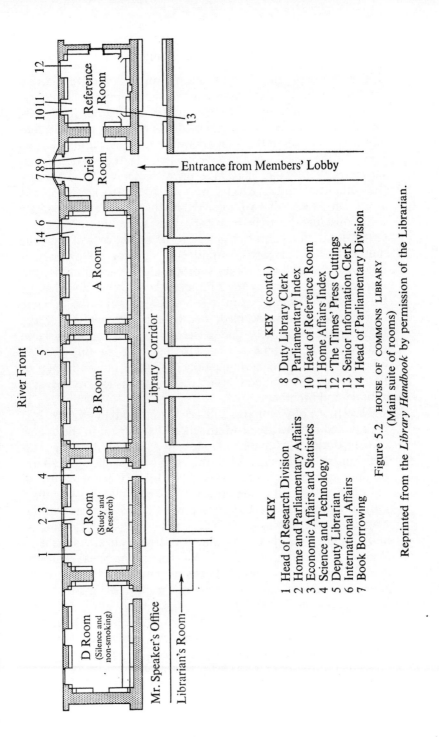

Figure 5.2 HOUSE OF COMMONS LIBRARY
(Main suite of rooms)

Reprinted from the *Library Handbook* by permission of the Librarian.

KEY

1 Head of Research Division
2 Home and Parliamentary Affairs
3 Economic Affairs and Statistics
4 Science and Technology
5 Deputy Librarian
6 International Affairs
7 Book Borrowing

KEY (contd.)

8 Duty Library Clerk
9 Parliamentary Index
10 Head of Reference Room
11 Home Affairs Index
12 'The Times' Press Cuttings
13 Senior Information Clerk
14 Head of Parliamentary Division

deal with the organisation of, and the provision of services in, the Library do have the assistance of the Librarian'.[1]

At present the Library Subcommittee consists of four MPs, all of whom are also members of the Services Committee. The Librarian reports to the Subcommittee at regular intervals, and may also be called upon to give evidence to the Services Committee. Any Member may take up a matter with the Library Subcommittee; alternatively, he may prefer to approach the Librarian direct, who will refer the matter to the Subcommittee if he considers this to be necessary. The Subcommittee will then either decide the course of action to be taken, or will refer the matter to the Services Committee if a major policy issue is involved. Thus, the Library's proposals for computerisation were considered first by the Library Subcommittee and then by the Services Committee; in a less technical vein, the Services Committee recently decided, on the recommendation of the Library Subcommittee, that a second of the Library's large rooms should become a non-smoking area. In this way an official channel of communication has, since the setting up of the Services Committee in 1965, been established between the Library and Members.

The House of Commons Library is not a public library. It is maintained for the use of Members of Parliament in the course of their duties. It is manned from 9.30 a.m. each morning until the rising of the House. When the House is not sitting, staff are on duty from 10 a.m. until 5 p.m. The Library is not staffed on Saturday afternoons, Sundays and public holidays. Members may of course use the Library's premises and services without restriction. Additionally, Officers of the House of Commons, and Commonwealth Clerks and Librarians on attachment to Westminster, may use them. By courtesy of the Speaker, Peers, and Officers of the House of Lords may avail themselves of the Library's services, subject always to the prior claims of Members. Limited use of, and access to, the Library at certain times is permitted to a small number of Members' research assistants (a maximum of fifty in 1973).[2] Members' secretaries, however,

[1] See, for example, *Votes and Proceedings* (5 November 1971).

[2] The Boyle Committee's recommendation on payment for research assistants undoubtedly means that more Members will be using research assistants in the future. This presumably will mean more pressure on Library facilities. *Boyle Report*, p 40, para. 123 (f).

who frequently telephone the Library for information on Members' behalf, are not normally allowed into the Library.

5.3   ACCOMMODATION AND HOLDINGS

One beneficial effect of the fire of 1834 was that it enabled Sir Charles Barry and Augustus Welby Pugin to build the fine suite of four large, tall apartments, each sixty feet long, and a smaller entrance hall named the Oriel Room after its window, which still form the main accommodation of the House of Commons Library. Adjoining the Oriel Room is the small galleried Reference Room which was added to the other apartments shortly after the latter came into use in 1852. (For a diagram of the room arrangement, see Figure 5.2) Smoking and conversation are allowed in all rooms except *D* Room (silence and non-smoking) and *C* Room (non-smoking). Overlooking the Terrace and the River Thames, and at the same time close to the chamber on the principal floor, the Library is ideally situated to perform its several functions.[1] A former Librarian has described the scene thus:

'... whatever the defects of Barry's library, it has served its purpose tolerably well. He evidently intended it as the principal amenity for Members outside the Chamber for both work and recreation. There is already an historic quality about it. Ministers have their rooms, but much of the work of the Opposition and of backbenchers is done in the library. Many famous speeches have been written at the long tables and many political jests whispered among the green armchairs. ... Sometimes, in clear sunlight, the river scene through the tall windows has the detailed brilliance of a painting by Canaletto; and often the green velvet curtains are comfortably drawn against winter fogs. But the view which many Members prefer is of the moonlight and yellow lamps glittering on the river on a fine night.'[2]

[1] Marsden has said that the Library rooms 'occupy what is undoubtedly the finest position in the whole Palace of Westminster'. Philip Marsden, *The Officers of the Commons 1363–1965*, p 177, Barrie and Rockliff (1966).
[2] Strathearn Gordon, 'The Library of the House of Commons', in Irwin and Staveley, *op. cit.*, p 95.

As the number of private rooms, with telephones, for the use of Members increases, it is possible that the extent to which Members will avail themselves of the Library's writing tables will diminish. However, it seems unlikely that the Library's function as a place for Members to meet, relax and converse will lose any of its importance as long as the 'club' atmosphere of the House of Commons persists, and as long as the Library itself seeks to provide those facilities traditionally associated with the best 'club' libraries: a reasonably quiet environment, comfortably and appropriately furnished for reading, writing and discreet conversation.

A Member entering the Library from the chamber is most likely to do so by way of the Oriel Room. Here, books held by the Library may be borrowed against the Member's signature on a borrowing card; here, too, requests are made for books not in stock to be obtained on loan. The Library possesses some 120,000 bound volumes and a Member may borrow any book for one month, except that books constantly and instantly required by Members[1] may be used only inside the main Library suite. Exceptionally, any book or other document may be taken into the chamber or a committee room for a short period for purposes of quotation and consultation. Almost any book not held by the Library (except a work of fiction) can be borrowed for a Member, although the loan is sometimes made subject to conditions imposed by the lending library. About 5,000 book loans are transacted by the Library in an average year.

From the Oriel Room the remainder of the main Library suite is visible; it comprises, when one faces the river, four large rooms to the left and a small one to the right. This last is the Reference Room and is the main repository of current and recent numbers of the national, and some regional and foreign, newspapers and journals.[2] Telephone directories, annual reports of a wide range of organisations, travel guides, timetables, Government circulars and press notices, dictionaries, maps, university calendars, year books and other such items are also

[1] This category includes law books, reference works, some pamphlets and all official publications.

[2] More than 120 newspapers and about 1,400 journals are taken, although, for reasons of space, by no means all are kept in the Reference Room.

located here. The material held in the Reference Room is not available for loan. For the most part this diversified range of reference material is held in a simple alphabetical subject sequence that runs in a clockwise order around the lower shelves and continues similarly in the gallery above. Staff are available here – as everywhere else throughout the Library – to help Members. A special service provided in the Reference Room is a cuttings service for *The Times*, with holdings extending back over a rolling period of two and a half years.[1] Still older material can be retrieved by means of *The Times* indexes.

To the left of the Oriel Room are the four large apartments called, in receding sequence, *A*, *B*, *C* and *D* Rooms, and it is in these rooms that the Library's main book holdings are located. There are no galleries here, so that Members and staff must use ladders whenever a volume from one of the upper shelves is required. The detailed arrangement of the books on the shelves in these rooms has been dictated by tradition, partly by the specialised needs of Members and partly by the serious shortage of shelf space. As in the Reference Room, a simple alphabetical system of subject location is followed. Shortage of shelf space means that a fairly high proportion of the stock has to be kept in 'reserve' locations situated outside the main suite of rooms. A diagram showing the lay-out of the Library's accommodation and the locations of the various book sections is posted in the Oriel Room; here, too, are the principal author and subject card catalogues which may be freely consulted by Members.

Within its annual budget the Library sets out to provide good collections of printed books in those subject areas likely to be of the greatest value and interest to Members in their work. Parliament, modern history, law, biography, economics and the social sciences generally comprise the more important of the various book sections. Some classical literature, English and foreign, and a small selection of books on the fine arts, travel and topography are also held; but works of modern fiction are neither purchased nor borrowed.

The number of volumes held (120,000) understates the extent of the holdings, for the Library is rich in British official publications. The 9,000 volumes of Parliamentary Papers alone contain

---

[1] Cuttings are classified: (a) under various topics and (b) as they refer to individual Members.

some 125,000 separate documents. The Library lists the main classes of official publications held as follows:[1]

Parliamentary Papers. These comprise Public Bills, House of Commons Papers and Command Papers. The Library's bound set dates from 1801, and is virtually complete: the Abbot Collection of miscellaneous 18th century Papers, in 110 volumes, is also held.

House of Lords Papers constitute a separate series, and are held by the Commons Library from 1870.

The printed *Journals* of the House of Commons (1547 to date) and of the House of Lords (1509 to date).

Sessional Papers ('The Vote'). These day-to-day records of the House of Commons are bound up in their respective series; Votes and Proceedings, Notices of Motions, &c. The Library has bound volumes dating back to the early 19th century.

Non-Parliamentary Publications of HM Stationery Office. The Library receives and catalogues a wide selection of these documents.

State Papers (on political and commercial affairs), published by the Foreign Office since 1812.

Statutes Revised (to the end of 1948), and subsequent annual volumes of Public General Acts. The Library regularly annotates and updates one set of these Acts.

Statutory Instruments, formerly Statutory Rules and Orders.

Local & Personal Acts from 1798; *Road Acts* 1760–1796.

Parliamentary Debates. The best part of seven complete sets of *Hansard* are held, together with alternative sources, such as the *Mirror of Parliament* (1828–41), for some of the earlier periods.

In addition, two other categories of documents which are not normally published in the official parliamentary series are received in the Library:

'*Unprinted Papers*' are copies of certain Reports, Accounts, Orders, &c., presented under Statute or (less frequently) by Command. The term 'unprinted' refers only to the fact of their

---

[1] *Library Handbook*, pp 7–8.

non-publication as Parliamentary Papers: many are in fact printed by HM Stationery Office. Copies presented to the House have been preserved since 1851.

Deposited Papers are documents placed in the Library by the Speaker or by Ministers, for consultation by Members.

With the increasing specialisation of function within the Library, particularly within the Research Division, there has gone a tendency for a number of important specialist collections to grow. This has happened in statistics,[1] education, agriculture, science and technology and – most significantly in terms of bulk alone – international and foreign affairs. All the published documents of the United Nations and its agencies are handled by the Library's International Affairs Section, together with a substantial selection of publications from other international organisations and certain foreign governments, including a large collection from the United States. The United Kingdom's accession to the European Communities has already enhanced considerably the scale and complexity of the documentation and indexing commitments of this Section, which now includes a special European Communities Desk.

5.4 THE PARLIAMENTARY DIVISION

The Library is organised in two Divisions – Parliamentary and Research – each under the supervision of an Assistant Librarian. The former Division, which has retained its old, historical designation of 'Parliamentary', is in fact the general or 'reference' library. Its staff and holdings occupy most of the principal suite of rooms, and it is responsible for the intake, arrangement, cataloguing and indexing of by far the greater part of the Library's material resources. The Oriel Room, in which parliamentary enquiries and book borrowing are dealt with, the Reference Room, Cataloguing Section, Intake Office and the important International Affairs Section all form a part of the Parliamentary Division.

---

[1] For a view of the problems involved in building up and handling this type of material, see G. F. Lock, 'Statistics for Politicians', *Statistical News*, No. 12 (February 1971).

In addition to acquiring and holding books and other documents, the Library, in particular the Parliamentary Division, has the task of organising this material in order to make particular items and specific information immediately available to Members on demand. As regards book material, there are the author and subject catalogues. There remains, however, a vast amount of *non-book* material – official papers, debates, press and periodical comment, etc. – any single item of which may have to be traced very quickly. In this context the House of Commons Library has since 1955 pioneered the use of a number of visible strip indexes. These are vertically mounted panels containing sequences of variously coloured strips which denote the different categories of current and recent material incorporated. These indexes are placed at several strategic enquiry points in the main suite of rooms for use by Members or, more frequently, by Library staff working on behalf of Members. The indexing is undertaken by members of the staff. Many of the tens of thousands of documents received annually by the Library are entered on one or more of these specialised indexes, and most of the latter are subsequently photocopied and bound up as permanent records.

The main visible strip indexes are as follows:

1   *Parliamentary Index.* This arranges, alphabetically by subject, references to current British Parliamentary Papers, debates and statements in both Houses, Notices of Motions and certain other categories of official United Kingdom material.
2   *Public Bill Index.* This lists by title the various stages of current and recent legislation in both Houses.
3   *Parliamentary Questions Index.* This lists all recent Questions answered in the House of Commons. The listing is chronological under the names of the various Government Departments.[1]

These three indexes are located in the Oriel Room. All are updated on a daily basis, and together they aim to provide a complete, 'at-a-glance' word-picture of the parliamentary history of any given topic.

---

[1] These and the other visible strip indexes are discussed in D. C. L. Holland, 'Parliamentary Libraries: Indexing of Material', *The Parliamentarian*, **50** (1), pp 28–32 (January 1969).

Another visible strip index is the *Home Affairs Index*, which is located in the Reference Room. This major Library facility contains extensive references to comment on public affairs in the United Kingdom, selected by the staff from national newspapers and periodicals. References are also included to relevant Government circulars and press notices – an important aspect of a Member's information requirements – and to documents produced by the Central Office of Information and other organisations. The strips on which the individual references are typed are arranged chronologically under a large number of subject headings. A prominent feature of the Home Affairs Index is that cuttings corresponding to the press and periodical references are filed in special envelopes and kept in filing cabinets adjacent to the index. These cuttings are available for on-the-spot consultation, and can be quickly reproduced on the Reference Room's photocopying machine if a Member wishes to have copies for his personal use. This combined indexing and cuttings service, geared by the Library to Members' specialised requirements, is much used.

A further visible strip index is the large *International Affairs Index*, which is located in *A* Room. Here, references to the many thousands of documents of foreign and international organisations handled by the Library are listed on strips, together with selected references to British books, periodical articles and official United Kingdom papers bearing on overseas affairs. This index, like the Home Affairs Index, is supplemented by a press cuttings service. Another strip index contains references to the secondary legislation (regulations, directives and decisions) of the European Communities. This index is compiled from the Communities' *Official Journal* and the reports and debates of the European Parliament, and is located at the recently instituted European Communities Desk in *A* Room.[1]

A final visible strip index is the *Scientific Index*, which is located in *C* Room. This compilation is the work of the Scientific Section of the Research Division. Scientific, technical and medical subjects, plus some aspects of agriculture, are indexed in one alphabetical subject sequence. The material covered

[1] For further details about this service see the Memorandum by the Librarian to the Select Committee on European Community Secondary Legislation. H.C. 143, 1972–73, Appendix 2, pp xix–xxii.

consists mainly of British official reports and papers, pamphlets, selected United States government and research reports, international scientific documents and journal articles. A collection of press and periodical cuttings is also maintained by the Scientific Section.

The Parliamentary Division provides a rapid information service for Members in connection with their parliamentary duties. There are three main reception points for inquiries that do not involve written research: the Oriel Room, the Reference Room and the International Affairs Section in *A* Room.

In the Oriel Room staff deal with numerous inquiries from Members concerning parliamentary affairs, parliamentary papers, debates in both Houses, statutes, delegated legislation and all other British official material. The book borrowing service is also based in this room. Many Members place their inquiries in person; others telephone their requirements or send their requests by letter; others approach the Library staff by telephone through their secretaries or research assistants. As elsewhere in the Library, the principal collections and the strip indexes are indispensable aids to this information service; but a great deal still depends on the active, personalised attention that the staff endeavour to offer Members.[1]

Staff working in the busy Reference Room deal with a wide range of general reference inquiries. The International Affairs Section in *A* Room handles all short-term inquiries from Members on foreign or international matters and on matters related to the European Communities. In addition the staff of this Section, which includes three graduate Library Clerks, answer a number of the longer-term, more complex inquiries from Members which involve a certain amount of research and a written reply. Many of these longer-term inquiries, however, are dealt with by subject specialists in the Research Division.

Staff in the Parliamentary Division as a whole answer some 50,000 inquiries from, or on behalf of, Members during the course of a year. These inquiries may be made in person or by telephone. 'Inquiries' in this context range from very simple requests for information or references, to the considerably more complex and difficult type of oral inquiry.

[1] See, *inter alia*, David Menhennet, 'Parliamentary Libraries: Information and Research Services', *The Parliamentarian*, **50** (2), p 111 (April 1969).

5.5 THE RESEARCH DIVISION

The 1945–46 Select Committee on the Library recommended the appointment of 'two Research Assistants, with special qualifications in the Social Sciences'. This number rose to four almost immediately, two of those appointed being statisticians, but the senior complement of the Library's Research Division had increased to only six by 1964. There followed a period of relatively swift and substantial expansion, with the result that today the senior research staff, including two professionally qualified supporting librarians, number sixteen in all. Two clerical officers and four secretaries make up a total establishment of twenty-two.

Staff are organised into four sections, which deal with inquiries from Members involving research and (usually) requiring a written reply. The sections are: Economic Affairs, Home and Parliamentary Affairs, Scientific, i.e. science and technology, and Statistical. A fifth section, International Affairs, is also partly a research unit although, for administrative and other reasons, it falls within the ambit of the Parliamentary Division (see section 5.4).

In the Research Division each section is headed by a senior researcher, graded as a Deputy Assistant Librarian, and the Division itself comes under the day-to-day supervision of one of the two Assistant Librarians. For the most part, the graduate staff have specialist qualifications and experience (for example in economics, political science, statistics or scientific policy), in addition to a good honours degree. Further, individual Library Clerks are expected to specialise in one or several broad areas of public affairs such as agriculture, higher education, housing, immigration and race relations and transport. Such specialisation involves keeping abreast of current developments and making useful contacts with outside bodies and individuals.

Over 2,000 written answers to inquiries from individual Members are produced each year by the Library's Research Division. Requests for information may be placed in several ways: through the staff of the Parliamentary Division, by telephone or by correspondence. It is also possible for a Member to make a direct approach to a member of the section which will handle his inquiry, since staff from the four sections of the Research

Division work at desks in *C* Room. This procedure is often most desirable, since uncertainties regarding the precise meaning and scope of a Member's inquiry can easily arise if it has to pass through several intermediaries before reaching the person who will provide the actual answer. Great importance is attached to this 'direct contact' between research staff and their clientèle.

Members using the Library's research services are asked to bear in mind three important provisos:

1 Only those inquiries may be undertaken that bear directly on a Member's official duties.

2 As much time as possible should be allowed to the researcher to do the work given to him or her. It is not realistic to expect a detailed and considered reply at an hour or so's notice.

3 Research staff work largely from published material supplemented by such oral information and advice as they can glean from external sources. They are thoroughly competent in the handling of these sources, but they are unlikely to get free access to as yet restricted, unpublished information. This is especially true in the defence field where, almost invariably, the researcher will be asked to put the inquiring Member into direct touch with the Ministry.

However, to offset some of these limitations, the Library's service does offer Members tangible advantages. In the first place, research answers can cover subjects for which there is no ministerial responsibility and thus no likelihood of a parliamentary question being accepted. Second, inquiries of an historical character may be placed. Third, the service is available, albeit in a restricted form, for as long as the House is sitting. Fourth, the staff acquire over the years a valuable experience of the requirements and habits of work of busy Members. Within reason, therefore, it is possible for Members to put almost any inquiry to the research staff in the expectation of receiving a better than merely routine reply. Geoffrey Lock, Head of the Statistical Section, has commented on the work of his Section:

'The Statistical Section of the House of Commons Library meets a growing need on the part of Members (and to some extent Peers) for statistics more extensive than can be obtained by a parliamentary question, without the publicity involved and without the need for a wait of some days. (We have no set rules about notice and can often reply quickly; naturally we prefer to be given a reasonable time to reply as rushed work can lead to mistakes.) Enquiries can only rarely be answered by the straightforward extraction of figures from a single source. We usually have to bring together figures from a wide range of different sources, do calculations on them, annotate them on conceptual points, and generally adapt them to the Member's specific needs. Only very rarely can we give to one Member material prepared for another; the inquiries all differ, so the replies are individually tailored. We work largely from printed material, of which we maintain a large collection, and for recent figures *Hansard* answers and press notices form an important source. . . . The clientèle consists mainly of backbenchers and some frontbenchers of the Opposition of the day, though it is not unknown for Ministers to consult us, even on matters connected with their own Departments. The work can vary from the supply of figures to a front-bench spokesman for a winding up speech in a major debate, through such things as assistance with a note of dissent to a Report of a Royal Commission, to (as it turned out) provision of material for a filibuster in Committee.'[1]

Turning to specific examples, the following are typical research inquiries put to the Library staff:

An outline of the special taxation provisions for blind persons. (*Economic Affairs Section*)

An explanation of the criteria for selecting scheduled gaming areas under the Gaming Act of 1968 and under subsequent delegated legislation. (*Home and Parliamentary Affairs Section*)

Technical comment on, and a summary of the law pertinent to, the US Army's proposal to dump surplus chemical weapons in the Atlantic. (*Scientific Section*)

A 'layman's guide' to methods of measuring changes in the standard of living, with statistical illustrations for the United Kingdom during the period 1960 to 1970. (*Statistical Section*)

Do any EEC countries give interest-free loans to developing countries? (*International Affairs, Parliamentary Division*)

[1] 'Statistics for Politicians', *Statistical News*, No. 12, pp 5–6 (February 1971).

In addition to answering questions from individual Members, research staff regularly provide a number of services for Members as a whole. These are:

1 *Reference Sheets*. These are annotated reading lists produced before major items of legislation come before the House, or when some important topic is in the air. The actual material listed on the Reference Sheets is additionally provided in the Library as special 'working kits'. Subjects treated in this way in recent sessions have included: the Third London Airport, International Monetary Reform, a Scottish Parliament, Shipbuilding Industry Grants, the Steel Industry, the Parliamentary Commissioner for Administration, the *Criminal Justice Bill, 1971–72*, the *Coal Industry Bill, 1972–73*, and the *Water Bill, 1972–73*. Between twenty and thirty Reference Sheets are produced in an average year for internal distribution to Members only.

2 *Science Digest*. This is a fortnightly series of summarised articles from the scientific and technical press. Well over 100 Members are on the standing distribution list for this compilation.

3 *Background Papers*. These are pamphlet-length, factual 'briefs' on topics of current concern to Parliament. Background papers in recent sessions have dealt with Inflation and Incomes Policy, Value-Added Tax, Murder Statistics, the *Housing Finance Bill, 1971–72*, Ministerial Salaries and Social Security Benefits. In addition, the International Affairs Section produced during 1970–72 a whole series of Background Papers on the Common Market negotiations, and a further paper on the situation in Rhodesia.

Background Papers have proved to be a significant and popular innovation. However, insofar as these documents are prepared for general distribution among Members, with the consequential impossibility of controlling their circulation in any effective way, they do expose Library staff to possible criticism in a way that the great majority of research answers – prepared for one Member only – do not.[1]

---

[1] A Background Paper on the Civil List, although containing no confidential information, achieved a degree of celebrity in 1971 through its novel presentation of information already in the public domain. See *The Guardian* (29 May 1971) and *Sunday Mail* (6 June 1971).

Another important aspect of the Research Division's work which has been greatly extended in recent years is the aiding of select committees and, in particular, specialist committees such as those dealing with science and technology, agriculture, education, race relations and overseas aid. The Library's role might be defined as a source of technical back up for the committee, its Clerk, or any outside advisers the committee may appoint. Library staff are able to provide services ranging from the compiling of annotated bibliographies and the supply of press and periodical literature to suggesting witnesses and assisting (if asked to do so) with the drafting of the committee's report. In certain exceptional circumstances, and for limited periods of time, committee work can amount to almost 50 per cent of a Library Clerk's time.[1]

Finally, mention should again be made of the responsibility of at least two sections – Scientific and Statistical – to maintain adequate, up-to-date special collections of books, journals and other relevant materials. Comparative statistics on the cost of living or on regional unemployment may be required at very short notice and late at night. On such occasions, when Members turn for help to the Research Division staff on duty, the immediate availability of essential source material is a crucial factor.

5.6 PROPOSALS FOR MECHANISATION

The interest of the House of Commons Library in mechanised systems, and in particular in the prospects of a computer-aided information system, goes back over a number of years. This early interest culminated in 1968 when, in conjunction with the Office for Scientific and Technical Information (OSTI), the House of Commons sponsored an experimental production of weekly Current Literature Bulletins in the Library. Index entries for items on British domestic affairs, prepared in the Library, were fed into the existing computer system of the Culham Laboratory Library of the United Kingdom Atomic Energy Authority. The principal result was a weekly series of Current Literature Bulletins in thirty-six subject fields, which

---

[1] For more details, see the chapter by G. F. Lock, 'The Role of the Library', in Hanson and Crick, *op. cit.*

were distributed to over 400 MPs and to a number of outside libraries and other organisations which had agreed to participate in the experiment.

The main purpose was to provide, for the limited period of the experiment, a current awareness service based on the stated subject interests of the Members and other participants. The bulletins – ranging from 'Agriculture', 'Air Transport' and the 'Arts' through 'Employment' and 'Environment' to 'Social Services', 'Taxation' and 'Wales' – offered a simple form of regularly updated Selective Dissemination of Information (SDI) service. It was found that Members tended to express their current awareness interests in fairly broad terms (such as 'Agriculture'), and that it was in any case possible to provide a more narrowly tailored SDI service *within* each Current Literature Bulletin by dividing it into sub-groupings. Thus, the weekly bulletin on 'Central Government' carried eight sub-groupings as follows: Government and Central Administration, Cabinet, Civil Service, Parliamentary Commissioner, Patronage, Prime Minister, Royal Family and Security.[1]

In retrospect, the three most significant aspects of this brief but successful experiment appear to have been as follows:

1   An attempt was made to provide individual Members with *regularly* updated lists of references to sources of information in one or more subject fields in which they themselves took a continuing interest. On average, each participating Member received some eight or nine subject bulletins each week.

2   Whilst there were already in existence a number of well-known mechanised information services in the natural sciences, there was at the time no equivalent computer-based service for the social sciences.

3   Certain Commons Library staff – with substantial help from the staff of Culham Laboratory Library – had the opportunity of studying and helping to operate a system involving the machine-handling of information, a new and increasingly important feature of information technology.

[1] For fuller accounts of the 1968 computer experiment, see J. B. Poole, 'Information Services for the Commons: a Computer Experiment', *Parliamentary Affairs*, 22, p 161 (Spring 1969); and J. L. Hall, J. Palmer and J. B. Poole, 'An Experimental Current Awareness Service in the Social Sciences', *Journal of Documentation*, 26, p 1 (March 1970).

At the end of the 1968 experiment a detailed questionnaire was sent to the Members concerned, and 260 of them replied. Of these, 85 per cent said that they had found the service either 'very useful' (26 per cent) or 'useful' (59 per cent). In June 1969 the Librarian of the House of Commons applied for a grant of money 'to support a feasibility study of the application of computer techniques to the Library's information processes', and it was subsequently agreed that a twelve-month feasibility study should be paid for jointly by the House of Commons and OSTI. A team from Aslib carried out a detailed survey of the Library's information processes and of Members' present and likely future requirements, and prepared a report for the Librarian in January 1971.[1]

This 276-page report, although not strictly confidential, has not been published; consequently, it has had only a very limited circulation outside the Library, up to the present time. However, it is no secret that its central recommendation was that the Library of the House of Commons 'should move towards automation', and that it proposed that a development programme on the following lines, to be spread over a number of years, should be considered:

1 The preparation in machine-readable form of entries which are at present being fed into the Library's conventional visible strip indexes.
2 Compilation and distribution to Members of current awareness bulletins as a permanent feature of the Library's work.
3 The automatic production of various kinds of cumulative or specially produced indexes (covering, for example, all the Parliamentary Questions asked by a particular Member).
4 Eventually – and perhaps most important of all – the setting up of visual display terminals in the Library which would give direct on-line access to references stored in the computer file.[2]

The principle of computer support, and the economic acceptability of such a development, are of course matters for the

[1] B. C. Vickery and H. East, *Computer Support for Parliamentary Information Service*, Aslib Research Department (1971).
[2] For an example of the potential value of such a service see A. E. Negus and J. L. Hall, *Towards an Effective On-Line Reference Retrieval System*, UKAEA Research Group Library Memorandum (1971).

Services Committee to decide on behalf of Members. Accordingly, the Librarian referred the Aslib report to the Library Subcommittee for its consideration. Subsequently, in July 1971, the Subcommittee made its own report, based on the Aslib report's recommendations, to the Services Committee. In April 1972 the Services Committee resolved

'That in view of the considerable costs involved the full proposals contained in the Library Sub-Committee's Report on computer techniques for the Library's information services of July 1971 should not be implemented at this stage; but that it is essential that the Library should maintain an informed and continuing interest in computer applications, particularly as regards the indexing of Hansard and Parliamentary Papers, and that the Librarian should therefore seek, through the Staff Board, to add a suitably qualified person to the present permanent establishment.'[1]

Approval for such an appointment was subsequently given.

Computer support is of course only one aspect, albeit a major one, of current developments in library and information technology. The Commons Library is actively considering a programme of acquiring microfilm and the appropriate apparatus for its use; and in time the acquisition of much newspaper and periodical literature on microfilm will achieve considerable savings in shelf space, in addition to enabling the Library to complete many of its serial holdings through the purchase of microfilm. The possibility of providing video-cassette recording facilities for Members has also been investigated. However, there appears for the moment to be no regular means of making available – except at disproportionate trouble and expense – recordings of very recent television and sound broadcasts which Members might wish to view or hear at short notice, as a part of the Library's service.

Photocopying is, of course, no longer a new facility in libraries. It is an established service which enables the user to take away for personal reference that part of a particular book or document which interests him. In 1972 about 150,000 items were copied in this way in the House of Commons Library for Members and staff.

[1] H.C. 72–iii, 1971–72, p iv.

5.7 CONCLUSION

The House of Commons Library is by no means the only source of information on which Members of Parliament can and do draw in the course of their duties. It constitutes, however, the principal *official* information service available at Westminster. Barker and Rush have claimed that 'the term "parliamentary information services" is 95 per cent synonymous with the work of the Library'.[1] It might perhaps be argued that the recommendation of the Boyle Committee in 1971 that up to £300 of a Member's allowance could be spent on employing a research assistant recognised the existence of an alternative 'information service' paid for out of public funds. However, developments in this direction are still at an early stage, and research assistants are likely in any case to complement – rather than in any way replace – the Library's role.

The Library, moreover, has four important advantages in its function as a collective information service:

1 The general nature and scope of its services are controlled by the House itself on Members' behalf.
2 It has the obvious convenience of being on the spot, and available at all hours of the working day and night.
3 Every effort is made to ensure that its services are free of any selectivity or bias which might attach to material or information emanating from the Government, a political party or an organised pressure group. Within its resources the Library is committed to serving Members in the best possible objective manner.
4 It has the major advantage of being based upon, and integrated with, a good *library* of historical and (above all) current affairs documentation.

In terms of parliamentary libraries, the House of Commons Library is still not very large. Its staff compares unfavourably, in terms of size, with that of some other parliamentary libraries (see Chapter 9). Further expansion of the Library's staff and services over the next ten years appears therefore to be a

[1] Barker and Rush, *op. cit.*, p 290.

reasonable probability, although the problem of finding accommodation for such additional staff may not be easy. One thing is certain: in the future (as in the past), it is likely that the sort of use which Members make of their Library and the critical interest which they take in its affairs will do much to determine the scope and nature of its services.

CHAPTER 6

SALARIES, ALLOWANCES
AND PENSIONS

6.1 HISTORY OF SALARIES

The figures in Table 6.1 provide a general picture of the history of the payment of Members of Parliament. It is clear from these figures that most of the changes in Members' remuneration that have occurred since its introduction in 1911 have been concentrated in a relatively short period of time. All six changes have taken place within a span of thirty-five years, four within twenty years and three within fifteen. Moreover, by implication it may be assumed that an important factor in the increasing salaries paid to MPs, especially in the post-war period, has been

Table 6.1 *Members' Salaries, 1911–73*

Date	Salary, £
1911	400*
1937	600*
1946	1,000*
1954	1,000†
1957	1,750‡
1964	3,250§
1972	4,500

* From 1912 £100 was exempt from income tax, being regarded as an average allowance for necessary parliamentary expenses. In practice Members could (and still can) claim expenses for tax purposes up to the total of their parliamentary salaries.

† The £100 tax-free allowance was abolished in 1954 and a sessional allowance, exempt from tax, of £2 per sitting day was substituted. Members could still claim additional expenses on their salaries, however.

‡ The sessional allowance was abolished in 1957 and replaced by an additional sum of £750, which was regarded as an appropriate amount to cover necessary parliamentary expenses.

§ £1,250 of this salary was regarded as an appropriate amount to cover necessary parliamentary expenses, but as before additional expenses could be claimed on the remainder of the Member's salary.

the impact of inflation. A number of further considerations are not explicit in the Table. For example, the Table does not illustrate the principles on which the remuneration of Members of Parliament have been based and how they have changed over time; nor does the Table throw much light on the particular circumstances in which remuneration was introduced and has subsequently changed. These questions are vital to an understanding of the present financial position of Members.

Although the present system of an annual salary for Members of Parliament dates from 1911, the general question of remuneration has a much longer history, both in practice and in principle. In the earliest Parliaments Members were paid expenses by their constituents and this form of remuneration continued until at least the later part of the seventeenth century, though by this time only in some boroughs.[1] The reluctance of constituents to meet these expenses, however, meant that payment was neither regular, nor was it systematically applied over the whole country. Under the impact of property qualifications for Members, which were first introduced in the reign of Henry V, the payment of expenses became largely obsolete, since it became increasingly necessary for MPs to have private means or to have the support of a wealthy patron. Moreover, as the system of 'rotten' and 'pocket' boroughs developed and as elections that were contested tended to be decided by bribery and other corrupt practices, the expense of becoming a Member of Parliament increased considerably. In addition, once elected, a Member required financial support considerably greater than these early payments would have provided. It is not in fact surprising that it should have been particular boroughs which continued to provide some financial support for their representatives, since the county constituencies were more likely to be represented by wealthy men, and it was in a limited number of boroughs that elections were least corrupt and thus less financially demanding upon candidates.

Quite apart from the expense of securing election to Parliament and of maintaining himself once elected, a Member was also faced with the system of influence by which the House of Commons operated before the *Reform Act 1832*. Ironically, in a

[1] See T. F. T. Plucknett, *Taswell-Langmead's English Constitutional History*, pp 578–9, Sweet and Maxwell (eleventh edition, 1960).

sense MPs were paid during the eighteenth century, but the manner and purpose of such payments militated against the introduction of any regular remuneration of Members: by the payment of pensions, the giving of bribes, the granting of various favours, and other financial inducements the Government of the day sought to secure parliamentary support for its policies. This system of political corruption was largely open and was widely considered to be a necessary and legitimate part of government.[1] Such a system could not survive the regular and adequate remuneration of Members, who, according to the philosophy of the time, would have been continually beholden to the Government of the day and would have lost the degree of independence that the system of bribery and corruption genuinely afforded.

Nonetheless, the principle of the payment of Members was not entirely forgotten and some reformers regarded it as a means of giving MPs effective independence of the executive. In 1780 a parliamentary committee reported in favour of the principle of payment of Members and in 1830 Lord Blandford included the payment of Members in a Reform Bill he presented to the House of Commons.[2] Similarly, the payment of Members was one of the demands made by the Chartists in 1838, but it was not until 1891, when the Liberals included it in their 'Newcastle Programme', that the principle of remuneration of MPs was openly espoused by a major political party. It was not a very firm commitment, however.[3] Nor was it pursued with any great enthusiasm by the Liberal governments of 1892–95, although resolutions in favour of paying Members were passed by the Commons in 1893 and 1895, only to be rejected by the Lords.

It was not, in fact, until ten years after the creation of the Labour Representation Committee in 1900, and four years after the creation of the Labour Party itself in 1906, that the Liberal Party firmly committed itself to the introduction of

[1] Plucknett, op. cit., pp 568–9; and Sir Lewis Namier, The Structure of Politics at the Accession of George III, pp 262–4, Macmillan (second edition, 1957).

[2] H.C. Deb., 2nd Series, xxii, c. 678.

[3] Sir Robert Ensor, England, 1870–1914, p 207, Clarendon Press (1936). For the text of the Newcastle Programme, see H. J. Hanham, The Nineteenth Century Constitution, 1815–1914, Documents and Commentary, p 219, Cambridge University Press (1969).

payment of MPs. Two important events lay behind the conversion of the vague promise of 1891 into the firm commitment of 1910. The first of these was the Osborne Case, in which a trade union branch secretary successfully sought an injunction preventing his union from supporting Members of Parliament by means of a compulsory levy on union members. After December 1909, when the House of Lords upheld the decision, injunctions were obtained against a number of unions: the means by which a significant number of Labour Members had been financially supported was effectively cut off and, since efforts to continue such support through voluntary contributions from trade unionists were largely unsuccessful, the very existence of the Labour Party as a parliamentary force was threatened.

The second important event was the general election of January 1910, in which the Liberal Party lost the huge overall majority it had won in 1906, but retained office with the support of the Irish Nationalists and the Labour Party. Because the Irish Nationalist and Labour parties supported the policies of the Liberal Party in general, and its policies on the House of Lords and Home Rule for Ireland in particular, Asquith's Government was not in constant danger of defeat, nor was it constantly forced to moderate its policies or make concessions in return for parliamentary support. The decision to pay Members was not, therefore, forced upon the Liberal Government by the Labour Party; it arose from the problems that the Osborne judgement had created and from the fact that payment offered not only a partial solution to these, but would facilitate co-operation with the Labour Party in the political situation created by the election of January 1910 and confirmed by that of December 1910. Furthermore, the introduction of the payment of MPs should be seen in conjunction with the passing of the *Trades Union Act 1913*, which reversed the Osborne judgement and allowed trade unions to establish political funds. These funds could be used for various political purposes, including the financial support of MPs and candidates, and the objections which led to the Osborne Case were met by allowing any union members to contract out of paying the political levy. This legislation enabled trade unions not only to sponsor and give financial support to particular MPs, but to give general financial support to the growing Labour Party. The *Trades Union Act 1913*, was thus the wider and somewhat delayed response to the Osborne decision; the payment of Members was the specific and more immediate response.

These were the circumstances which led to the announcement by the Prime Minister in November 1910 that if the Government was returned at the forthcoming election it would propose the payment of Members of Parliament. Following the return of the Liberal Government in December, the promise to introduce payment was confirmed in Lloyd George's budget statement in May 1911 and implemented by a resolution of the House of Commons and a Supplementary Estimate the following August. These laid down that Members should be paid an annual sum of £400, of which from 1912 £100 was exempt from income tax, being regarded as an average allowance for necessary parliamentary expenses.

The original salary of £400 remained unchanged until 1937, but the question of the remuneration of MPs did receive some attention during the intervening period. The increase in the cost of living between 1911 and immediately after the First World War led to the appointment of a select committee of the House of Commons in 1920 to consider the salaries and expenses of Members. The committee took the view that the salary of £400 was now inadequate, but because of the current economic situation it felt unable to recommend an increase. Nevertheless, the committee recommended that the financial position of MPs should be reconsidered in the near future. The Government adopted a more sympathetic view towards the financial difficulties in which some MPs found themselves and proposed that the whole of the £400 be treated as an allowance exempt from tax. This proposal met with considerable public and parliamentary opposition, however, and was defeated on a free vote in June 1921.

After 1921 the cost of living began to fall and this, combined with the introduction of free travel facilities in 1924 (see section 6.2), resulted in little or no pressure for an increase in salary. The economic crisis of 1931 actually led to a *reduction* by 10 per cent in Members' salaries, half of which was restored in 1934 and the remainder in 1935. In 1937, however, the Government decided to raise ministerial salaries and in the ensuing debate on the Ministers of the Crown Bill attention was drawn to the financial position of backbench Members. As a result the Prime Minister, Stanley Baldwin, agreed to make informal inquiries among MPs to ascertain their views on a possible increase in salary. These inquiries showed that some of the Members whose sole source of remuneration was their parliamentary salary were making 'undesirable economies [and] . . . were unable to keep within their means',[1] and the Government, now led by Neville Chamberlain, recommended that Members' salaries be increased to £600. This was approved by the House in June 1937.

The decision to raise the salary to £600 was taken for two reasons: the Prime Minister and his predecessor felt that a lesser sum 'still would not be sufficient for a certain number of Members, and that it would be better . . . to adopt a figure which would settle the matter for an indefinite period'.[2] This indefinite period, however, was inevitably curtailed by the inflationary impact of the Second World War and in 1945 a Select Committee was appointed to consider once again the salaries and expenses of Members. The Committee recommended in 1946 that the salary should be raised to £1,000, of which £500 should be allowed for parliamentary expenses. The Government accepted the increase to £1,000 but rejected the recommendation on allowable expenses.[3]

The cost of living continued to rise and the position was reviewed by a Select Committee on Members' Expenses in 1953–54. This Committee recommended a salary increase of £500 and the abolition of the automatic tax-free allowance of £100. Because of the economic situation the recommendation placed the Government in some difficulty, which was heightened when the House approved an increase of salary to £1,500 on a free vote. Following discussions with the Opposition, the Government proposed that instead of an increase in salary MPs should be entitled to draw a sessional allowance of £2 per sitting day, excluding Fridays. This was approved by the House in July 1954. As a result of the introduction of the sessional

[1] *Report of the Committee on the Remuneration of Ministers and Members of Parliament*, November 1964, Cmnd 2516, para. 16. Hereafter referred to as the *Lawrence Report*.

[2] H.C. Deb., 22 June 1937, 325, c. 1052.

[3] Ministers with an annual salary of less than £5,000, who were also MPs, were paid a parliamentary salary of £500. See Appendix A.

allowance the tax-free deduction of £100 from Members' salaries was abolished. From the Government's point of view the advantages of the sessional allowance were that it avoided a direct increase in MPs' pay, that not all Members would necessarily draw the allowance, that it was related to 'productivity', and, most important of all, it would cost less than the £500 increase proposed by the Select Committee. This last point is borne out by Peter Richards' estimate that the allowance would amount to £280 in an average session.[1]

Although the introduction of the sessional allowance did something to alleviate the difficulties of less well-off MPs, considerable dissatisfaction remained, particularly on the Opposition benches. Labour Members criticised the Government for rejecting the Select Committee's recommendation after it had been passed in a free vote and, 'for a short while, they refused to "pair" with Government supporters'.[2] Pressure for a further review continued to grow, as Richards points out:

'Within eighteen months [of the introduction of the sessional allowance] the question of Members' pay was again a source of public discussion: Earl Attlee, soon after he had resigned the Leadership of the Labour Party, told the Cardiff Business Club that Members were grossly underpaid and some were "walking about in the House and really dying on their feet". In June, 1956, the Leaders of the Labour and Liberal Parties wrote to the Prime Minister (Sir Anthony Eden) urging the establishment of an independent extra-parliamentary committee to investigate Members' claims for more pay; this was turned down by the Government. A further debate the following month merely brought forth another refusal from the Treasury Bench, because of the general economic situation, to ease the hardship that it was admitted some Members were suffering.'[3]

An easing of the economic situation in 1957 enabled the Government to relent, however, and it proposed an increase in salary of £750. This was the amount that the Select Committee of 1953–54 had found to be the average level of Members' expenses. The

[1] Peter G. Richards, *Honourable Members*, p 248, Faber (second edition, 1964).
[2] Richards, *op. cit.*, p 248.
[3] Richards, *op. cit.*, pp 248–9.

Government proposed that this sum should replace the sessional allowance, so that Members were now paid a total salary of £1,750.[1]

This salary remained unchanged until 1964, but there were the inevitable demands for a further increase in the intervening period. An important development was the appointment in 1963 of a Committee on the Remuneration of Ministers and Members of Parliament. The chairman of the Committee was Sir Geoffrey Lawrence, who was also chairman of the National Incomes Commission. The other Committee members were H. S. Kirkaldy, a barrister, and W. J. M. Mackenzie, then Professor of Government at the University of Manchester. To assist them in their inquiries the Committee had an advisory panel consisting of two Peers and five MPs. This Committee, usually known as the Lawrence Committee, marks an important departure from earlier reviews of the payment of Members, since for the first time the task of conducting the review was given to a body outside the Government and Parliament. Hitherto all reviews had been made either by the Government of the day or by a select committee, and the precedent of the Lawrence Committee gave added strength to those who wished to see Members' salaries subject to periodic and regular review (see section 6.4).

The Committee recommended increases in the salaries of both Ministers and Members of Parliament. However, whilst the incoming Labour Government accepted the recommended salary of £3,250 for MPs, it proposed a reduction in the suggested increase for Ministers, although a Minister's *parliamentary* salary was increased to £1,250. The new salary for MPs of £3,250, of which £1,250 was regarded as an appropriate amount for parliamentary expenses,[2] was approved by the House in December 1964 and implemented with effect from the previous October.

Between 1964 and 1970 there were again demands for increases to keep pace with the rising cost of living. In January 1969 it was announced that an increase in salary of 18·1 per cent would be necessary to take account of the rise in the consumer price index since 1964.[3] By September 1970 the purchasing

---

[1] From 1957 all Ministers who were also MPs were paid a parliamentary salary of £750. See Appendix A.

[2] As before, claims had to be substantiated with the Inland Revenue.

[3] H.C. Deb., 30 January 1969, 776, c. *378* written answers.

power had fallen from £3,250 to £2,495, an annual average decline of 4·4 per cent since 1964, and by October to £2,467, a total decline in purchasing power of 24·1 per cent since 1964.[1]

The pressure for a salary increase in the latter half of the 1966–70 Parliament was not abated by the change of government in June 1970. The following December the Government announced that Members' pay would be referred to one of the three review bodies it proposed to establish to advise on the pay of various groups, such as the boards of nationalised industries, the judiciary, senior civil servants and members of the armed services. In May 1971 the Review Body on Top Salaries was formed; it was chaired by Lord Boyle, a former Cabinet minister and Member for Birmingham Handsworth from 1950–70. Assisted by staff from the Office of Manpower Economics, the Boyle Committee undertook its review of Members' salaries, allowances and pensions and presented its report the following December. The Committee recommended a salary of £4,500 and important changes in the allowances paid to Members. These recommendations were accepted and implemented with effect from 1 January 1972.[2]

Of much greater significance than the increase itself, however, were the two premises on which the most important recommendations were based. The first of these was that a clear distinction should be drawn between salaries and expenses so that 'it should not normally be the responsibility of the individual Member to finance the facilities he needs to do his job'.[3] The second premise was that 'the job of an MP has become increasingly full-time, and ... it is essential that the level of remuneration should be adequate to provide for full-time Members without other sources of income'.[4] These two premises mark an important change in the philosophy of Members' remuneration – a change that is the culmination of earlier changes in the provision of Members' expenses, allowances and pensions.

[1] H.C. Deb., 27 October 1970, 805, c. *29* written answers; and H.C. Deb., 14 December 1970, 808, c. *254* written answers.
[2] *Review Body on Top Salaries: Ministers of the Crown and Members of Parliament*, December 1971, Cmnd 4836. Hereafter referred to as the *Boyle Report*. See also: H.C. Deb., 20 December 1971, 828, cc. 1129–1252.
[3] *Boyle Report*, para. 33.
[4] *Boyle Report*, para. 36.

6.2 EXPENSES AND ALLOWANCES

The relationship between the salary paid to Members of Parliament and the expenses they may incur in carrying out their parliamentary duties is complex, partly because Members receive certain allowances which are not part of their salaries, and partly because Members do not receive a separate allowance for expenses but may, like other taxpayers, claim expenses for income tax purposes against their salaries.

At present Members of Parliament may claim seven allowances in cash or kind in connection with their parliamentary duties, which, with two exceptions, are not regarded as part of the Member's income and not therefore subject to income tax. These are: certain free travel facilities, a subsistence allowance, free stationery, free postage, free telephone calls, a secretarial allowance, and the allowance for drafting assistance on Private Members' Bills.

The provision of free travel on parliamentary duties was first recommended by the Select Committee on Members' Expenses of 1920 and its recommendations were finally accepted and implemented in 1924. Members were originally entitled to travel vouchers (exchangeable for first class tickets) for rail journeys on parliamentary duties between London and their constituencies. This provision was subsequently extended to include journeys between the Member's constituency and his home, and between his home and London. In 1932 Members were allowed to claim for third class sleeping berths; and from 1936, for first class berths. In 1945 free travel was extended to public air and sea services, and more recently to chartered air services and private aircraft, provided in the last case that the cost does not exceed the cost of public transport. By certifying that they intend to travel from their place of residence to the House of Commons at least four days a week during the parliamentary session, Members can secure a railway season ticket, but, unlike the arrangements for travel vouchers, this facility is not available during the summer and Christmas recesses. Members may also claim reimbursement of bus fares for journeys between Westminster and their constituencies, Westminster and their homes, and their homes and their constituencies.

In April 1971 Members' wives became entitled to free first-class rail travel. Specifically, they became entitled to four return tickets a year so that they could visit their husbands at Westminster or go with them to their constituencies. This facility also applies to the husbands of women Members.[1] Following the *Boyle Report* the number of return journeys was increased to ten.[2]

Those Members who prefer to use their cars may claim a car allowance for the types of journeys described above. Originally MPs could claim only for the cost of petrol and there was an upper limit equal to the relevant first-class rail fare. This meant that the amount a Member could claim depended on the type and condition of his car and, in the view of the Lawrence Committee, made the calculation unnecessarily complicated. The Committee recommended that a flat rate of $4\frac{1}{2}$d per mile be substituted; this was the then general rate per mile of first class rail travel.[3] This recommendation was implemented by a resolution of the House in December 1964. The rate was increased to 6d per mile in 1969[4] and to its present level of 5p per mile in 1970.[5]

Since the *Boyle Report*, Members have also been able to claim travelling expenses for journeys made *within* their constituencies. They may also claim for journeys to central and local government authorities concerned with their constituencies when such authorities are located outside their constituency boundaries.[6]

The Boyle Committee further recommended that two special funds should be established to provide MPs with assistance in making journeys 'to inform themselves on subjects of relevance to their work'. One fund would provide for travel within the United Kingdom; the other, for travel abroad. The funds would be administered by a committee of the House of Commons and

[1] Resolution, H.C. Deb., 7 April 1971, 815, c. 640.
[2] *Boyle Report*, para 42(c); and Resolution, H.C. Deb., 20 December 1971, 828, c. 1250. A proposal that this facility should be extended to companions of the opposite sex of single Members was rejected in 1972. H.C. Deb., 12 July 1972, 840, c. *351* written answers.
[3] *Lawrence Report*, para. 63.
[4] Resolution, H.C. Deb., 18 December 1969, 793, cc. 1693–1722.
[5] Resolution, H.C. Deb., 3 November 1970, 805, cc. 1038–44.
[6] *Boyle Report*, para. 42(a); and Resolution, H.C. Deb., 20 December 1971, 828, c. 1250.

financed by the Exchequer. The sort of journeys envisaged by the Boyle Committee were those that a Member might make to inform himself on an industry of importance to his constituency, or to gather information in connection with the sponsoring of a private bill, or, in the case of Opposition spokesmen, in connection with their front-bench responsibilities.[1] So far the recommendation on the special funds has not been implemented.[2]

Prior to the implementation of the recommendations of the Boyle Committee, Members received no subsistence allowance in connection with their parliamentary duties, except as members of official delegations or of select committees working outside Westminster.[3] The Boyle Committee recommended that Members representing London boroughs, and those provincial Members who opt to be regarded as resident in London, should receive a London supplement of £175 per annum to meet the extra cost of living in London. This supplement would be subject to income tax. The Committee also recommended that provincial Members should be paid a daily subsistence allowance, whilst engaged on parliamentary duties, of £5·25 when staying in London and £5 when in their constituencies. Provincial Members could nominate either London or their constituencies as their place of residence and usual place of work, and would be eligible to claim a subsistence allowance for expenses incurred in attending their other place of work. The allowance would be available, in the case of Members who nominate London, provided they did not possess a season ticket or claim mileage allowance for journeys between their homes and London, when Parliament is in session.[4] The Government accepted these recommendations in general. The Government accepted the proposal for a London supplement of £175, and introduced a subsistence allowance for provincial Members.

[1] *Boyle Report*, para 42(b).

[2] In August 1972 the Government tabled a motion to establish the two funds, but the motion was withdrawn following opposition from Conservative and Labour backbenchers. A proposal to contribute up to £60 towards the cost of language study courses for individual Members was also withdrawn. It was reported that the Government hoped to secure sufficient support in the House for the travel funds at a later date. *Daily Telegraph* (4 August 1972).

[3] For details of parliamentary delegations and travel by select committees see Chapter 8.

[4] *Boyle Report*, paras 39–41.

The allowance for provincial Members covers additional costs incurred in living away from the Member's main residence; the allowance is claimed quarterly, in arrears, subject to a maximum of £750 per annum. This sum is based on the calculation that Parliament sits for about thirty-four weeks a year and that MPs spend four nights a week in London when Parliament is in session. It also allows for some time spent in London during parliamentary recesses. The allowance came into effect from 1 January 1972.[1]

Members have been entitled to some free stationery since 1911, but since April 1972 they have been entitled to an un-limited supply of free stationery. It had been found that the *cost* of collecting the money for extra stationery from MPs was not much less than the amount of money recovered. Members may also secure up to twelve photocopies (previously six) of docu-ments concerned with their parliamentary duties. Where one Member is having photocopies made for colleagues, the number of copies may be appropriately increased according to the number in the group. The provisions relating to stationery and photocopying were introduced following the recommendations of the Services Committee.[2]

The Services Committee also recommended that MPs should be provided with free postage and telephone facilities. These recommendations were accepted by the Government and came into effect in October 1969.[3] Previously MPs had been entitled to limited free postage and could make free telephone calls within the London area.[4]

Finally, from October 1969, Members were able to claim a secretarial allowance of up to £500 a year, payable quarterly in respect of secretarial expenses actually incurred. This provision, like those on stationery, postage and telephone calls, was originally recommended by the Services Committee;[5] and it was accepted in principle by the Government in July 1969. The

[1] Resolution, H.C. Deb., 20 December 1971, 828, c. 1249.

[2] 6th Report, Services Committee, 1968–69, H.C. 374, para. 13; and H.C. Deb., 22 March 1972, 833, c. 332 written answers. Prior to 1972, MPs were entitled to note paper and envelopes to an annual value of £25 and to 100 file pockets per year. It might also be noted that Members may have stationery sent to their home address free of charge. H.C. Deb., 9 May 1972, 836, c. 363 written answers.

[3] H.C. Deb., 24 July 1969, 787, cc. 474–6 written answers.

[4] For further details concerning postal and telephone facilities see Chapter 8.

[5] 6th Report, 1968–69, H.C. 374, paras 4–5.

allowance was increased to £1,000 as a result of the *Boyle Report*, and it was additionally provided that £300 of the allowance could be used towards the cost of employing a research assistant.[1]

With the exceptions of the London allowance and the cash allowances for car journeys between home and Westminster and home and constituency, these allowances in cash and kind are not normally subject to income tax. It is in fact extremely difficult to calculate, even in the case of those allowances which take the form of cash payments, the value of these allowances to Members. Quite apart from the fact that their use undoubtedly varies considerably from one Member to another, their use almost certainly varies over time. An obvious case in point is travel: some Members represent constituencies very close to Westminster, others represent constituencies a considerable distance from London; some Members live in or near their constituencies, others need to undertake journeys between home and constituency, home and Westminster, and constituency and Westminster; some Members travel at least once a week to their constituencies, others less frequently. Even a relatively constant expense, such as secretarial assistance, varies considerably according to the particular secretarial arrangements of the Member. Although some details of the cost to the Exchequer of providing these facilities are available (see section 1.2), the average expenditure per Member is not especially meaningful and there is no way of calculating the value per Member of these allowances. Nonetheless, it is clear that they are of considerable value and importance to MPs. The most important point about these various allowances in terms of a Member's salary and expenses is that in general they are *not* met from the Member's salary.

All other expenses that a Member incurs in the performance of his parliamentary duties must be met out of his official salary or from such other income as he may possess. Like any other individual who incurs expenses in connection with his occupation, a Member of Parliament may claim expenses which are deducted from his gross income. As the Lawrence Committee pointed out, in the cases of both Members and Ministers these expenses must be incurred 'wholly, exclusively and necessarily

[1] For further details of secretarial arrangements and facilities, see Chapter 7.

in the performance' of their respective offices. However, the revised system of allowances that followed the *Boyle Report* removed most of the more onerous expenses which formerly had to be·met from a Member's salary.

What remains in dispute are various expenses which have been specifically excluded by the Inland Revenue. The Lawrence Committee noted that the following could not be claimed as deductible expenses:

1 Literature issued for canvassing purposes.
2 Election expenses.
3 Periodicals, books, newspaper cuttings, etc.
4 Charitable subscriptions or donations.
5 Entertaining.
6 Extra costs arising out of late night sittings.
7 Expenses incurred by wives of Members, e.g. in deputising for or accompanying Members.
8 Payments to political organisations for political purposes.
9 Generally, expenses which the Member incurs not as a Member of Parliament but as a member of a political party.[1]

The distinction drawn by the Inland Revenue between allowable and non-allowable expenses led the Lawrence Committee to comment: 'The effect of these rules is that by no means all the reasonable expenditure of a Member is deductible for tax purposes'.[2]

As has already been noted (see Table 6.1), for the greater part of the period since payment of Members began, a proportion of the salary has been regarded as an average allowance for necessary parliamentary expenses. Between 1912, when the allowance was first agreed by the Treasury, and 1954, when it was replaced by a sessional allowance, the amount was £100. Between 1954 and 1957 Members were allowed a sessional allowance of £2 per sitting day, excluding Fridays. In 1957 the salary was increased to £1,750, the increase of £750 being regarded as an appropriate amount to cover necessary parliamentary expenses. This amount had in fact been found by the Select Committee on Members' Expenses of 1953–54 to be the

[1] *Lawrence Report*, para. 45.
[2] *Ibid.*, para. 46.

average level of Members' expenses. Then, in 1964 the salary was raised to £3,250, of which £1,250 was regarded as an appropriate amount to cover expenses.

The practice of regarding a proportion of a Member's salary as an allowance to cover expenses tended to confuse the question of expenses and allowances for a number of reasons. Firstly, although the original £100 allowance was a flat-rate deduction exempt from tax, a Member, following the Finance Act of 1913, could claim a larger amount than this up to the total of his parliamentary salary, and this provision still applies.[1] Secondly, and because of this provision, the amount of expenses varied considerably from one MP to another. Consequently there was no meaningful relationship between that part of the salary which was regarded as an appropriate amount for expenses and the actual amounts claimed by Members and allowed by the Inland Revenue. Thirdly, it was reasonable to argue that the majority of Members devote a larger proportion of their salaries to necessary expenses than is the case with most occupations, and that therefore the real or net salary of most Members was not only considerably below the then gross salary of £3,250, but also considerably below the £2,000 left after the deduction of the notional sum of £1,250 for expenses. The Boyle Committee found that in 1969–70 the average net pay after meeting necessary expenses, but before tax, was £1,920.[2]

The Lawrence Committee found the average amount of expenses claimed and allowed by the Inland Revenue for the tax year 1962–63 was £1,132. It is thus clear that however appropriate a figure of £750 might have been in 1957, by 1962–63 it was clearly inadequate and as early as 1960 a majority of Members were claiming more than this figure. By 1969–70 the average amount of expenses, before deduction of the newly introduced secretarial allowance, had risen to £1,788.

Following in the steps of the Lawrence Committee, the Boyle

[1] Details of expenses allowed to Members by the Inland Revenue, as noted in Appendix B of the *Lawrence Report*, actually show eighteen Members in 1961–62 and twenty-three in 1962–63 with expenses of *more* than £1,750. This was due to the fact that a part of the car allowance counted as taxable income, and these Members were allowed the full parliamentary salary as expenses plus the taxable part of the car allowance.

[2] *Boyle Report*, paras 4–6.

Committee pointed out that expenses varied considerably according to the type of constituency a Member represented, and showed this by an analysis of expenses allowed according to whether the Member sat for a London borough, an urban constituency (defined as a borough outside Greater London), or a rural constituency (defined as a county constituency).

Table 6.2   *Expenses allowed to Members (excluding Ministers) according to type of constituency, 1969–70*

Expenses allowed, £	London, %	Urban, %	Rural, %
Over 1,000	40·6	87·4	96·1
Over 1,500	6·2	55·2	76·0
Over 2,000	–	30·5	43·8
Over 2,500	–	13·0	24·9
Over 3,000	–	3·6	7·7
Over 3,500	–	–	0·4
NUMBER	32	223	233
AVERAGE	£941	£1,694	£1,991

Source – Adapted from *Boyle Report*, Appendix D, Table 1.
Note – These figures are for expenses before the deduction of the secretarial allowance. The average expenses after the deduction of the secretarial allowance were £1,562.

Table 6.2 makes clear the greater expenses likely to be incurred by a Member representing the relatively scattered population of a rural constituency compared with a Member representing a more compact urban area. The Table also makes clear the greater expenses likely to be incurred by a Member sitting for a constituency some distance from Westminster compared with a London Member. Doubtless other differences in the amount of expenses allowed would emerge if constituencies were analysed according to such criteria as distance from Westminster; accessibility by road, rail, air and sea services; size of electorate; and area of constituency. Further differences would emerge in relation to the Members themselves. Does the Member employ any secretarial help, and, if so, is it on a full-time or part-time basis? Is the Member a full-time or part-time MP? Does the Member find it necessary to maintain more than one residence?

The expenses allowed to Members in recent years have increased significantly. Thus the proportion with expenses of less than £1,000 declined from 17 per cent in 1966–67 to 13 per cent in 1968–69 and the proportion with expenses of £3,000 or more increased from 2 to 5 per cent. Similarly, there was a decline in those with expenses of between £1,000 and £1,999 and an increase in those with £2,000, but less than £3,000. This general increase is also shown by the range of expenses allowed during each of these years: in 1966–67 one MP was allowed expenses of less than £100, in the following two years there were none at this level; in 1967–68 the lowest allowance was between £100 and £199 and in 1968–69 between £300 and £399. The maximum allowance was over £3,100 in 1966–67 and over £3,200 in 1968–69. The situation was partly eased by the introduction of the secretarial allowance and free postal and telephone facilities in 1969, but MPs were still expected to meet a considerable proportion of their expenses from their parliamentary salaries.

Table 6.3   *Expenses allowed to Members (excluding Ministers) in 1969–70, expressed as a proportion of the Member's salary*

Expenses allowed as approximate proportion of salary	Before deduction of secretarial allowance		After deduction of secretarial allowance	
	%	MPs	%	MPs
Up to $\frac{1}{4}$	6·4	31	10·7	52
$\frac{1}{4} - \frac{1}{2}$	36·7	179	45·7	223
$\frac{1}{2} - \frac{3}{4}$	22·1	108	17·8	87
More than $\frac{3}{4}$	34·8	170	25·8	126
TOTAL	100·0	488	100·0	488

Source – Adapted from *Boyle Report*, Appendix D, Table 3.

It is clear from Table 6.3 that in 1969–70 nearly three-fifths of backbench MPs were allowed expenses amounting to more than half of their salaries, and a third to more than three-quarters of their salaries. Even after deducting the secretarial allowance, nearly three-fifths of Members were allowed expenses amounting to up to half their salaries, a further fifth between half and three-quarters of their salaries, and a quarter more than three-quarters of their salaries. Allowing for inflation, there has undoubtedly been an increase in the *real* expenses allowed to Members and, since the rules applied by the Inland Revenue have not been relaxed, this can only be attributed to a *real* increase in expenses by Members. It is not unreasonable therefore to argue that the salary increase of 1964 enabled MPs to increase their expenses to a level which they regarded as more appropriate to their duties – duties which had not significantly altered since the increase in salary. What is also abundantly clear, however, is that what Members regard as an appropriate amount of their salary to devote to their expenses varies considerably.

As was suggested earlier, MPs could and did claim amounts larger than that part of their salaries regarded as an appropriate amount for expenses; the latter is therefore merely a notional sum. Thus in 1962–63 only 16 per cent of Members were allowed expenses which were within the notional sum of £750 and in 1968–69 only 30 per cent kept within the notional sum of £1,250. It is also clear that the net salaries before tax of the majority of Members were significantly lower than the gross £3,250. Translated into real or net salaries, the 1969–70 figures in Table 6.3 mean that 11 per cent of backbench Members had a net salary of between £2,346 and £3,250, 46 per cent of between £1,624 and £2,346, 18 per cent of between £812 and £1,624, and 26 per cent a *maximum* net salary of £812. Thus in 1969 R. J. Ledger (former Labour Member for Romford) claimed that after deduction of expenses his income had been 'working out at only £1,700 to £1,800 a year',[1] whilst Dr Michael Winstanley (former Liberal Member for Cheadle) claimed that after expenses his salary amounted to £240.[2]

It was these considerations that led the Boyle Committee to examine closely the question of Members' expenses and allowances, and to recommend that 'in future a clear separation should be observed between salary, on the one hand, and provision for expenses on the other'.[3] Through its survey of Members the Committee found that three major items contributed to Members' expenses: the additional cost of living away from home, amounting on average to £685 in 1969–70; office expenses and secretarial assistance over and above the secretarial allowance, amounting to £288; and travel within constituencies, amounting to £245. These expenses, together with on average a

---

[1] *Daily Telegraph* (31 December 1969).
[2] *The Guardian* (4 April 1970).
[3] *Boyle Report*, para. 33. Original italics.

further £112 for other expenses, produced a total of £1,330.[1] The fact that these expenses were tax deductible alleviated the burden to some extent, but they still had to be met from Members' salaries. This led the Boyle Committee to recommend that this should no longer be the case and that expenses should be met entirely or substantially by new and extended allowances.

The Boyle Committee recognised that a separation of salary and expenses 'is not capable of perfect application'[2] and that Members would still claim additional expenses against income tax; but the Committee argued that its recommendations would reduce these expenses on average 'to little more than £300'.[3] Accordingly there will still be Members who spend a substantial part of their salaries on parliamentary work, but their numbers will have been reduced by the implementation of the *Boyle Report* and, for the first time, a meaningful distinction has been drawn between Members' salaries and their expenses. Nonetheless, the attitude of the Boyle Committee towards Members' expenses and allowances remains in other respects firmly in the tradition of past arrangements.

6.3 PENSIONS

The problems associated with providing pensions for former Members of Parliament are not difficult to discern. First, there are philosophical questions concerning the nature of membership of the House of Commons, such as whether membership ought to be regarded as a career with appropriate pension rights, or whether membership ought to be a full-time or part-time occupation, or whether being an elected representative is compatible with ultimately receiving a pension other than the normal state pension. Secondly, there are practical problems. How, for example, should a pension scheme for Members be funded? Should it be contributory or non-contributory? If it is contributory, should it also be supported from public funds? To what extent should it be linked with the length of a Member's service, given the fact that the average parliamentary career is considerably shorter than most other careers? Should pensions

[1] *Boyle Report*, para. 5.
[2] *Ibid.*, para. 33.
[3] *Ibid.*, para. 47.

be related strictly to age, given the considerable variation in the ages at which Members enter the House of Commons? Should account be taken of special circumstances that might apply to MPs, such as electoral defeat or loss of constituency through redistribution? Should a pension scheme take account of need, given the known variation in Members' incomes and personal circumstances?

In view of the history of the remuneration of Members it was perhaps inevitable that it was this last consideration which first received attention – the *needs* of those Members who suffered financial hardship after resignation or retirement from the House. Thus, following the report of a Departmental committee in 1937, a scheme was established for this purpose by the *House of Commons Members' Fund Act 1939*. Under this Act grants based on an assessment of needs could be made to ex-Members and to their widows and children. These grants could take the form of an annual pension, but the Members' Fund did not and does not constitute a fully-fledged pension scheme, since only those ex-Members (and their dependants) in need are eligible to benefit under its terms.

The fund is administered by six trustees drawn from current Members of Parliament. The trustees have the power to invest the fund's capital, to make grants within the limits laid down by the scheme, and they are required to submit an account annually and report at five-yearly intervals to Parliament. Until 1957 the scheme was funded by compulsory Members' contributions (originally £12 a year). Since 1957 the scheme has been funded by compulsory Members' contributions and an annual Exchequer grant.

The grants that may be made have always been subject to specified maxima and to maximum income limits. The original maximum grant to an ex-Member was £150 a year, provided the recipient's *total* income (including the grant) did not exceed £225 per annum, whilst for a Members' widow the maximum grant was £75, with an income limit of £125. The ex-Member had to be at least 60 years of age or incapacitated, and have served in the Commons for ten years.

Since most retirements occur at general elections, there was little call on the fund between 1939 and 1945. Furthermore, the policy of the then trustees was one of caution and by 1946 a sum of £48,000 had accumulated. The trustees therefore felt able to recommend increased benefits and some relaxation of the rules regarding eligibility. Accordingly the following changes were made by the *House of Commons Members' Fund Act 1948*: widowers of ex-Members became eligible; provision was made for the children of deceased Members; and special grants could be made to ex-Members and their dependants who were otherwise ineligible. The 1948 Act also allowed variations to be made by a resolution of the House; such variations could affect the benefits payable and the level of contributions.

The working of the fund was referred to the Select Committee on Members' Expenses of 1953–54. The Committee recommended the establishment of a non-contributory pension scheme, but this proposal was rejected. At the same time, the financing of the Members' Fund was reorganised. The Member's contribution was raised, and from 1957 an annual grant was made from the Exchequer. Since 1962, moreover, the trustees have had wider powers to invest the fund's capital. The present Member's contribution is £24 per annum, whilst the Exchequer grant was £5,000 in 1957 rising to £10,000 in 1958, £15,000 in 1961 and £22,000 in 1962. The fund is further supplemented by investment income which in 1968 realised more than £10,000 and in 1969 more than £9,000. The present benefits are shown in Table 6.4.

Table 6.4   *Benefits payable to ex-Members or their dependants from the Members' Fund*

Beneficiary	Maximum grant payable p.a.		Income limits (including grant)	
	Normal	Discretionary	Normal	Discretionary
Ex-Member	£660	£1,190	£1,000	£1,500
Widow or Widower	375	595	750	925
Children	30–100	–	–	–

Source – Resolution, H.C. Deb., 1 August 1972, 842, cc. 489–90.
Note – Grants larger than the normal maxima, up to the amount specified in the Table, may be made at the discretion of the trustees, having regard to the need of the prospective recipient and length of service in the case of an ex-Member.

In spite of the increase in benefits and the relaxation of the conditions regarding their payment, the Members' Fund applies in practice to only a small minority of ex-Members and their dependants, i.e. to those in need. Nevertheless, as Richards has pointed out, the increased contributions and the Exchequer grant have enabled the trustees to assist a larger number than previously. The number of grants increased from forty-four in 1955 to seventy-five in 1960.[1] A further increase occurred after 1960, as Table 6.5 shows.

Table 6.5   *Number of grants made from the Members' Fund*

Year	Grants to ex-Members	Special hardship cases	Grants to widows/widowers	Grants to children	Total
1960	29	8	35	3	75
1965	39	6	41	2	88
1969	37	8	38	–	83

Source – H.C. 183, 1969–70.

The terms of reference of the Lawrence Committee did not specifically include any consideration of the Members' Fund nor the question of pensions for Members. Nonetheless, after consulting its advisory panel of MPs and Peers the Committee asked the then Prime Minister, Sir Alec Douglas-Home, whether it should consider either or both of these matters. After consulting the leaders of the other two parties Sir Alec replied that it would be 'desirable' for the Committee to consider both the Members' Fund and pensions.[2] The Committee subsequently reported that 'the large majority of those who have submitted evidence or expressed views to us favoured the establishment of a pensions scheme for Members of the House of Commons'.[3]

After due consideration of the evidence the Lawrence Committee recommended the establishment of a pension scheme. This recommendation was effected in the *Ministerial Salaries and Members' Pensions Act 1965*, and the scheme took effect from 1964. Later, important changes were made as a consequence of the *Boyle Report*. A revised scheme was introduced by the *Parliamentary and Other Pensions Act 1972*, the main provisions of which are as follows:

[1] Richards, *Honourable Members*, *op. cit.*, p 262.
[2] *Lawrence Report*, para. 3.
[3] *Ibid.*, para. 73.

1   Membership is compulsory.

2   Each Member pays a contribution equal to a maximum of three-eighths of the total cost, which amounts to 5 per cent of salary. Any deficiency is met from public funds.

3   Full pension benefits are payable from the age of sixty-five (or the date of ceasing to be a Member if retirement occurs after sixty-five), subject to a minimum membership of the House of four years. Members may, however, retire with reduced benefits between sixty and sixty-five. Reckonable service is assessed on the basis of completed days.[1]

4   Pensions are payable to the widows, incapacitated widowers, children or orphans of Members or ex-Members with not less than four years' service. Pensions payable to widows or incapacitated widowers are equal to half the pension entitlement of the former Member. Where there are surviving children under sixteen (or under twenty-two if receiving full-time education), the pension is augmented by one-eighth of the pension entitlement of the Member for each child, up to a maximum of four children. Where a former Member leaves one orphan (or where the widow subsequently dies), a pension equal to one quarter of the Member's pension entitlement is payable, subject to the age limits noted above, and equal to half for two or more orphans.

5   The pension payable to qualifying ex-Members accrues at the rate of one-sixtieth of the final salary, averaged over the last twelve months of service, for each year of service. Members have the option, however, of commuting a proportion of the payable pension into a lump sum equal to three-eightieths of the final salary for each year of service. The rates of benefit are subject to a biennial review to take account of increases in the cost of living.

6   The payment of a pension is *not* subject to either need or means.

7   Full credit is given to those Members who were elected before 1964, up to a maximum of ten years, and the additional cost of this is met from public funds.

8   In the event of a Member leaving the House of Commons with less than four years' service or before the age of twenty-six, the former Member is entitled to repayment of

[1] Reckonable service was previously assessed on the basis of completed years.

his contributions plus interest at 3 per cent per annum. Members who have completed four years' reckonable service on ceasing membership of the House are not entitled to any refund of contributions, but qualify for preserved pension rights.

9   If a Member with less than four years' but more than twelve months' service dies whilst still a Member, his estate is entitled to a sum equivalent to twelve months' pay or the repayment of his contributions with interest, whichever is the greater,

10 Pensions are not payable to Members who hold the offices of Prime Minister, Speaker or Lord Chancellor. Their contributions are repayable.[1]

The changes introduced as a result of the *Boyle Report* took effect from 1 April 1972.

A report on the Parliamentary Contributory Pension Fund is submitted to the House at five-yearly intervals and accounts are presented annually. Table 6.6 shows details of income and expenditure.

Table 6.6   *Income and expenditure of the Contributory Pension Fund, 1964–71*

Year ending March*	Income			Expenditure paid to		
	Members' contributions £	Exchequer contributions £	Investment income £	Retired MPs £	Widows and widowers £	Children £
October 1964 to March						
1966	131,663	329,663	16,205	750	1,102	147
1967	93,819	225,819	35,620	14,804	2,114	107
1968	93,443	225,443	51,961	15,849	3,805	157
1969	93,577	225,577	73,028	19,524	5,808	219
1970	93,413	225,413	83,727	20,698	8,330	695
1971	88,426	220,428	109,246	57,278	10,534	671

Source – Annual accounts of Contributory Pension Fund.
   * The first accounting period was eighteen months.

[1] For further details on Members' pensions see the *Lawrence Report*, paras 70–82 and Appendix *D*; the *Ministerial Salaries and Members' Pensions Act 1965*, sections 4–15 and Schedules 2 and 3; the *Boyle Report*, paras 53–74 and Appendix *H*; and the *Parliamentary and Other Pensions Act 1972*.

The Exchequer contribution consists of (a) a sum sufficient to meet the cost of the scheme after the deduction of Members' contributions and retirement income, (b) £122,000 per annum to meet the cost of pensions for MPs with up to ten years' reckonable service before October 1964,[1] and (c) £10,000 to cover the costs arising from the fact that contributions from each Member are uniform irrespective of age on entering the scheme. The fund is divided into two parts: a closed fund for MPs with service before October 1964 and an open fund for MPs with service only since that date. By 31 March 1970 thirty-eight pensions had been awarded to ex-Members under the scheme, but only thirty-three were in payment at that time since five former Members had died. In addition twenty-eight pensions were being paid to widows and dependants, whilst fifty-four former Members who had not reached the age of sixty-five retained an interest in the fund.[2]

With the introduction of the pension scheme the importance of the Members' Fund is bound to diminish, since the majority of MPs retiring at general elections will qualify for pensions either immediately or on reaching the minimum qualifying age of sixty. This has been recognised by the trustees of the Members' Fund who anticipate that during 1974–79 drawings on the fund will amount to £90,000, falling to £40,000 by 1984–89 and to £25,000 after 1989. Nonetheless, the Members' Fund continues to assist ex-Members (and their dependants) who are excluded from the contributory pension scheme because they ceased to be Members before October 1964. The fund can also be used to assist ex-Members who, though qualified in terms of service, may not have reached the qualifying age, or those who – on retirement, resignation or defeat – have served less than four years in the House. In all cases, however, the criterion of need still applies.

The pension scheme introduced in 1965 effectively fulfilled its most important aim of providing pensions, either immediately or on reaching the original qualifying age of sixty-five, for the overwhelming majority of retiring MPs. Of the Members retiring at the 1966 and 1970 general elections 89 per cent

[1] This will lapse after twenty-five years.
[2] House of Commons Members' Contributory Pension Fund Report, H.C. 59, 1970–71.

qualified immediately for pensions, or would do so in due course.[1] Had the scheme been in operation at earlier elections 82 per cent would have been qualified in 1964, 71 per cent in 1959, 82 per cent in 1955, but only 32 per cent in 1951 and 42 per cent in 1950. Those who failed to qualify in 1966 and 1970 (and those who would have failed to do so at earlier elections) did so because they had less than ten years' service, but most retired voluntarily knowing that they would not qualify under the ten-year rule. Although there were cases of former Members who had served just under ten years, most had served considerably less, and together they constituted only 11 per cent of retiring Members in both 1966 and 1970.

Much the largest category of ex-Members who failed to benefit under the original pension scheme and the Members' Fund, except for the provison of special grants in cases of need, were those who were *defeated* at general elections and had less than ten years' service. Fifty-five per cent of those defeated in 1966 failed to qualify under the Ten-Year Rule. Had the scheme been in operation in 1964, 70 per cent would not have qualified. Whilst this presents a marked contrast with the figures for retiring Members, the matter received little attention until the election of 1970, when 88 per cent of the defeated Members failed to qualify and only 4 per cent qualified for immediate pensions. Most of those defeated in 1966 were Conservative Members and it is likely that the majority suffered little or no financial hardship as a result of their defeat, but most of those defeated in 1970 were Labour Members and immediate attention was focused on the financial problems that they faced. Some suffered short-term difficulties because of the abruptness with which electoral defeat terminated their salaries;[2] others suffered longer-term hardship because they found it difficult to secure an alternative form of employment or were obliged to accept a considerable reduction in income. They were not eligible for unemployment benefit,[3] nor redundancy payments. The only

---

[1] In 1966 55 per cent were fully qualified and 34 per cent were qualified by service but not age. The corresponding figures for 1970 were 62 per cent and 27 per cent.

[2] Strictly speaking a Member's salary ceases from the date of the dissolution of Parliament.

[3] Prior to the *Boyle Report*, MPs were classed as self-employed for National Insurance purposes and therefore ineligible for unemployment benefit, but they

state assistance ex-Members could claim was supplementary benefit or, where appropriate, sickness benefit. Furthermore, it should be stressed that former Members are not entitled to any refund of their contributions to the Members' Fund nor, under the original scheme, could their contributions to the pensions fund be returned until they had ceased to be Members for five years or reached the age of sixty-five, regardless of length of service. Most of these former Labour Members had first been elected in 1964 or 1966 and had, at most, six years' service and it was recognised by the Boyle Committee that in order to serve for ten years Members had in practice to serve in at least three Parliaments.[1]

Apart from the problems of defeated Members, there were complaints that the original scheme lacked flexibility in that, unlike many occupational pension schemes, it did not provide for retirement earlier than the age of sixty-five and that there was no provision for allowing part of the pension entitlement to be converted into a lump sum payable on retirement. It was felt that the option of early retirement would help Members such as those who were defeated in their late fifties or early sixties or whose health precluded or militated against a further parliamentary term during which they would become sixty-five. Similarly it was felt that the option of commuting part of the pension into a lump sum would assist former Members whose immediate need was a capital sum.

There was also criticism of the general level of the pensions and the effect of increases in the cost of living since the inception of the scheme. It seems likely that these criticisms will be largely met by the fact that Members' pensions now consist of earnings-related benefits and are subject to periodic review to take account of inflation, in accordance with recommendations of the Boyle Committee.

Of much greater importance, however, were the Committee's recommendations that the qualifying period should be reduced

---

were not regarded as self-employed for tax purposes since they were assessed under Schedule E as holding an office. H.C. Deb., 6 April 1971, 815, c. *93* written answers. The Boyle Committee suggested that the position of Members under National Insurance should be re-examined, and this was being done by the Government in 1972. H.C. Deb., 17 May 1972, 837, cc. *118–9* written answers.

[1] *Boyle Report*, para. 56.

to four years, that Members should have the option of retiring between sixty and sixty-five, and that they could opt out for a proportion of the pension entitlement to take the form of a lump sum.[1] Moreover, in order to alleviate the problems created for Members whose parliamentary salaries are their only source of income, the Committee recommended that Members should continue to be paid throughout the period of a dissolution.[2] This was also intended to help Members who were defeated. Additional assistance was envisaged in the recommendation that a terminal grant equal to three months' salary should be payable to defeated MPs and the further suggestion that they should be eligible to claim unemployment benefits.[3] The acceptance of these recommendations has met the major criticisms of the pension scheme introduced in 1964 and, as far as the conditions peculiar to being an MP allow, have brought the scheme into line with pension arrangements in other occupations.

6.4 REVIEWS OF SALARIES, ALLOWANCES AND PENSIONS

Since 1911 one of the basic problems concerning Members' remuneration has been the question of reviewing it in relation to the general rise of incomes and expenses. This problem is important not only in respect of the actual method by which salaries and other payments should be reviewed, and whether such reviews should be regular or *ad hoc*, but also in respect of the extent to which changes and proposed changes in remuneration have been related to the national economic situation.

The national economic situation has been an important factor in leading governments to reject proposals for increased salaries and expenses for Members – even when they have been recommended by select committees – and in their resisting proposals for regular or periodic review by an extra-parliamentary body. Consideration of the economic situation has not been confined to governments, however. In 1920 a select committee felt unable to recommend an increase in salary because of the economic

---

[1] *Boyle Report*, paras 56–66.
[2] *Ibid.*, paras 48–52.
[3] *Ibid.*, para. 52.

situation, although it maintained that the salary of £400 was inadequate; when the Government of the day sought to have the whole £400 treated as an allowance exempt from tax the proposal was defeated in a free vote in the House of Commons.

It is not difficult to see why governments, or, occasionally, parliamentary opinion, should be sensitive to the relationship between Members' remuneration and the national economic situation, since any proposal to increase salaries or allowances during a period of economic difficulty places the Government and MPs in the embarrassing position of having to decide whether Members (and on some occasions Ministers) constitute a special case.[1] It matters little whether the decision is taken by the Government or whether by a free vote of the House; in the past Members have played the part of counsel, judge and jury in their own cause, and even with the creation of the Review Body, they remain judge and jury. Thus in 1931 the Government felt it necessary to propose a temporary reduction of 10 per cent in Members' salaries which lasted until 1935. In 1946 the Government felt unable to accept a select committee's recommendation on allowable expenses. In 1954 the Government felt unable to accept another select committee's recommendations, which had been approved in a free vote, for a salary increase of £500. In 1956 on economic grounds the Government resisted new demands for a review of salaries and allowances. Similarly, for the greater part of the 1966–70 Parliament, the Government refused either to increase Members' salaries or to establish a system of review. Of course, it has been largely because of inflation that salaries and allowances have increased since 1911, and it has invariably been because of an easing of economic problems that concessions have been obtained. Nonetheless, both Ministers and Members remain sensitive to their unique position of legal and political responsibility, which makes the review of Members' remuneration a more complex subject than it might at first appear. It is instructive that while establishing a Review Body the Government has retained a right of veto

[1] See, for example, the comment of a Labour Member following the publication of the *Boyle Report*: 'I know from experience it is practically impossible to convince ... [constituency parties] we need the money. Now that expense allowances are to be introduced it is going to be more difficult than ever. They will tell me, "You are to get about £90 a week, with four months' holiday a year." ' *Daily Telegraph* (8 December 1971).

by committing itself to accept its recommendations 'unless there are clear and compelling reasons for not doing so'.[1]

Until the appointment of the Lawrence Committee in 1963 the financial position of MPs had always been dealt with by a select committee of the House or by the Government of the day. Thus in 1920, 1945–46 and 1953–54 select committees considered the problem of Members' salaries and expenses and made recommendations to the House. On other occasions, as in 1937 and 1957, the Government took the initiative and brought proposals before the House, usually after informal consultations.

Inevitably there have been demands that salaries and allowances should be subject to regular and periodic review, either in their own right or by being linked to salaries in the civil service. The Lawrence Committee commented:

'One suggestion repeatedly made to us was that the remuneration of Members in the House should in some way be linked to a level of salary in the Civil Service on the ground that this approach would not only indicate some comparative level of salary to be initially adopted but would ensure that as and when salaries in the Civil Service were adjusted in accordance with the established principles affecting those salaries, the salaries of Members of the House would likewise be maintained at an appropriately up-to-date level. *This is a suggestion which we firmly reject.* In the first place we are fully satisfied that *there is no basis of comparison at all between the two types of service.* Secondly, we are far from accepting the principle that the remuneration of Members of the House should be linked to any external scale: it should be determined on its own and should not enjoy any automatic built-in protection. A third point which can be made against the suggestion is that any link between salaries of Members of the House and salaries in the Civil Service might involve the latter at times in political controversy.'[2]

Despite this categorical rejection, pressure for some form of regular and periodic review of Members' remuneration by an extra-parliamentary body continued and, indeed, increased as inflation continued. For most of its period of office the Labour

---

[1] *Boyle Report*, para. 121.
[2] *Lawrence Report*, para. 39. Author's italics.

Government of 1964–70 rejected such proposals as inappropriate, specifically rejecting the suggestion that Members' pay and expenses should be referred to the Prices and Incomes Board.[1] In 1969 however, the Government changed its mind and announced that salaries would be referred to the PIB in the next Parliament.[2] This was followed by a further change of policy when Barbara Castle, then Secretary of State for Employment and Productivity, said: 'It is only right and proper that all public servants, including ourselves, who have no normal negotiating machinery, should have their pay and conditions reviewed at regular intervals by an independent body.' She announced that the Government now intended to refer the question to its proposed Commission for Industry and Manpower.[3]

The defeat of the Labour Government in June 1970 plunged the whole question of review into a state of uncertainty and prompted Douglas Houghton (Labour Member for Sowerby) to introduce a Private Members' Bill which sought to establish a review body for Members' pay, allowances, pensions and conditions of service.[4] During the debate on the motion for second reading of Mr Houghton's Bill, William Whitelaw, Leader of the House, announced that Members' and Ministers' pay, allowances, expenses and pensions would be referred to one of three bodies, each of which would deal with defined groups of individuals whose remuneration came from public funds.[5] The body reviewing Members' remuneration had eight members: Lord Boyle, the Chairman; Harold Atcherley, former Group Personnel Co-ordinator of Shell and a consultant on recruitment to the Secretary of State for Defence; Gerard Young, Chairman of the Tempered Group and a former member of the Prices and Incomes Board; Anthony Lloyd, a barrister; Peter Menzies, Deputy Chairman of ICI; Lord Beeching, former Chairman of British Railways; Sir George Coldstream, former

[1] See, for example, H.C. Deb., 17 March 1969, 780, c. 37.
[2] Statement by the Leader of the House (T. F. Peart) on the 6th Report of the Services Committee, H.C. Deb., 24 July 1969, 787, cc. *474–6* written answers.
[3] H.C. Deb., 8 April 1970, 799, c. 568–9.
[4] House of Commons (Conditions of Service) Bill, Bill 30, Session 1970–71. The Bill was presented in November 1970 by Mr Houghton and two other senior Conservative and Labour Members.
[5] H.C. Deb., 4 December 1970, 807, cc. 1721–5.

Clerk of the Crown in Chancery; and Sir Mark Turner, Deputy Chairman of Kleinwort Benson.

The Boyle Committee recommended that 'there should be a major comprehensive review at intervals of four years, ie. corresponding roughly to once in the lifetime of each Parliament of normal length. However, we do not wish to exclude the possibility of an intermediate adjustment between major reviews'.[1] This was in line with a Government statement during the debate which led up to the establishment of the Boyle Committee. In the debate the Government stated that it was its intention that a 'review should be made once in every Parliament of normal length'. This pledge was repeated in the debate on the second reading of the Ministerial and Other Salaries Bill of 1972 and the resolutions which implemented most of the Boyle Committee's recommendations.[2] Only time will tell whether these pledges will result in fact in a pattern of regular, periodic reviews of Members' remuneration.

6.5 THE PHILOSOPHY OF MEMBERS' REMUNERATION

In announcing the decision in 1911 to pay MPs £400 a year, David Lloyd George, the Chancellor of the Exchequer, insisted on calling the intended payment 'an allowance to a man to enable him to maintain himself comfortably and honourably, but not luxuriously, during the time he is rendering service to the state'.[3] Moreover, Lloyd George specifically rejected such alternative descriptions as 'remuneration', 'recompense' and 'salary', although the actual resolution authorising payment of Members used the term 'salary', and it is by this term that payment is generally known. Lloyd George's insistence on the use of the term 'allowance', however, is indicative of the importance of the philosophy of Members' remuneration. Similarly, the circumstances in which MPs first received payment in 1911 illustrate the basic problem of the philosophy – *its purpose*.

The pressures which led to the payment of Members in 1911 stemmed principally, as we have seen, from the election of an

---

[1] *Boyle Report*, para. 123. For a general discussion of salary review see J. A. Cross 'Reviewing the pay of MPs', *The Parliamentarian*, pp 273–6 (October 1966).

[2] H.C. Deb., 20 December 1971, 828, c. 1244. The pledge was repeated again during the committee stage of the bill. H.C. Deb., 18 January 1972, 829, c. 378.

[3] H.C. Deb., 10 August 1911, 29, c. 1382.

increasing number of Members who found it difficult to support themselves financially as members of the House of Commons, and in particular from the rise of the Labour Party. Hitherto the great majority of Members either had private means or could earn sufficient money outside Parliament (and sometimes both) to enable them to serve as Members of Parliament un-aided by financial support from the state; but the working class MPs who began to be elected in the last three decades of the nineteenth century, and many of the Labour MPs elected in the first decade of the twentieth, had neither private means nor occupations which they could combine with membership of Parliament.

This situation was reflected not only in the individual circum-stances of Members, but in their attitudes towards their re-muneration. These attitudes may be briefly described as a dichotomy between those Members who regarded membership of the House as a public service, voluntary in nature and un-tainted by payment, and those who, whilst accepting member-ship as a public service, regarded payment as a necessary condition of membership; between those who felt payment would attract recruits for its own sake, and those who felt that payment was essential if the House of Commons was to become a more socially representative body; and, increasingly, between those who regarded a job or activity outside Parliament as a useful adjunct to their role as Members, and those who regarded such activities as a distraction from their parliamentary duties. Broadly speaking, the argument was between those who regarded their roles as Members of Parliament as part-time and those who regarded them as full-time. Thus, in spite of the fact that from the outset payment to Members has been liable to tax as earned income, the attitude that salaries are provided to enable Members to carry out their duties rather than sustain them in a political career retains a wide currency.[1]

It is because of this dichotomy of attitudes that the question of Members' remuneration has always been approached in a pragmatic and piecemeal fashion. There has never been broad agreement at any time as to the appropriate level of salary for

---

[1] See, for example, the speeches by Enoch Powell (Conservative Member for Wolverhampton South-West) and Ivor Stanbrook (Conservative Member for Orpington) in H.C. Deb., 20 December 1971, 828, cc. 1150–8 and 1214–6.

Members. Allowances have been introduced sparingly and with little or no regard to consistency. Expenses are confined to what the Inland Revenue regards as appropriate expenditure in pursuance of a Member's parliamentary duties and are allowances against income tax, not additions to Members' salaries. Pensions are a recent innovation, preceded only by special provision to meet cases of hardship and need among former Members. Finally, the lack of periodic reviews has been a major factor in the unsystematic development of Members' remuneration.

The absence of an agreed purpose concerning the remuneration of Members has prevented the question of salaries, allowances, expenses and pensions from being considered as a unified whole, quite apart from any consideration of remuneration in relation to parliamentary services and facilities. Even the Lawrence Committee, despite fairly wide terms of reference[1] and the use of a reasonably extensive questionnaire to Members, stopped short of amending, or suggesting any modification in, the original principle concerning Members' remuneration enunciated by Lloyd George. The Lawrence Committee did, however, analyse the implications of that principle and concluded that the principle recognises:

'. . . the existence of candidates for parliamentary service who have neither the private means nor the opportunity of earnings outside Parliament which will enable them to assume this form of political life . . . for such persons the payment offered should not be so high as to include any elements of "luxurious" living but should recognise that parliamentary service calls for and should be willingly accorded a measure of personal sacrifice. At the same time the payment should not be so low as to deter such persons for financial reasons from entering or remaining in the House.'[2]

[1] These were 'To review, and to recommend what changes are desirable in, the remuneration of Mr Speaker, Ministers of the Crown and Members of the House of Commons and also the allowance for Members of the House of Lords, *having regard to their responsibilities, to the place of Parliament in the national life and to the changes which have taken place, since the existing emoluments were fixed, in general standards of remuneration, and to the increases in expenses borne by Members of both Houses in the discharge of their duties.' Lawrence Report*, para, 1. Author's italics.

[2] *Lawrence Report*, para. 29.

The Lawrence Committee concluded 'that this analysis of the principle provides the only practical working basis on which we can proceed'.[1] Thus the committee recognised that some Members were able to pursue occupations outside the House and in this way supplement their parliamentary salaries and, above all, that whilst some Members regarded their parliamentary work as a full-time occupation, others felt equally strongly that, notwithstanding any financial considerations, the pursuance of a part-time occupation outside the House was a positive contribution to their parliamentary work. The Committee therefore concluded that:

'This lack of homogeneity is a central feature of membership of the House and it necessarily precludes the fixing of a salary at a level which will exactly meet the needs of all Members, simply because these needs are by no means uniform.'[2]

The Lawrence Committee firmly rejected the introduction of a system of differential salaries which would vary according to the circumstances of particular Members. Nonetheless, this proposal retains support in some quarters. James Wellbeloved (Labour Member for Erith and Crayford) has suggested that MP's pay should 'be related to participation in the work of Parliament measured by attendance, voting record and service on committees'.[3] Another proposal, by James Dickens (former Labour Member for Lewisham West), envisages the creation of a two-tier system of membership. One tier would consist of full-time Members, who would be paid £4,500 a year and have full and free supporting services; the other would consist of part-time Members, who would be paid £2,250 and share free services, such as a secretary, with other part-time Members. In order to enforce the two-tier system there would be an attendance register and fines for Members who did not meet their responsibilities.[4]

Whatever the merits of such proposals, one thing is apparent from any examination of Members' remuneration: quite apart from any consideration of private income enjoyed by individual

[1] *Lawrence Report*, para. 30.
[2] *Ibid.*, para 34.
[3] Amendment to Early Day Motion 60, Session 1967–68, November 1967.
[4] See *The Times* (26 September 1969) and *The Guardian* (3 November 1969).

Members or the ability of some Members to supplement their parliamentary earnings by work outside the House, until the acceptance of the *Boyle Report* no clear picture had emerged of how much Members of Parliament earn. This was largely because Members were expected to meet a considerable proportion of their expenses from their parliamentary salaries and because the circumstances of Members vary. Because it is a matter for the personal decision of the Member what expenses he incurs, the real salary of Members before tax varied enormously. Although individuals other than MPs who pay income tax under Schedule E and who claim expenses against tax are no different from Members of Parliament in theory, as far as tax and expenses are concerned, the position of MPs differed in practice because of the much greater expenses which Members tend to incur, for which there was no special or separate allowance and which had, therefore, to be met from their salaries. With some feeling, but not without an element of truth, Eric Lubbock (now Lord Avebury) could comment that as an MP 'the harder one works the less remuneration one receives'.[1]

The report of the Boyle Committee is, therefore, a watershed in the history of Members' remuneration, since, as was pointed out earlier, it marks a fundamental change in philosophy by drawing a basic distinction between Members' salaries and their expenses. Furthermore, unlike the Lawrence Committee which effectively avoided the question of whether Members should be regarded as full-time or part-time,[2] the Boyle Committee argued that 'it is essential that the remuneration should be adequate to provide for full-time Members without other sources of income'.[3] It is, however, a pertinent commentary on the economic and political sensitivity of the question of Members' remuneration that the Boyle Committee should feel obliged to keep their 'recommendations for increases and improvements to the absolute minimum which we consider to be necessary'.[4]

[1] H.C. Deb., 11 March 1969, 779, c. 1163.

[2] *Lawrence Report*, para. 31.

[3] *Boyle Report*, para. 36.

[4] *Ibid.*, para. 121. See also the speech by Joseph Kinsey (Conservative Member for Birmingham Perry Barr), H.C. Deb., 20 December 1971, 828, cc. 1195–8. It is also interesting to note that in August 1972 it was announced that three Members were drawing *reduced* salaries from 1 January 1972. H.C. Deb., 9 August 1972, 842, c. *498* written answers.

CHAPTER 7

SECRETARIAL AND RESEARCH ASSISTANCE

We have already seen that Members are, if they wish, provided with somewhere to work in or near the Palace of Westminster, either in the form of single or double rooms or writing spaces in desk rooms (see section 3.1). We have also seen that there are various ancillary facilities – lockers, filing cabinets and file pockets, stationery and photocopying facilities, postal and telephone facilities, and, since 1969, an allowance towards the cost of employing a secretary, part of which may now be spent on employing a research assistant. One of the major assumptions of the Services Committee in its Third Report of 1968–69[1] was that each Member would want a room of his own, together with accommodation for his secretary. This will be realised with the completion of the new parliamentary building.

The situation has changed dramatically since 1951. In 1951 only a handful of Members had desks in or near the Palace of Westminster; most Members had only a locker in which to put their personal papers and belongings; stationery was officially limited to a daily quota and photocopying facilities were non-existent; free telephone calls were limited to the London area, and free postage to correspondence with Ministers, Government Departments and other official persons and bodies; and Members had to meet the full cost of secretarial or personal research assistance. The position has now been reached in which it is envisaged that each Member will have his own properly equipped office, will enjoy adequate postal and telephone facilities (see Chapter 8) and will be provided with assistance from public funds towards the cost of secretarial and research assistance (see Chapter 6).

In this chapter we shall give detailed attention to one dimension of this changing pattern. We shall examine the services that

[1] H.C. 295.

MPs receive from three groups of persons who are not officials of the House of Commons. They are Members' secretaries, Members' personal research assistants and specialist advisers who work with select committees. Because these aides may receive remuneration from the House of Commons vote and use official facilities, we regard it as within our brief to devote a chapter to them. In the case of secretaries and research assistants we found it necessary to conduct a survey of Members in order to obtain a full picture of the existing situation.

7.1 SECRETARIAL ASSISTANCE

When the £500 secretarial allowance was introduced in 1969, it was of course recognised that it would not be sufficient to meet the cost of employing a full-time secretary, and it was therefore regarded as a contribution towards Members' secretarial expenses. Thus it could be used to meet part of the cost of employing a full-time or part-time secretary; or it could be used for the services provided in the Palace of Westminster by Ashworth and Company, the official secretarial agency to the Houses of Parliament.[1] The Boyle Committee recommended that not only should the allowance be increased to £1,000, but that Members should be able to use up to £300 of the amount towards the cost of employing a research assistant.

Although Members were not paid any secretarial allowance before October 1969, as long ago as 1895 arrangements were made for typing to be done for members of both Houses of Parliament. Furthermore, as has already been noted, since 1912 MPs have been able to claim secretarial expenses against income tax and this remains true for any such expenses incurred over and above the £1,000 secretarial allowance (see Chapter 6). Nonetheless, the actual employment of a secretary or research assistant is a matter for each individual Member, and it is the Member who is responsible for paying the salary and social security contributions of any secretary or research assistant he employs. It is partly because Members are left to make their own secretarial arrangements that these arrangements vary

---

[1] Ashworth's closed down in December 1973 and was succeeded in January 1974 by Max-Muller's Secretarial Agency, which provides a similar service to Members.

considerably, but it is also important to take into account the varying needs of Members and the level of secretarial assistance that they feel able to afford. Moreover, some MPs receive assistance from their constituency parties, or from businesses or professional offices with which they are associated outside Parliament, or, in the case of union-sponsored MPs, from their trade unions. Not infrequently, they receive assistance from their wives or other relatives.

In order to ascertain the various levels of secretarial assistance employed by Members we conducted a survey of all backbench MPs and Opposition frontbenchers, other than the Leader of the Opposition and the Opposition Chief Whip.[1] The survey, which was conducted in July 1971, shows clearly that the amount

Table 7.1   *Secretarial arrangements of Members of Parliament, 1971*

Secretarial arrangement	%	MPs	
No secretarial help	1·3	5	
Uses Ashworth's Agency only	4·7	18	
Shares a secretary with three or more MPs	2·6	10	
Shares a secretary with two other MPs	12·7	49	
Shares a secretary with one other MP	18·4	71	67·4%
One secretary working exclusively for the MP *part-time*	33·7	130	
One secretary working exclusively for the MP *full-time*	20·7	80	
Two or more part-time secretaries working exclusively for the MP	2·6	10	26·6%
Two or more full-time secretaries	2·3	9	
Combination of full-time and part-time secretarial assistance	1·0	4	
TOTAL	100·0	386	

Notes – (a) The response rate to the questionnaire was 69·8 per cent. For further details of the survey see Appendix B.

(b) Where a Member employed two or more secretaries *part-time*, this was included in the overall total of those having full-time secretarial assistance.

(c) The survey of Members conducted on behalf of the Boyle Committee found that 97 per cent of Members either employed or shared in the employment of a secretary, and that 13 per cent used secretarial pool facilities. *Boyle Report*, Appendix A, Table 9.

[1] At the time of the survey the Leader of the Opposition and Opposition Chief Whip were the only Opposition Members to receive official salaries in addition to their parliamentary salaries. As a result of the *Boyle Report*, two additional Opposition whips are now paid official salaries. *Boyle Report*, para. 108.

and type of secretarial assistance employed by MPs varies considerably.

As Table 7.1 makes clear, only a very small proportion of respondents had no secretarial help at all, usually preferring to deal with their correspondence themselves. Moreover, less than 5 per cent relied entirely on the secretarial services provided by Ashworth's. Thus nine out of every ten respondents employed a personal secretary on a part-time or full-time basis.

Although the overwhelming majority of Members employed a personal secretary, the actual arrangements varied considerably. In general, it may be noted that approximately two-thirds of the respondents had some form of part-time assistance, and about a quarter had full-time secretarial assistance or its equivalent. Apart from the personal preferences of Members, the major factor in determining the extent of secretarial assistance is financial. There is little doubt that the introduction of the secretarial allowance enabled more Members to employ full-time assistance or more extensive part-time assistance.

Nevertheless, the service provided by Ashworth's is both important and comprehensive. The provision of a typing service for MPs was, as mentioned earlier, introduced in 1895 following requests to the First Commissioner of Works for such a service. Tenders were invited and that of Ashworth and Company was accepted by the First Commissioner, who then placed the control of the service under the jurisdiction of the Serjeant at Arms. Since 1895 Ashworth's has been the only organisation within the parliamentary precincts providing Members with secretarial assistance. Between 1925 and 1950 Ashworth's was located in the Westminster Hall Annexe, but since 1950 the agency has been provided with accommodation on the West Front of the House of Lords. At present this accommodation consists of two rooms on separate floors, together with space for a duplicating machine in a third shared room. The present staff numbers twelve and the present limited accommodation precludes any increase in staff.

As the survey shows, some MPs rely entirely on Ashworth's and are provided with a full secretarial service, which 'covers collecting post, dealing with routine letters, filing, meeting constituents, arranging tickets [for the public galleries], guides, booking lunches and dinners, and in general anything we are asked to do'.[1] Other Members, though still relying entirely on Ashworth's in that they do not employ a personal secretary, simply use the agency's dictation and typing services. There are, however, Members who use Ashworth's to supplement their secretarial assistance. This may occur when Members' personal secretaries are unable to cope with the volume of work, or when their secretaries are ill or on holiday, or during recesses (especially the summer recess) when some Members do not employ secretaries. Similarly, some Members have their duplicating and printing done by Ashworth's.

The services provided by Ashworth's are available all the

Table 7.2   *Comparison of secretarial and research assistance, 1967 and 1971*

Assistance	1967			1971		
	%	MPs		%	MPs	
No secretarial help	3·7	4		1·3	5	
Use Ashworth's Agency only	8·2	9		4·7	18	
Shares a secretary with three or more MPs	6·4	7		2·3	9	
Shares a secretary with two other MPs	15·6	17	63·2%	12·4	48	62·6%
Shares a secretary with one other MP	18·3	20		16·6	64	
One secretary working exclusively for the MP *part-time*	22·9	25		31·3	121	
One secretary working exclusively for the MP *full-time*	15·6	17	24·8%	19·7	76	31·3%
More than one full-time secretary or *assistant*	9·2	10		11·6	45	
TOTAL	99·9	109		99·9	386	

Notes – (a) The figures for 1967 are taken from the survey of MPs conducted by Anthony Barker and Michael Rush on behalf of the Study of Parliament Group and Political and Economic Planning in preparation for their book *The Member of Parliament and His Information*, Allen & Unwin (1970). A brief discussion of secretarial assistance is found in Barker and Rush, p 191.
(b) No distinction was drawn in 1967 between secretarial and research assistance. The 1971 figures have been adjusted to include research assistants, and the figures shown do not therefore correspond exactly with those in Table 7.1. Thus a respondent who employed a secretary *and* a research assistant is included among those having more than one secretary or assistant.

[1] Letter to the editors from the Administrative Secretary of Ashworth and Company.

year round from Monday to Friday between 10 a.m. and 6 p.m. and may be used by MPs and Peers. On average the services provided by Ashworth's are used by between seventy and eighty MPs and Peers each month. Ashworth's thus provides a small proportion of Members with all their secretarial assistance and a rather larger proportion with supplementary assistance. No precise figure is available of the number of MPs who use Ashworth's to supplement their normal secretarial assistance, but 10 per cent of the survey respondents reported that they used Ashworth's for this purpose. A Member using Ashworth's pays directly to the agency for the services rendered.

A comparison of the results of the 1971 survey with those obtained in a similar survey conducted in 1967 reveals significant trends (see Table 7.2). For example the proportion of Members employing full-time assistance increased from less than a quarter in 1967 to nearly a third in 1971. Moreover, although the proportion employing part-time assistance remained constant, the proportion sharing a secretary with one or more other MPs declined and the proportion employing exclusive part-time help, often amounting to more than half-time, increased significantly. There was also a small increase in the proportion of Members with more than one secretary or assistant.

The doubling of the secretarial allowance from £500 to £1,000 will almost certainly lead to a further extension of the secretarial assistance used by Members. The new allowance provides for greater flexibility, however, in that Members may now use the allowance to meet 'both secretarial and general office expenses',[1] whereas previously it could be used only for the employment of a secretary. Furthermore, as already mentioned, up to £300 of the allowance may be used to employ a research assistant.

The extent to which the secretarial allowance has been welcomed can be gauged by the proportion of Members claiming it (see Table 7.3). During the first six months of the 1970–71 accounting period 87 per cent (546) of the 624 Members (including Ministers) serving throughout the period claimed at least £200, 8 per cent (48) claimed less than £200, and, by 1 July 1971, only 5 per cent (30) had made no claim at all.[2] It is clear from these figures that a considerable majority of Members claim the full

[1] *Boyle Report*, para. 45.
[2] H.C. Deb., 20 July 1971, 821, c. *264* written answers.

Table 7.3   *Members of Parliament* (*including Ministers*)
drawing the secretarial allowance, 1969–70

Amount claimed	%	MPs
Full allowance (£500)	70·2	328
Less than £500	28·9	135
No claim	0·9	4
TOTAL	100·0	467

Source – H.C. Deb., 20 July 1971, 821, c. *264* written answers.
Note – The accounting period for the allowance is 1 October to 30 September. Since a general election intervened in the first year of the allowance's operation, the Table gives figures only for those Members who served throughout 1969–70.

allowance, that most of the rest claim some of it, and that only a handful claim none. This is hardly surprising, since as one survey respondent remarked: 'In London a good experienced secretary expects to earn at least £1,300 a year with Luncheon Vouchers, and may get £1,400 or £1,500'. Another respondent asserted: '£500 per annum buys less than half a secretary at London rates'; and another: 'I pay £1,000 over the allowance for a full-time secretary'. This situation was, of course, recognised when the allowance was introduced, as the then Leader of the House remarked:

'I recognise that this sum will by no means meet the costs of Members who employ a secretary full-time in their parliamentary duties. But it will be a considerable contribution to the secretarial expenses incurred by a substantial majority of Members.'[1]

Given the extent, notwithstanding the secretarial allowance, to which secretarial arrangements depend on the financial position of individual Members, it is not surprising to find that there are significant differences between the parties (see Table 7.4). The dichotomy between the two major parties is marked, with one Conservative in three employing full-time help, compared with only one Labour Member in six. Moreover, a further analysis shows that Labour MPs are more likely to share a secretary with two or more colleagues, whereas Conservative MPs are more

[1] H.C. Deb., 11 December 1969, 793, c. 655.

Table 7.4 *Secretarial arrangements of Members of Parliament by party, 1971*

Secretarial arrangements	Conservative		Labour	
	%	MPs	%	MPs
No secretarial help	1·0	2	1·6	3
Use Ashworth's only	4·7	9	4·8	9
Part-time secretary	58·6	112	77·6	146
Full-time secretary	35·6	68	16·0	30
TOTAL	99·9	191	100·0	188

Note – Of the six Liberal Members, five employed full-time secretaries and one a part-time secretary.

likely to share a secretary with only one colleague. Similarly, Conservative Members are more likely to have secretarial assistance in addition to a full-time secretary (see Appendix B, Table B2). The principal reason for this party difference is almost certainly financial: in general Conservative MPs are financially better off than their Labour colleagues, either because they are more likely to come from a wealthy background or because they are in a better position to supplement their parliamentary salaries with earnings outside Parliament.[1] Conservative MPs are more likely to have occupations which they can pursue on a part-time basis whilst serving in the Commons. For instance, although a higher proportion of Labour MPs are members of the professions, the largest single group are former teachers and lecturers, occupations which cannot normally be continued on a part-time basis, whereas the largest professional group amongst the Conservatives consists of barristers and solicitors. More importantly, however, Conservatives are far more likely to continue previously existing business interests or to develop such interests whilst Members.

Apart from the party difference there are also significant differences in the secretarial arrangements of Members according to length of service. The figures in Table 7.5 show that

[1] The Boyle survey found that 70 per cent of the respondents had regular or occasional occupations in addition to their parliamentary duties. These extra-parliamentary jobs earned (after allowing for expenses but before tax) up to an additional £999 for 34 per cent of the respondents, between £1,000 and £4,999 for 46 per cent, and £5,000 or more for the remaining 20 per cent. *Boyle Report*, Appendix A, Table 16.

Table 7.5   *Secretarial arrangements of Members of Parliament by length of service, 1971*

Secretarial arrangement	First elected					
	Before 1964		1964–70		1970 or later	
	%	MPs	%	MPs	%	MPs
No secretarial help	1·7	3	1·0	1	0·9	1
Uses Ashworth's	7·4	13	1·9	2	2·8	3
Part-time secretary	61·1	107	69·5	73	75·5	80
Full-time secretary	29·7	52	27·6	29	20·8	22
TOTAL	99·9	175	100·0	105	100·0	106

Members elected before the general election of 1970 are more likely to have full-time secretarial assistance than those elected in 1970 or later, a much greater proportion of whom employ part-time assistance. Although a higher proportion of those elected between 1964 and 1970 employ part-time secretaries than those elected before 1964, this is partly because a slightly higher proportion of the latter have no secretarial help at all, but more especially because a much higher proportion of these longer-serving Members rely entirely on Ashworth's. It is important to note that in spite of these two differences similar proportions in both groups employ full-time assistance. Since the Barker-Rush survey also found that more recently-elected MPs were less likely than their longer-serving colleagues to employ full-time assistance, it seems likely that newer Members prefer limited secretarial assistance until they have some experience of parliamentary life and of the financial commitments involved. It may also be, of course, that there is a tendency for a Member's parliamentary workload to increase with service compared with his early years in the House and with it his secretarial needs.

The secretarial arrangements described above are by no means exhaustive in that it was clear from the replies to the survey questionnaire that a number of Members enjoy varying degrees of supplementary assistance in addition to their principal full-time or part-time secretaries. The main sources of such additional help (apart from Ashworth's) are local party organisations, Members' wives (and occasionally other relatives), and Members' business or professional interests. Survey respondents were asked to specify any secretarial arrangements not covered by the alternatives suggested, and one Member in six said that they received supplementary assistance from one of the foregoing sources. Since these were 'write-in' responses, it may well be that the proportion of Members with such supplementary assistance is underestimated. Nonetheless, assuming no underestimation, it is clear that a significant minority of Members receive supplementary secretarial assistance. Labour Members were slightly more likely to receive help from their local party organisations and much more likely to get additional secretarial help from their wives, while, not surprisingly, Conservatives were much more likely to receive help from business or professional sources (see Appendix B, Table B5).

A further variation in the secretarial arrangements of Members concerns the secretary's place of work. The variety of arrangements derives in part from the fact that there is insufficient accommodation for all Members' secretaries in or near the Palace of Westminster, and partly from the fact that not all Members wish their secretaries to work at Westminster. Some MPs prefer their secretaries to work in their constituencies since a great deal of their work is concerned with constituent's problems; others find it more convenient to use their business or professional offices, which may be located in London or in the Member's constituency or wherever these interests are based; and a few Members maintain their own private offices, usually in London, solely or primarily for their political work. In cases where a Member would prefer his secretary to work in the Palace of Westminster, but no accommodation is available for her, she may work in the Members' London house or flat or in her own home.

To facilitate the work of secretaries for whom there is no parliamentary accommodation, there are interview rooms and dictating cubicles on the Lower Ground Floor of the House of Commons below the Commons chamber, though these are also available for Members to receive visitors or hold small meetings. In 1973 there were 210 desks available for Members' secretaries in or near the Palace of Westminster.[1] Some of these are situated in the Palace itself – in the Westminster Hall Annexe, the Upper Committee Corridor and above the Members' Lobby. Other desks are nearby in 7 Old Palace Yard, 1 Bridge Street and 2 Abbey Gardens.

[1] 1st Report, Services Committee, 1972–73, H.C. 196, pp 2–3.

Table 7.6 *Location of Members' secretaries, 1971*

Location	%	MPs
Palace of Westminster and adjacent buildings	58·0	208
Elsewhere	41·2	148
Both	0·8	3
TOTAL	100·0	359
No answer		4
Respondents employing secretaries		363

Note – The fact that the number of Members claiming that their secretaries work in the Palace of Westminster and adjacent parliamentary buildings (208) exceeds the number of desks available (197), quite apart from the secretaries of Members who did not reply to the questionnaire, is probably explained by the fact that some secretaries work in the single or double rooms allocated to Members, whilst others may share one desk.

Nearly three-fifths of the secretaries employed by MPs in 1971 worked in the Palace and adjacent buildings, and two-fifths worked elsewhere (see Table 7.6). At the same time, whereas more than three-fifths (63 per cent) of Conservative Members' secretaries worked in the Palace and adjacent buildings, this was the case with little more than half (53 per cent) of the secretaries employed by Labour Members. There is some evidence from the survey that more Labour Members than Conservative Members preferred to have their secretaries working in their constituencies rather than at Westminster.

Whether accommodation is available at Westminster or not, the majority of Members find it convenient to make arrangements for their secretaries to have access to the Palace. All secretaries who work in or near the Palace or regularly visit the Member or Members for whom they work must have a pass which is issued by the Serjeant at Arms and is renewable annually. In April 1971 the Serjeant at Arms' Department had issued approximately 400 passes, which, in the context of the information obtained by the survey, would suggest that approximately four out of five Members' secretaries had passes to enter the Palace of Westminster.

Secretaries in possession of passes may enter the Palace by St Stephen's Entrance or by the carriage gates in New Palace Yard or by the subway entrance from Westminster underground station. The pass admits the holder to the secretaries' typing rooms, to the Members' Post Office for the collection of mail and to the Strangers' Cafeteria. When the House is not sitting, secretaries may enter the Members' Lobby to go to the Post Office, to obtain Members' *Hansards* and other publications from the Vote Office, and to go to the Members' Letter Board. They may also visit the Library door to collect books or documents for Members; and they may enter the Interview Floor, the Galleries (if they have an Admission Order), the rooms allocated to the Members employing them, and the Table Office (to hand in a Member's parliamentary question). Secretaries may not enter the Members' Dining Room, Smoking Room, Tea Room, Lounges, Desk Rooms, Writing Rooms, Television Rooms, Wireless Room or the House of Commons Library.

There are a number of additional secretarial and related facilities available, including photocopying machines for the use of secretaries, which are located in the Sale Office (Palace of Westminster) and at 1 Bridge Street; filing cabinets in Members' Rooms, Desk Rooms and secretaries' rooms; and Members' lockers in the Ways and Means and Library corridors. In addition free stationery is provided in the Library, Writing Rooms, the Cloisters, Members' Rooms and secretaries' typing rooms. Finally, copies of Vacher's *Parliamentary Companion* may be purchased from the Superintendent of the Members' Cloakroom.[1]

7.2   RESEARCH ASSISTANCE

Apart from any assistance they may receive from their party headquarters or from other outside organisations, Members may receive research assistance in three ways: through the services provided by the House of Commons Library, through the services of a research or personal assistant, or as a member of a select committee which employs specialist assistance. The services provided by the Library are described elsewhere,[2] and

---

[1] These details are taken from *Information for Members' Private Secretaries* (May 1968) and *Accommodation for Members and Secretaries* (April 1970). Both are issued by the Department of the Serjeant at Arms.

[2] For an account of the research assistance provided by the House of Commons Library see Chapter 5 above and Barker and Rush, *op. cit.*, pp 290–337. For an account of the research assistance provided by party organisations, see *ibid.*, pp 233–64.

this section therefore deals with research assistants employed by individual Members or groups of Members and with specialist assistance for select committees.

7.2.1 Personal Research Assistants

Whereas the overwhelming majority of survey respondents said they employed a full-time or part-time secretary in 1971, only a few said they had the services of a research assistant (see Table 7.7).

Table 7.7 *Members of Parliament employing research assistants, 1971*

Employing a research assistant	Conservative		Labour		Total	
	%	MPs	%	MPs	%	MPs
Full-time research assistant	8·9	17	4·8	9	7·2	28
Part-time research assistant	2·1	4	2·1	4	2·1	8
No research assistant	89·0	170	93·1	175	90·7	350
TOTAL	100·0	191	100·0	188	100·0	386

Notes – (a) Two of the six Liberal respondents had research assistants.
(b) The Boyle survey found that 9 per cent of MPs had research assistants. *Boyle Report*, Appendix A, Table 14, Note (b).

The fact that less than 10 per cent of MPs employed a research assistant can be mainly attributed to financial considerations. This is not to say that every Member would employ a research assistant had he the financial means to do so, but it is clear from earlier research that many more would do so if they could.[1] As with secretarial assistance, the fact that a Member may now use up to £300 of the secretarial allowance to employ a research assistant will almost certainly result in an increase in the number of research assistants employed by MPs. Also facilitating an increase in the number of research assistants is a scheme initiated recently by the Joseph Rowntree Social Service Trust.

[1] Barker and Rush, *op. cit.*, pp 326–332. Thirty-five per cent of the respondents in the Barker–Rush survey mentioned their wish to have or share the services of a research assistant, although no specific question on this matter was put to respondents. In two separate surveys in 1963 and 1964 Malcolm Shaw found that more than two-thirds of his respondents favoured some form of research assistance other than that provided through the House of Commons Library. See Malcolm Shaw, *Proposals for Research Assistance for Members of Parliament: An Interim Report* (June 1964) and *Assistants for Members of Parliament* (October 1964), both published by the Institute for Social Research.

Under this 'fellowship' scheme several Members (ten in 1973) are being provided with assistants (for details see Appendix B).

In view of the primacy of financial considerations it is hardly surprising to find that more Conservative than Labour Members have research assistants; nor is it surprising, in view of the competition for parliamentary accommodation, that only two-fifths of the research assistants work in official facilities in or adjacent to the Palace. Apart from the functional distinction between a secretary and a research assistant,[1] the distinction is also of some importance in that, not only may research assistants use the same facilities in the Palace of Westminster as secretaries, but unlike secretaries a limited number (fifty at present) may also make use of the House of Commons Library. They are only admitted to certain parts of the Library, and the times at which they may use the Library during session are restricted.[2] Nevertheless, this is an extremely useful facility, and has probably led more than one Member to register his personal assistant as a research assistant rather than a secretary. The principal disadvantage of such a course is that a Member's secretary is likely to be given preference over a research assistant in the allocation of accommodation in the Palace of Westminster.

The future of secretarial and research assistance for Members depends on two factors: the future development of Members' salaries, expenses and allowances; and the development of more extensive parliamentary accommodation. The introduction of the secretarial allowance in 1969 marked the acceptance of the principle that Members should be provided with secretarial assistance at public expense. This decision undoubtedly reflects the attitudes of Members themselves. The Services Committee reported in 1968–69 that 'there is a growing feeling that such a basic facility as the provision of a secretary is essential', and recommended that 'regardless of any possible later revision of salary, provision should be made at public expense for secretarial assistance or an allowance to meet up to one full-time secretary per Member'.[3]

[1] This distinction is not necessarily as clear-cut as the terms suggest. At least five Members employing research assistants also use them to do their secretarial work.

[2] Even on its present modest scale the admittance of research assistants to the Library poses important questions as to the privacy of Members in the Library.

[3] 6th Report, Services Committee, 1968–69, H.C. 374, para. 5.

Whilst accepting this principle, the Government felt unable to agree to an allowance that would cover the full cost of employing a secretary, but clearly left open the question of an increase in the allowance in future which would be sufficient to meet the cost of a full-time secretary. The Services Committee in fact envisages that in due course each Member will have his own secretary and, furthermore, that in the new parliamentary accommodation there will be space for all Members' secretaries.[1] It also seems clear that for the foreseeable future secretarial assistance at public expense will take the form of an allowance, rather than the provision of secretaries employed by the public service or some form of more centralised secretarial service. As the Leader of the House said when he announced the secretarial allowance in 1969:

'The great majority of Members wish to continue to make their personal arrangements. Many Members stressed the confidential nature of their work, and the obvious advantages of having secretarial assistance familiar with their personal and constituency arrangements.'[2]

7.2.2. Specialist Advisers for Select Committees

Whilst individual Members may have the services of their own research assistants, as members of select committees they may, in addition, have the services of outside specialist advisers. Committee advisers began to appear on the Westminster scene in an important way after 1966, although they have not become very numerous. Nevertheless, their numbers have been increasing, and they may be said to provide a significant new service to the House. Between 1966 and January 1972 a total of twenty-eight appointments of advisers had been made to select committees and their subcommittees.

The specialist adviser is an unusual servant of the House in that he is neither a part of the official Westminster establishment nor even, like a Member's secretary, a regular employee. He is an outsider, normally with a full-time job outside the House, who has been recruited by a select committee to do a specific task during a specific time period. In the process he

[1] 3rd Report, Services Committee, 1968–69, H.C. 295, para. 4.
[2] H.C. Deb., 11 December 1969, 793, c. 654.

supplements traditional services provided by Clerks and by the research staff of the House of Commons Library. A typical authorisation to a select committee to appoint such advisers is:

'That the Committee have power to appoint persons with specialist knowledge for the purpose of particular inquiries, either to supply information which is not readily available or to elucidate matters of complexity within the Committee's order of reference.'[1]

The practice of attaching a specialist adviser to a select committee is not strictly new. An adviser worked with the Select Committee on the Organisation and Administration of the Telephone Service in 1921 after the Committee had been given the power to appoint persons 'for the purpose of obtaining special expert or scientific information or advice upon the subject matter of their orders of reference'.[2] A further precedent was the case of the Select Committee on House of Commons (Rebuilding) of 1944, which had a professional adviser.[3] But these early examples were isolated cases.[4] When the Estimates Committee acquired its first specialist adviser in 1966, this was to mark the beginning of a chain reaction. As other select committees have subsequently asked for authority to appoint advisers, and have appointed them, the outside specialist has become a familiar, while not universal, figure among the select committees. In every session since 1966 there have been a number of outside specialists attached to the various select committees.

There was of course a precedent of a very different kind. The Public Accounts Committee has long been serviced by the Comptroller and Auditor General and his staff of more than 500, who have direct and continuing access to the departments in Whitehall. This Committee is thus furnished with an unrivalled

[1] 4th Special Report. Select Committee on Overseas Aid, 1969–70, H.C. 154, p 3.
[2] David Coombes, *The Member of Parliament and the Administration*, p 78, Allen & Unwin (1966).
[3] Martin Partington, 'Parliamentary Committees: Recent Developments', *Parliamentary Affairs*, 23, p 367 (1970).
[4] Between 1872 and 1914 there were twenty-five payments to individuals for services performed on behalf of Commons committees. Erskine May, *Treatise on the Law, Privileges, Proceedings and Usage of Parliament*, p 639n, Butterworth (eighteenth edition, 1971).

source of advice independent of the executive. As Crick has noted, while some committees of the Commons have brains and teeth, 'only the Committee of Public Accounts has had hands and feet to work for them'.[1] As John Boyd-Carpenter (formerly Conservative Member for Kingston-on-Thames) said during the Commons debate on the Government's Green Paper on Select Committees of the House of Commons: 'If the Public Accounts Committee achieved any measure of success, it was due almost entirely to the fact that the necessary research work . . . was done in advance for the Committee regularly throughout the year'.[2] But it should be kept in mind that in recent years select committees have not been seeking assistance as ambitious as is available to the Public Accounts Committee.[3] What they have been seeking, and getting, is authority to attach to their committees from time to time someone with special expertise who can help them deal with certain specific questions.

Although in 1966 the Estimates Committee became the first post-war committee of the Commons to receive authorisation to appoint specialist advisers, another select committee requested such authorisation seven years earlier and was turned down. In 1959 the Nationalised Industries Committee made the request after canvassing the whole subject of what kind of assistance it needed.[4] While failing to obtain a specialist adviser, the Committee succeeded in obtaining the services of an extra Clerk.

The request by the Estimates Committee for authority to appoint specialist advisers was made in April 1965:

'Your Committee appreciate that the assistance they obtain from witnesses and from their Clerks may often be all that they

[1] Bernard Crick, *The Reform of Parliament*, p 83, Weidenfeld and Nicolson (second edition, 1968).

[2] H.C. Deb., 12 November 1970, 806, c. 632.

[3] Nevertheless, the Procedure Committee of 1968–69 envisaged the possible use by the new Expenditure Committee of the Comptroller's staff. 'Your Committee recommend that, if it proves to be the case that Sub-Committees need extra help in their enquiries, it should be examined whether the valuable knowledge and experience of the [Exchequer and Audit] Department can be of use to them, quite apart from the assistance given to the Public Accounts Committee; or whether they require additional expert assistance.' 1st Report, Select Committee on Procedure, 1968–69, H.C. 410, p xvii.

[4] Special Report, Select Committee on Nationalised Industries, 1958–59, H.C. 276.

require. They consider, however, that there may be occasions on which it would be valuable for them to engage the services of someone with technical or scientific knowledge on an *ad hoc* basis for the purpose of a particular enquiry or part of an enquiry either to supply information which was not readily available or to elucidate matters of complexity within the Committee's order of reference.'[1]

The Committee went on to say that the adviser 'would have no power to vote or examine witnesses'. He would attend meetings of the relevant subcommittee, 'conducting the inquiry when invited to do so'. This last suggestion is ambiguous, as Coombes has pointed out, inasmuch as it is difficult to see how one can 'conduct' an inquiry without examining witnesses.[2]

The Procedure Committee endorsed the request for specialist assistance.[3] The matter then went to the House where the Leader of the House (Herbert Bowden) announced that the request could not be granted directly. Instead, he referred the matter to the Services Committee.[4] The Services Committee, in turn, approved the Committee's request:

'Your Committee have considered the question of allowing select committees conducting enquiries to employ specialist assistants either to act as expert assessors or for the purpose of undertaking particular tasks for them, and find no reason why permission should be withheld. Anyone so engaged should be entitled to attend meetings of the committee ... whether the committee were meeting to take evidence or to deliberate. He would, however, have no power to vote or to examine witnesses.'

But this did not constitute authorisation for all select committees to appoint specialist advisers. The House would have to authorise the use of this power in each case. At the same time, a broader enabling procedure was envisaged for the future:

[1] 5th Special Report, Estimates Committee, 1964–65, H.C. 161, para. 4. A decade earlier the Stokes Committee had recommended that the Estimates Committee be empowered 'to secure the assistance of an accountant, actuary or other qualified person'. H.C. 184, 1953–54, p xii.
[2] Coombes, *op. cit.*, p 209.
[3] 4th Report, Select Committee on Procedure, 1964–65, H.C. 303.
[4] H.C. Deb., 27 October 1965, 718, cc. 185–6.

'Consideration might well be given in future Sessions to the desirability of including this power in the order of reference of select committees likely to require it'.[1]

In February 1966 the Commons formally authorised the Estimates Committee 'to appoint persons with technical or scientific knowledge' on terms as set out in the Committee's original request. This authorisation has been in the Committee's order of reference ever since, and the successor to the Estimates Committee – the Expenditure Committee – has inherited the power.

After the Estimates Committee obtained authorisation, a number of other committees requested it. The second committee to be authorised to engage specialists was the committee which had been turned down in 1959 – the Nationalised Industries Committee. Additional authorisations were made to the Science and Technology Committee, the Agriculture Committee, the Education and Science Committee, the Committee on Overseas Aid and Development, and the Scottish Affairs Committee. All committees which have applied for authorisation have been given it, but there were delays in granting authorisation in three cases (Agriculture, Science and Technology, and Education and Science), and as we have seen there was also a delay with the Estimates Committee. In all instances, moreover, a case had to be made out. Once granted, however, the power has been renewed each session. Moreover, committees of both the 'departmental' and 'subject' types have been given authorisation. Nevertheless, there appears to be a reluctance on the part of Governments to make a blanket extension of the power to select committees.

Committees that are authorised to engage specialists have all done so. In some cases – particularly the Estimates and Expenditure committees with their subcommittees – two or more advisers have worked simultaneously for the same committee. Many of the advisers have been university teachers. Professor P. G. Pyatt of the University of Warwick assisted the Estimates Committee's Subcommittee on Government Statistical Services. Another Estimates Committee adviser was Michael Blackburn, an accountant, who helped with an inquiry into the public building programme. Among the advisers who have worked

[1] 1st Report, Services Committee, 1965–66, H.C. 70, p 4.

for the Science and Technology Committee are Professor D. D. Eley (coastal pollution), Professor R. W. Cahn and Dr Bryan Harris of Sussex University (carbon fibres), and W. R. Thomas of Elliott-Automation and Christopher Harlow of Political and Economic Planning (defence research). The Nationalised Industries Committee has engaged Professor Maurice Peston for inquiries concerned with North Sea Gas, the National Coal Board and ministerial control of the nationalised industries. The late Professor A. H. Hanson of the University of Leeds also assisted this Committee. The Agriculture Committee appointed four outside advisers during the short time that it was in a position to do so.

The Expenditure Committee, which has attached several specialist advisers to its subcommittees, submitted a request in 1971 for further 'supporting staff'. The Committee reported that its members have need:

'... not only of temporary specialists but also some general guidance from more permanent technically qualified staff ... [so that] Members' attention can be drawn to important developments in the broader field of their activity. This we think can only be assured by the establishment of a small staff of qualified persons, in touch with the affairs of all the Subcommittees, and able to assess and advise on the significance of new ideas and political decisions.'

To fulfil such a need, the Committee asked the House for 'a small, full-time, properly qualified, secretariat, consisting of say, a Head of Section and two subordinates'. This secretariat would be within the establishment of the Clerk of the House.[1] The Government did not accede specifically to this request, although in November 1971 a former civil servant was appointed as 'special adviser' to the Expenditure Committee, with the rank of Principal Clerk. This appointment differs from the appointment of other advisers in being (a) full-time, (b) in the Clerk's Department and (c) filled by a 'generalist' rather than a specialist.

In 1973, following a visit by one of its subcommittees to Washington, the Expenditure Committee renewed its request

[1] 2nd Special Report, Expenditure Committee, 1970–71, H.C. 436, pp 6–7.

for additional assistance.[1] Several suggestions were put forward. One was to create an 'investigating staff', which would examine the estimates, call attention to points requiring further examination and, if so requested by a subcommittee, undertake an investigation. The Committee also renewed the suggestion of the Procedure Committee of 1968–69 that the staff of the Comptroller and Auditor General might assist the Committee. The Expenditure Committee noted that one of its subcommittees had already approached the Comptroller and Auditor General with a view to arranging for the secondment to the subcommittee of one or two officials from his Department.

Thus one can envisage the use of different kinds of committee aides. Specialist advisers, Clerks and the staff of the Library have all served committees in various ways, and it may be useful to consider them in conjunction.

Crick has pointed to the wide range of services which Clerks provide. 'Their duties in practice extend far beyond procedure, keeping the minutes and drafting the reports: they may have to organise research and may find themselves asked for advice by the chairman of the committee or subcommittee, much as a senior civil servant may talk both formally and informally to his Minister.'[2] A former Clerk of the House, Sir Edward Fellowes, put it this way: 'Though not experts in accounting or finance, the staff [of the Clerk's Department] who serve the Estimates Committee can claim to be intelligent laymen with the necessary knowledge of where the information sought by the Committee can be obtained, and the experience to know what to look for when the facts and figures are put before the Committee'.[3]

The House of Commons Library provides a further dimension of assistance to select committees. A member of the senior Library staff wrote in 1970 that 'A field that has widened considerably in the last two years or so has been the Library's activities in connection with select committees'.[4] Some authorities indeed maintain that the Library is the logical place for

[1] 9th Report, Expenditure Committee, 1972–73, H.C. 269, pp ix–xi.
[2] Crick, *The Reform of Parliament, op. cit.*, pp 92–3.
[3] 'Parliament and the Executive: Financial Control of the House of Commons', *Journal of the Parliaments of the Commonwealth*, **43**, p 227 (July 1962).
[4] Geoffrey Lock, 'The Role of the Library', in A. H. Hanson and Bernard Crick (editors), *The Commons in Transition*, p 141, Fontana (1970).

select committees to go for the specialist help that Clerks cannot provide. In fact the Library has close working relationships with a number of select committees. Library research staff have some advantages over outside advisers: they have more experience of the House; they provide continuity; they do not have to contrive an academic sabbatical to be available. But on the other hand, 'they are not numerous enough, or wide-ranging enough in their subject specialities, to enable committees always to dispense with outside assistance hired on a temporary basis for specific enquiries'.[1]

In considering the contributions that can be made to select committees by specialist advisers, Clerks and Library research staff, respectively, different authorities have given different weighting to the various elements. In the debate on the 1970 Green Paper on procedure, Mr Boyd-Carpenter envisaged an ambitious role for specialist staffs:

'If the new [Expenditure] committee is to work efficiently, this is not just a question of giving it one or two extra clerks. . . . It involves equipping it with a real investigatory staff of its own . . . who can get at work on the books and accounts of the Departments of State.'[2]

On the other hand, Ian Mikardo (Labour Member for Poplar) has said:

'I fear that, if the committees were to build up large, subject-expert staffs, their authority would be weakened, not strengthened. There would be a real danger of their simply rubber-stamping reports drawn up by their expert advisers. I hope that the Select Committee on Nationalised Industries will continue to be primarily staffed by committee clerks.'[3]

[1] Hanson and Crick, *op. cit.*, pp 144–5. 'The degree of involvement [by the Library] with committee work varies with the requirements of the committee and with the amount of time that the Library researcher is able to devote to it.' *Ibid.*, p 143.

[2] H.C. Deb., 12 November 1970, 806, c. 632.

[3] Ian Mikardo, 'The Select Committee on Nationalised Industries', in Alfred Morris, *The Growth of Parliamentary Scrutiny by Committee*, p 66–7, Pergamon (1970).

Geoffrey Lock sees a useful role for all three types of aides to select committees:

'The principal advisers and servants of committees must of course always be their Clerks, but it is clear that there is also a place for both expert consultants and research assistance. ... Some subjects of enquiry are so narrow that only an academic specialist could provide the service that a Committee would want. ... On others there is no reason why a member of the Library staff should not provide a service at least equal to that which would be given by an outside specialist.'[1]

In any event, a factor that will have much to do with the use that is made of specialist advisers is the amount of money available to pay for their services. So far only a small amount has been allocated for this purpose. In the 1972–73 estimates, £11,000 was provided for committee advisers.[2]

7.3 CONCLUSION

In regard to the three services discussed in this chapter – those provided by secretaries, personal research assistants and advisers to select committees – one sees once again the tendency in recent years to enlarge the ancillary services available to Members. The allowance for secretaries and research assistants is of particular importance as a new facility. These developments have occurred in a piecemeal way and illustrate the essentially pragmatic approach which is characteristic of such developments in the House. In all three cases, the enlarged services and facilities were acquired independently in the first instance, with little or no regard apparently being paid to other services and facilities.

[1] Hanson and Crick, *op. cit.*, p 144.
[2] Supply Estimates, 1973–74, Class I, 2. The estimate for 1973–74 is £12,000.

CHAPTER 8

OTHER SERVICES AND FACILITIES

A number of arrangements remain to be discussed. Because they cannot be conveniently included under the earlier chapter headings, they are dealt with in this chapter. The first matters to be taken up are postal services and telephone facilities. These discussions are followed by a consideration of Members' travel arrangements. Such arrangements relate to travel abroad by select committees, travel by delegations to such bodies as the North Atlantic Assembly and the European Parliament, travel by delegations to make presentations to Commonwealth Parliaments, and travel to conferences sponsored by the Commonwealth Parliamentary Association and the Inter-Parliamentary Union. Services provided by the Transport Office are discussed. Finally, refreshment facilities are considered, as well as the Crypt Chapel.

Looked at historically, postal and telephone arrangements have certain things in common. In both cases Members originally enjoyed free services and facilities, only to have them subsequently curtailed and then later restored. In both cases their curtailment and restoration illustrate changes in attitude towards the provision of services and facilities for MPs. The original arrangements were curtailed because the prevailing view was that MPs should not enjoy special privileges at the expense of the state. They were subsequently restored because the prevailing view was that their provision, if not a necessity, was a highly desirable contribution to the efficiency and effectiveness of Members.

8.1 POSTAL SERVICES

Prior to the introduction of the penny post in 1840 and from October 1969, Members of Parliament were allowed to send letters free of charge. But there the parallel ends, except perhaps for the fact that before 1840 this privilege was widely abused and since 1969 there have been accusations that it is being abused. Before 1840 Britain possessed a fairly extensive postal system, but it was expensive, not always reliable, and did not cover the whole country. Furthermore, various individuals and organisations enjoyed the privilege of franking, that is the right to send letters free of charge provided the sender signed the cover or outside of the letter. This privilege was established by a decree of the Council of State in 1652 and was claimed by the House of Commons in 1660 in a Post Office Bill, which included a demand that all correspondence *to and from* MPs should be carried free. The relevant clause was deleted by the House of Lords, but Members were allowed to receive and send inland letters free of charge for that session only. In fact the practice continued until 1764 when it was regulated and legalised, and MPs were allowed to send ten free letters per day, not exceeding one ounce each, to any part of the United Kingdom and to receive fifteen letters per day free of charge. In practice the restrictions were easily evaded, and the system was much abused. After 1784 free letters were required to bear both the signature and date of posting in the writing of the sender, but the restrictions on numbers were not enforced. In some cases MPs even supplied their friends with pre-franked envelopes. The system of franking was abolished with the introduction of Sir Rowland Hill's penny post in 1840.

No longer able to frank letters, Members' postal privileges went from one extreme to the other: from being able to send as many letters as they wished, quite apart from the receipt of letters, Members could now send none. Although franking had been abolished, the cost of all letters sent on official business by Government Departments was debited to departmental accounts; this facility was available to Ministers, but not to Members. As far as can be ascertained, however, from 1888 Members were allowed to send free correspondence to Ministers and Departments.[1] In due course Members were also allowed free postage when writing to nationalised industries, local committees and boards of the national health service, officials of the House of Commons, and, following a recommendation of the

[1] See *35th Report of the Postmaster-General on the Post Office*, 1889, c. 5850.

Lawrence Committee which was accepted by the Government in 1966, to the Clerks and heads of departments of local authorities.[1] Then in 1969 the Services Committee recommended that all correspondence on official business should be free. This was accepted by the Government and implemented with effect from October 1969.[2]

Free postage was facilitated by the introduction of 'Official Paid' envelopes. When they were introduced, 'no exact rules were formulated, beyond a general statement that Members should have free postage facilities [within the United Kingdom] in transacting their official business'.[3] In March 1970 William Hamilton (Labour Member for West Fife) complained that some MPs were using Official Paid envelopes to send circulars to new voters. Consequently the Leader of the House, Fred Peart, sent a letter to all Members informing them that they should not use free postal facilities to send circulars, 'even on non-party lines'.[4] At the same time Mr Peart announced that in the five and one-half months since free postage had been introduced nearly one million envelopes had been issued.[5]

From the figures on Official Paid envelopes given by the Leader of the House and the overall figures provided by the Services Committee a year after their introduction it appears that the monthly average was settling down to rather more than 100,000.[6] At the same time, the figure can be expected to vary according to the time of year and other factors which affect the size and nature of Members' correspondence.[7] Following accusations that the facility was being abused, the Services Committee investigated its working, and made further recommendations a year after its introduction. The Committee reported that there had been some confusion over the use of Official Paid envelopes and that 'some Members have inter-

[1] See *Lawrence Report*, para. 69; 3rd Report, Services Committee, 1965–66, H.C. 107, p 4; and H.C. Deb., 10 March 1966, 725, c. *650* written answers.

[2] See 6th Report, Services Committee, 1968–69, H.C. 374, para. 10; and H.C. Deb., 24 July 1969, 787, cc. *474–5* written answers.

[3] 2nd Report, Services Committee, 1970–71, H.C. 169, para. 2.

[4] *Ibid.*

[5] H.C. Deb., 18 March 1970, 798, c. *146* written answers.

[6] This pattern followed an initial flood during the early months of the scheme, especially the first month when more than 300,000 envelopes were issued.

[7] See Anthony Barker and Michael Rush, *The Member of Parliament and his Information*, pp 49–69, Allen & Unwin (1970).

preted the concession widely, others narrowly'.[1] The Committee recommended that the facility should *not* be used for (a) personal correspondence, (b) circulars to constituents, (c) circulars to Members and (d) correspondence by all-party committees which include persons who are not MPs. 'Otherwise', the Committee said, 'the decision about the use of these envelopes must continue to be left to the good sense of the individual Members'.[2]

In addition the Committee recommended that Official Paid postcards and acknowledgements cards should be made available. Previously only Official Paid envelopes were available. Finally, it recommended that second class envelopes should no longer be issued since 'only about 7,000 of these have been issued compared with nearly 1,400,000 of those stamped for first class post – clearly Members regard the greater part of their correspondence as urgent and important'.[3] A suggestion designed to make life easier for Members was that Official Paid envelopes should be of the self-seal type, but this was rejected on several grounds, including cost.[4]

Prior to 1833 the collection of outgoing mail was the responsibility of the Deputy Housekeeper who, for approximately £30 a year, gathered all letters for posting, put them into bags four times a day and sent them to the GPO. This system was criticised by the Select Committee on Establishments of 1833, which recommended the appointment of a Postmaster 'to take charge and to send and receive all Letters and Packets sent to and from the House of Commons by the General and Twopenny Post; also of all letters which may be given him for delivery by the Official Porter on Parliamentary business'.[5] Thus this Committee laid the foundations for today's system.

At present there are two Post Offices in the Palace. One is available for use only by Members and Officers of the House

---

[1] 2nd Report, Services Committee, 1970–71, H.C. 169, para. 3.

[2] *Ibid.*, para. 4. The Government subsequently rejected a request that Members should be allowed to send prepaid envelopes to constituents to enable them to send necessary information to Members. H.C. Deb., 20 January 1972, 829, c. 252 written answers.

[3] 2nd Report, Services Committee, 1970–71, H.C. 169, para. 6.

[4] *Ibid.*, para. 7.

[5] Quoted in Philip Marsden, *The Officers of the Commons 1363–1965*, p 163, Barrie and Rockliff (1966).

and is in the Members' Lobby; the other is in the Central Lobby. There is also a sorting office for letters and parcels, a telegraph service, a messenger service and a dispatch room. The two Post Offices are open from 8 a.m. until half-an-hour after the rising of the House on sitting days, and from 8 a.m. to 5 p.m. and 6 p.m. respectively during recesses.[1] The Postmaster is assisted by one deputy, sixteen postal and telegraph officers, six postmen, five telegraph messengers and a postman who supervises the messengers. Collections of mail are made frequently throughout the day.

Members and their secretaries may post letters at any one of thirty posting boxes in the Palace and nearby parliamentary premises, including two in the Bridge Street premises and others in convenient locations in the Palace such as the Library. Members' mail is available for collection from the Post Office in the Members' Lobby at any time after 8.15 a.m. from Monday to Friday until the rising of the House, or between 8.15 a.m. and 5 p.m. on Saturdays and during recesses. Mail may be collected by the Member or his secretary or some other accredited representative. In addition mail may be forwarded to Members in accordance with their instructions.

The House of Commons Post Office transacts normal public Post Office business, but there are several exceptions. Savings Bank service is available to Members only, and licences are not issued. Arrangements are made, however, to obtain licences on behalf of Members on request. The Commons Post Office will cash cheques for Members and Officers of the House, although this is not a normal Post Office service. There is also a telex machine in the Central Lobby Post Office for sending outgoing messages; it does not receive incoming messages because it is ex-directory.[2]

[1] The sorting office operates from 6 a.m. until half-an-hour after the rising of the House on sitting days and from 7 a.m. to 6 p.m. during recesses. The telegraph service is available from 8 a.m. until half-an-hour after the rising of the House on sitting days and from 8 a.m. to 6 p.m. during recesses. The messenger service is available from 8 a.m. to 8 p.m. on sitting days and from 8 a.m. to 5.30 p.m. during recesses. The despatch room operates from 6 a.m. until half-an-hour after the rising of the House on sitting days and from 8 a.m. to 6.30 p.m. during recesses.

[2] The question of the telex machine receiving incoming messages was to be reviewed by the Services Committee in 1972. H.C. Deb., 5 June, 1972, 838, cc. 24–5 written answers.

8.2   TELEPHONE FACILITIES

Telephones were first installed in the House of Commons in 1883 – one at the Members' entrance and the other in the Upper Waiting Hall. There was some dispute at the time as to how widely the availability of this service was known, leading one Member to point out that the 'one at the entrance is visible to the naked eye when you pass'![1] At this time all telephone lines were in private hands and MPs were allowed to make both trunk and local calls without charge. Thus originally Members enjoyed free telephone facilities, but, as in the case of postal services, these were subsequently curtailed, only to be restored in 1969. In 1896 *trunk* telephone lines were taken over by the Post Office from the National Telephone Company, but the latter continued to control *local* lines in the London area and continued to allow MPs to make London calls free of charge. It would appear that when, following a recommendation in 1889 by the Select Committee on Telephones, local services were taken over by the GPO between 1898 and 1911, Members retained their right to make free calls in the London area, while being charged for trunk calls. This remained the position until 1969.

Thus between 1896 and 1969 all telephone calls, other than those in the London area, had to be paid for by the Member concerned, although, as we have seen, they could be claimed against income tax as necessary expenses. Clearly, the provision of free calls in London was a considerable advantage to Members representing constituencies in or near London. The situation changed, however, when plans were approved for the introduction of a fully automatic telephone system, to begin operations in 1972.[2] This meant that from that date Members would be able to make free calls to any place in the United Kingdom. This was deemed feasible financially because of the saving to be achieved in the automatic system by a reduction in telephone staff. Moreover, the cost of collecting trunk call charges under the automatic system (estimated at £15,400 per

---

[1] H.C. Deb., 17 August 1883, 283, c. 961–2.

[2] In 1966–67 the Post Office investigated the Palace of Westminster's telephone system and recommended the installation of an automatic system, since the existing system would meet requirements only until 1972.

annum) would far exceed the revenue that would be realised (estimated at £6,750 in 1972).[1] In fact such calculations persuaded the Committee that there was no need to wait until 1972 to institute comprehensive free telephone service for Members. The Committee noted that under the existing (1969) system it cost more to collect the money payable on trunk calls than the amount collected.

Therefore in July 1969 the Committee recommended that free trunk calls should be introduced as soon as possible. This was agreed subject to four conditions:

1 That free trunk calls should be limited to Members and their secretaries.
2 That Members' private trunk calls as well as all international calls will be charged for as at present.
3 That it will be inadmissible for Members to accept any arrangement whereby charges are reversed on incoming trunk calls.
4 That the new system shall be subject to review after twelve months so that the position can be reconsidered if it has become apparent that the cost of these calls has risen unreasonably.[2]

These recommendations were accepted by the Government and implemented with effect from October 1969.

The automatic telephone service came into operation in August 1972. At that time there were over 1,300 extensions in the Palace and nearby parliamentary premises. Approximately 640 of these extensions were available for the use of Members; about eighty of them were in 'common areas', the remainder being in Members' desk rooms. The total telephone staff of the Palace consisted in 1972 of six supervisors and forty-seven telephonists.[3] The new exchange is not in the Palace itself, but is in the basement of the new building on the Broad Sanctuary site in front of the Central Hall, Westminster. Plans to install the exchange in the projected new parliamentary building in

[1] 6th Report, Services Committee, 1967–68, H.C. 289, paras 9–10.
[2] Ibid., 1968–69, H.C. 374, paras 6–9.
[3] Statistics relating to 1967 and 1957 give some indication of the use that is made of the telephone service. In 1967 the average number of calls was 13,134 per sitting day, an increase of 117 per cent on 1957.

Bridge Street had to be abandoned because of delays in constructing the new building.

Callers from outside the Palace of Westminster who know the extension number they require are able to make direct calls to that extension since each extension has its own telephone number. There is, however, a general House of Commons number for callers who do not know the extension number they require. In addition there is an Enquiry Bureau with a separate telephone number which may be used for calls to those Members who do not have their own extensions, to those who wish to restrict the circulation of their extension numbers and to those who are temporarily away from their rooms. Members using this 'absent service', which is controlled by a button on the Member's telephone, may have calls diverted to their secretaries or another extension or have their messages taken by the Enquiry Bureau. Messages are circulated by the doorkeepers and posted on the Letter Board; a copy of the message is retained by the Enquiry Bureau, and a 'message waiting' light is provided on each Member's telephone.[1] The Enquiry Bureau is open from 9 a.m. until the rising of the House on sitting days and from 9 a.m. to 5 p.m. during recesses.

For outgoing calls Members may, apart from using their own extensions, use any of the eighty or so extensions available in 'common areas'. Nineteen of these extensions are located in telephone cabinets or kiosks in the Members' Telephone Room, which is situated in the Cloisters and is open at all times.

The introduction of free trunk calls for Members and the extensive telephone services envisaged by the Services Committee in its Sixth Report of 1967–68 provide an important example of the considerable widening of Members' services and facilities in recent years. In particular, the Committee's aim of 'a room for every Member' is effectively complemented by its implicit aim of a telephone for every Member.

---

[1] The 'absent service' and 'message waiting' facilities are not available in the Bridge Street and Palace Chambers premises. They will be available on extensions in the new parliamentary building.

8.3   travel abroad by members

8.3.1.   *Journeys by Select Committees*

In the course of their inquiries select committees sometimes find it necessary to travel abroad. In recent years committees have visited India, Pakistan, Ethiopia, Hong Kong, Jordan and Malaysia. These are important occasions in that committees of the House are carrying out specific tasks entrusted to them by the House itself. However, they do not represent the House as a whole in the same way as delegations presenting gifts to Parliaments of newly independent countries of the Commonwealth. Nevertheless, the Foreign and Commonwealth Office gives appropriate assistance, as do any other British agencies or civil servants involved. The cost is borne on the House of Commons vote; £10,000 was included in the supply estimates for 1972–73 for this purpose.

The principle that select committees are entitled to travel abroad is now established, but it was not accepted until quite recently. In the 1950–51 session a subcommittee of the Estimates Committee examining the Foreign Service proposed to visit certain British embassies overseas to take evidence.[1] The then Clerk of the House, Sir Frederick Metcalfe, submitted a memorandum asserting that the proposed course was unconstitutional. He said:

'In my opinion this House should never seek to perform an act in a place where its writ does not run. For the House to authorise a Committee . . . to sit in the territory of a foreign State amounts to a claim to exercise authority outside British territory. It is an excess of jurisdiction and therefore unconstitutional. . . . If a Committee sits in a foreign country the House has no power to ensure respect for its authority, or even to protect its members from insult and molestation.'[2]

Although three overseas visits had taken place between 1945 and 1950, the Clerk advised that the only proper course was for the members of the subcommittee to make their visits unofficially.

[1] 7th Report, Estimates Committee, 1950–51, H.C. 242.
[2] *Ibid.*, p 284. The oral evidence of the Clerk is on pp 167–75.

The subcommittee decided not to go at all, but suggested that the House should consider the problem of supervision of overseas expenditure. The subcommittee pointed out that royal commissions made visits abroad without anybody raising objections about a lack of protection or conflicts of sovereignty.

In the 1953–54 session an Estimates subcommittee again wanted to investigate Foreign Service establishments abroad.[1] They proposed to travel as individuals, not as a committee, but wished to take their committee Clerk with them. It was ruled that this would only be possible if the House passed a motion giving the committee leave of absence.[2] The Government refused to be associated with such a motion and thought the proposal unconstitutional.[3] Once again the subcommittee did not go, and it said that as a result its inquiry had encountered considerable difficulties at every stage.

Two years later, however, a subcommittee dealing with service stores and ordnance depots succeeded in making an overseas visit, recording simply in its report: 'As all three Services hold a large quantity of their stores overseas, the subcommittee also visited [certain establishments] . . . in Malta'.[4] This visit was not held to constitute a precedent, and when in the early 1960s two inquiries were held into military expenditure overseas, difficulties were still encountered.[5] However, the subcommittee did in fact go abroad and took their Clerk with them.[6] The Members and the Clerk were invited as individuals by the Ministry of Defence, and their expenses were defrayed out of the Ministry's vote. No formal evidence could be taken overseas, and information collected abroad had to be confirmed by questions asked after the return to London. The subcommittee once again said that the whole problem of overseas visits merited urgent consideration by the House.[7]

[1] 7th Report, Estimates Committee, 1953–54, H.C. 290.
[2] 3rd Special Report, Estimates Committee, 1953–54, H.C. 149.
[3] 7th Report, Estimates Committee, 1953–54, H.C. 290, pp vi–vii.
[4] 3rd Report, Estimates Committee, 1956–57, H.C. 60, p iv.
[5] 10th Report, Estimates Committee, 1962–63, H.C. 282; 9th Report, Estimates Committee, 1963–64, H.C. 302.
[6] Presumably a new view was taken of the constitutional difficulties about the Clerk's going, as no motion for leave of absence was passed. Nine years earlier it had been held that only the passing of such a motion would make it possible for the Clerk to go.
[7] 9th Report, Estimates Committee, 1963–64, H.C. 302, p vi.

In 1964–65 the Estimates Committee made a special report on sittings of subcommittees overseas, recommending that they should be possible.[1] The Procedure Committee endorsed this view.[2] The right of committees to travel abroad was finally accepted in early 1966, and the next two years saw some tidying up of questions of finance and motions for leave of absence. The Services Committee recommended that when a motion for leave of absence was passed the travelling expenses of select committees abroad should be borne on the House of Commons vote. Formerly such expenses had been a charge on the service under investigation.[3] Subsequently, the Services Committee recommended that motions for leave of absence should be discontinued, and that expenditure on foreign travel should be authorised by committee chairmen meeting as a joint body.[4]

The system of administration of travel funds by a panel of committee chairmen had been recommended by the Agriculture Committee in the previous session.[5] This Committee had encountered intense difficulties over its proposal to visit Brussels to look into the staffing of the British delegation to the European Economic Community, and to have informal discussions with the staff of the E.E.C. Commission. At one stage the Committee was informed 'that the Government had strong objections to the visit being made and would not permit it to take place'.[6] After various delays, negotiations and procedural difficulties, the visit eventually took place. The Committee hoped that the 'misgivings [of the Foreign Office], which seemed to persist throughout the proceedings' were now at an end. As foreign visits by select committees have now been possible for more than six years, perhaps the anxieties of Ministers and civil servants, which held up developments in this field for fifteen years, have at last been allayed.[7]

---

[1] 6th Special Report, Estimates Committee, 1964–65, H.C. 162.
[2] 4th Report, Procedure Committee, 1964–65 H.C. 303 para. 13.
[3] 1st Report, Services Committee, 1965–66, H.C. 70, para. 3.
[4] 5th Report, Services Committee, 1967–68, H.C. 232.
[5] Report, Select Committee on Agriculture, 1966–67, H.C. 378–XVII, vol. 1, pp xii–xiii.
[6] *Ibid.*, p xi.
[7] For a review of the whole topic, see Sir Barnett Cocks, 'Parliament Goes Abroad', *The Parliamentarian*, **52**, pp 8–13 (January 1971).

8.3.2 *Delegations to Overseas Meetings*

In addition to making overseas trips as committee members, MPs make overseas trips as delegations from the House of Commons. These delegations of Members attend meetings of the Council of Europe, Western European Union and the North Atlantic Assembly. Such meetings may be at the plenary or committee level.

The delegations, which are nominated by agreement through the 'usual channels', attend plenary meetings of the three assemblies amounting to not less than six a year. They also attend meetings of committees at various times throughout the year but particularly during the autumn, early winter and the early part of the summer. As always when Members go abroad on official parliamentary business, they are assisted by Clerks. Clerks have also been providing procedural help for the Council of Europe and Western European Union ever since their creation, and more recently for the North Atlantic Assembly as well. The Services Committee has ensured by resolutions that the services of Clerks shall be available in all appropriate ways, including attendance at committees.

In the past, financial provision for Members came from the Foreign and Commonwealth Office, but recently a change in this arrangement has been effected. In December 1970 the House of Commons resolved that the cost of the attendance of Members at the three assemblies should be transferred to the House of Commons vote, with effect from April 1971.[1] This is a logical step so far as responsibility is concerned, but the expenditure of about £50,000 a year, with all the administrative responsibility involved, has increased considerably the work of the Overseas Office of the Clerk's Department as well as that of the Fees Office. As far as the expenses of Clerks attending on Members on official visits overseas are concerned, they have been met since before the resolution of 1970 from the House of Commons vote.

Economy class air travel is used in Europe but first class travel for elsewhere abroad (as sometimes is the case with the North Atlantic Assembly). Rail travel is first class, and reimbursement for travel by private arrangement is allowed. A daily subsistence

[1] H.C. Deb., 8 December 1970, 808, c. 355.

allowance is paid, calculated on the basis of French francs, for each period of twenty-four hours from time of arrival to time of departure, with proportionate allowances for periods beyond this. A limited miscellaneous expense allowance is also available, as well as a limited annual allowance for the entertainment of delegations.

8.3.3   The European Parliament

Since the accession of the United Kingdom to the European Communities, the United Kingdom Parliament has had the right to designate thirty-six Members as Members of the European Parliament. Initially twenty-one Members were so designated. A motion designating thirteen Members from the House of Commons was approved by the House in December 1972[1] and a similar motion designating eight Peers was approved by the House of Lords.[2] The motions were tabled by the Government.

The European Parliament meets eleven times a year for periods of between two and five days, amounting to about forty-five days in all. Plenary sessions are held in Strasbourg and Luxembourg while committee meetings are held in Brussels and other centres. Each Member generally serves on one or two committees, each of which meets at least a dozen times annually. British Members of the European Parliament receive the same assistance from Clerks as is given to members of the delegations to the other European assemblies.

Financial provision for these meetings is made by the European Parliament from its own budget. A travel and subsistence allowance is paid to Members by the European Parliament. In addition the Conservative members of the delegation who constitute a separate political group in the Parliament have a permanent secretariat financed directly from the Parliament's own budget. Other Members have joined existing political groups and are assisted by their secretariats, or have remained as independent or unattached Members.

8.3.4 Presentations to Commonwealth Parliaments

A further need for overseas travel occurs when delegations of Members present gifts to the Parliaments of newly-independent

[1] H.C. Deb., 19 December 1972, 848, cc. 1253–93.
[2] H.L. Deb., 20 December 1972, 337, cc. 1092–1114.

countries in the Commonwealth. This occurs later than the presentation by the Government of their own gift on the occasion of independence, with a Minister present at the celebrations, because it would be inappropriate for the House of Commons to become involved in the political occasion of independence. Moreover the old-style legislature often undergoes enlargement on independence, and may even change, as in the case of Fiji, from a unicameral to a bicameral Parliament.

Parliamentary presentations are therefore made about a year or more after independence and may very well take place much later. The actual date will depend on the time taken by consultations between the two countries about the kind of gift required and thereafter by the time factor of design and manufacture. A financial limit is imposed by the Treasury, but this has not yet prevented the presentation of appropriate gifts, which may vary from a Speaker's Chair or a Mace to a suitably rich inkstand for the Table of the House.

All gifts are presented by the House of Commons as being the elected House and the one responsible for the necessary finance. Where the recipient legislature is bicameral the presentation is always made to the lower house. The delegation from the House of Commons, which consists of from two to five Members and a Clerk, is the most important kind of parliamentary delegation to travel abroad because it is, in effect, the whole of the House itself on a mission to conduct the business of the House. For this reason the delegation travels first class and always, wherever possible, by a British airline; the VIP Lounge at Heathrow is reserved for its use and, if a halt is necessary en route, HM's Ambassador or High Commissioner attends upon the delegation. The cost of the gift, and all necessary travel and subsistence, is borne on the House of Commons vote.

8.3.5   CPA and IPU Conferences

Finally, Members travel abroad in connection with the Commonwealth Parliamentary Association and the Inter-Parliamentary Union. These are both international organisations, and the parent body in each case is independent of Parliament. The UK Branch of the CPA and the British Group of the IPU each receive an annual grant-in-aid.[1] These grants-in-aid, unlike

[1] These are found in Vote 6 of Class XI (Miscellaneous) of the Supply Estimates.

expenditure for the previously mentioned travel purposes, are not accounted for to the Comptroller and Auditor-General. Moreover, the secretaries of the Branch and the Group do not have to appear before the Public Accounts Committee as does, for example, the Clerk of the House in his capacity as Accounting Officer for the House of Commons Vote. Both the CPA Branch and the IPU Group have rooms in the Palace of Westminster.

The main purpose for which Members travel abroad in connection with these two organisations is the promotion of goodwill among Parliaments. There are, of course, reciprocal visits to the United Kingdom when the Westminster branches of the CPA and IPU act as hosts. Most visits, which are made as a result of direct invitations from host countries, take the form of a social and political tour. However those delegations attending conferences of the CPA and IPU have a crowded programme of working sessions. But even on these latter occasions, the host country tries to show its guests something of its local life.

The selection of Members to serve on such delegations is managed in both cases in a similar way. Members of all parties (including Peers) are notified of a proposed visit and are invited to apply to be considered for it. A committee which includes officers of the Branch or Group, which is balanced between the parties and on which the Whips have no influence, then selects the delegation. An object of the selection committee is to provide a delegation which is balanced from party and other points of view.

The UK Branch of the CPA, which has a full-time secretary and two assistant secretaries, sends about ten delegations abroad each year, involving approximately fifty Members. In addition a delegation attends the annual CPA conference, which in the past five years has been held in the Bahamas, Trinidad and Tobago, Australia, Malaysia and Malawi.

The UK Branch receives visits from delegations from individual Commonwealth countries, but its main effort is concentrated on organising two parliamentary visits and a parliamentary seminar. The two visits, in which perhaps forty legislators from twenty countries take part, introduce Commonwealth Members of Parliament to British parliamentary, social and industrial life. The seminar on parliamentary procedure and practice, attended by some twenty-four Members, including in particular Speakers and Deputy Speakers from some eighteen legislatures, is a longer and more comprehensive examination of parliamentary institutions. MPs, Peers and Officers of both Houses address the seminar.

The British Group of the Inter-Parliamentary Union, which has a full-time secretary, sends and receives delegations of legislators to and from member countries of the Union. In recent years there has been an average of perhaps four Westminster and four overseas visits per year. Countries visited have included Colombia, Indonesia, Italy, Japan, the Mongolian Peoples' Republic, the Soviet Union, Tunisia and the United Arab Republic. Delegations have come to Westminster from Belgium, Ethiopia, Iran, Nepal, Sweden, Turkey, the United States, Yugoslavia and other countries. In addition to such international exchanges, there are twice yearly conferences of members of the Union. A preparatory session is held for about a week in the spring and the annual Inter-Parliamentary Conference takes place for nine or ten days in the autumn. Since 1968 the spring meetings have been held in Dakar, Vienna, Monte Carlo, Caracas and Yaounde; while the autumn meetings have been held in Lima, New Delhi, The Hague, Paris and Rome.

8.3.6 The Transport Office

Thomas Cook and Son Limited first began operating a transport service for Parliament during the Second World War when in 1941 one of their staff began to make weekly visits to the Palace of Westminster. Later these visits became daily, and in 1950 he was appointed as the first full-time Transport Officer, with one assistant to help him. The Transport Office currently consists of the Transport Officer and seven assistants.

The service offered to Members of both Houses, originally restricted in many ways, is now as comprehensive as the service available in any other branch of Thomas Cook. The Office, which is not open to the public, keeps normal office hours except on Wednesdays and Thursdays when Parliament is sitting. On these days the Office remains open until 6 and 7 p.m. respectively. Although the Office devotes much of its time to arranging

Members' travel to and from their constituencies, it is also kept busy with all kinds of overseas travel arrangements for individual Members and for parliamentary delegations.

Although the Transport Office originally arranged only *official* journeys for Members, for some years Members have also been able to use it for their personal holiday arrangements. The usual travel facilities are available to Members. These include foreign exchange in most currencies, travellers' cheques, holiday insurance, and arrangements for shipping and forwarding goods. The Office does not normally provide travel facilities for the Commonwealth Parliamentary Association and the Inter-Parliamentary Union, which make their own arrangements.

8.4 REFRESHMENT FACILITIES[1]

The Catering Subcommittee of the Services Committee is, as was noted in Chapter 1, the successor to the former Select Committee on Kitchen and Refreshment Rooms (House of Commons). The Catering Subcommittee has been appointed sessionally since the 1965–66 session to control the provision to MPs of meals, drinks and banqueting facilities. As long ago as 1906, Speaker Lowther distinguished between the functions of the then Select Committee on Kitchen and Refreshment Rooms and those which rested with him personally as the custodian of the rights and privileges of the House, by explaining that the former was responsible for 'the provision of food and drink, salaries of waiters and employees, purchase of linen and all other accessories, character of the meals supplied, prices to be charged, and many other similar questions that must from time to time arise'. With Mr Speaker, however, rested (as now) the important decision as to which persons were permitted to avail themselves of the refreshment facilities.

When the House is sitting, MPs can obtain meals in the Members' Dining Room, the Strangers' Dining Room, the Members' Cafeteria and the Strangers' Cafeteria. A fifth dining facility is the Press Dining Room, to which Members are some-

[1] Much of the information in this section is taken, with permission, from a booklet issued by the Refreshment Department of the House of Commons, setting out the relevant *Information and Regulations* for MPs.

times invited by journalists.[1] The Members' and Strangers' dining rooms are open for lunch and dinner, when *table d'hôte* and *à la carte* menus are available. The two cafeterias are open whenever the House is sitting, although full cafeteria meals are not necessarily available at all hours.[2] The Members' Cafeteria opens at 12.30 p.m., whilst the Strangers' Cafeteria is open from 11 a.m. daily during session.

The facilities of the Members' and Strangers' dining rooms are available to Members and Officers of the House of Commons, who may entertain up to five guests in the latter. It is usually advisable to book a table in the Strangers' Dining Room in advance. The facilities of the Members' Cafeteria are available to Members (during recesses, to Officers as well); on sitting days a Member may bring up to three guests into this cafeteria at certain times. Members share the use of the Strangers' Cafeteria with all the staff of the Commons and with various other authorised persons such as Members' secretaries, members and officials of Commonwealth legislatures and visitors to the galleries who hold a refreshment pass.

Members and Officers can buy tea, coffee, soft drinks and snacks in the Members' Tea Room, which is conveniently situated close to the chamber and which is open on sitting days from 10 a.m. until just after the rising of the House. In addition, 'tea on the Terrace' is available to Members and Officers, with up to three guests, on sitting days from 4 until 5.30 p.m., Mondays to Thursdays inclusive. This popular facility is made available, weather permitting, from after the Spring Bank Holiday until the House rises for the summer recess.

Members and Officers may also entertain guests in the recently converted Harcourt Grill Room, which was opened in January 1973. There is no restriction on the number of guests. The Harcourt Room may also be used as a private dining room at weekends and during recesses. Members can entertain large

[1] This account is concerned only with facilities that are available wholly or in part to Members. In their Report on the accounts of the Refreshment Department for 1970–71, the Services Committee pointed out that there are no less than eighteen separate catering establishments within the Department. Some of these are for press and staff only. 3rd Report, Services Committee, 1971–72, H.C. 163, para. 2.

[2] If the House has not risen by 1 a.m., the cafeterias close from 1 a.m. to 2 a.m. to provide staff with a rest period.

dinner parties of not more than 106 persons and not fewer than eighty. Advance notice of such functions is essential and a booking fee is payable. This room is sometimes available for private entertaining on Mondays and Fridays at lunch-time during session, subject to the consent of the Serjeant at Arms. There are in addition four rooms fronting the Terrace which Members and Officers may reserve for smaller private luncheon and dinner parties.

The Members' Smoking Room, adjacent to the Commons Library on the principal floor, is reserved exclusively for the use of Members and Peers who were formerly Members. Drinks, coffee, tea and biscuits are served in the Smoking Room while the House is sitting. The Strangers' Bar, open from 11 a.m. until about the rising of the House, serves Members and Officers of *both* Houses and their guests. 'Annie's Bar' is for Members, Officers, Lobby representatives of United Kingdom newspapers and the BBC and ITA as well as certain other journalists and persons connected with the work of the House of Commons. No guests may be entertained.

The Refreshment Department is *not* one of the five permanent Departments of the House of Commons. The catering facilities are expected to be financially self-supporting, although grants have been received from the Treasury. These grants are intended to help in paying staff during recesses, when little income can be expected, and towards repaying the interest on a loan made by the Exchequer to the Department. Apart from this grant the Refreshment Department has to cover its costs from receipts from the sale of food and drink. At the same time, it has the free use of its premises, furniture, heating, lighting and some cleaning (as do staff canteens in Government Departments). In 1968, however, the Department made a loss of £3,400. The accounts show that whereas the Members' and Press dining rooms make substantial losses, the other establishments run by the Department make profits or only small losses, and thus serve to subsidise the meals in the Members' and Press dining rooms.[1] The result for 1969 was a 'profit' of £3,000 resulting from (a) a rise of £11,000 in the Exchequer grant and (b) a contribution

---

[1] 5th Report, Services Committee, 1968–69, H.C. 366. More recent accounts do not show financial results for separate establishments.

by the press of £2,000 towards the loss on press catering.[1]
During the period of fifteen months covered by the accounts for
1970–71, the Department sustained an operating loss of
£68,748, which was equivalent to 18·9 per cent of turnover.
This loss was reduced by an Exchequer grant of £47,000, and by
a sum of £2,994 to make good the Press Gallery losses. Thus
the net loss was £18,754.[2]

Constant attempts at rationalising the services are made, and
the Catering Subcommittee sometimes calls upon outside professional advice for this purpose. One obvious difficulty is, of
course, the need to cater for long, irregular hours of service
while the House is sitting, and at the same time to allow for
several months of the year when, staff of the Commons apart,
very few customers are available to use such facilities as are
kept open. In April 1971 Marcus Lipton (Labour Member for
Brixton) asked the Lord President of the Council 'why the firm
of J. Lyons Limited is taking over the Refreshment Department'.
The then Lord President (William Whitelaw) replied: 'Messrs.
J. Lyons Limited is not taking over the Refreshment Department, but I understand that Versa-Serve Limited, a subsidiary
of J. Lyons, has been asked to make an investigation of the
Refreshment Department's methods of administration, and to
advise the Catering Subcommittee'.[3] Mr Whitelaw went on to
emphasise that complete control would remain with the
Catering Subcommittee.

8.5   THE CRYPT CHAPEL[4]

The Crypt Chapel, more properly known as the Chapel of St
Mary Undercroft,[5] is a chamber situated to the east (river) side
of Westminster Hall. It is under the combined jurisdiction of the

[1] 3rd Report, Services Committee, 1970–71, H.C. 178.
[2] Ibid., 1971–72, H.C. 163.
[3] H.C. Deb., 1 April 1971, 814, c. 1678.
[4] This account is taken from information sheets issued by the Lord Great
Chamberlain, as reprinted from papers submitted to the Select Committee on
House of Commons Accommodation, 1953–54, H.C. 184, Appendix F, p 116.
[5] The Chapel of St Mary Undercroft was the lower chapel of a two-storied
building commenced by Edward I in 1292 and finished in 1346 under Edward III
The upper chapel was St Stephen's. After the fire of 1834 the Crypt Chapel was
restored by E. M. Barry, son of Sir Charles Barry.

Lord Great Chamberlain, the Lord Chancellor and the Speaker.[1] The Chapel can be hired by Members and Officers of both Houses for weddings and christenings, for a fee which is paid to the Lord Great Chamberlain, who is responsible for routine arrangements. The privilege of using the Chapel is extended to the sons and daughters of Members of both Houses and, in certain circumstances, to grandchildren. Notices in the press concerning the ceremony must include the name of the sponsoring Member.

The Chapel is not licensed for weddings and a special licence is therefore required. The marriage must be celebrated in accordance with the rites of the Church of England and will be entered in the marriage register of St Margaret's Church, Westminster. Fees are payable to the rector of St Margaret's, who is also usually the Chaplain to Mr Speaker, and to the vestry clerk who brings over the register. There is a small electric organ, and the Chapel has seats for 150 people.

In the case of christenings, the service can be performed by a clergyman of any Christian denomination. The certificate of baptism and the register are brought to the service by the Lord Great Chamberlain's Clerk.

[1] Statement by the Prime Minister, H.C. Deb., 23 March 1965, 709, c. 329.

CHAPTER 9

CONCLUSION

Having examined services and facilities in the Commons from various vantage points, we shall now attempt to put the analysis in a general and comparative perspective. In doing so, we shall keep to our brief by not recommending changes in existing arrangements, our task having been to construct a statement of what the present arrangements are. Any attempt to make recommendations would have to be buttressed by further field work in which, among other things, the opinions of Members on present arrangements would be obtained. This has not been done.

At the same time, it would seem appropriate to record some of the published comments that others have made concerning Members' services and facilities. Such comments are scattered through various documents and secondary works. By drawing them together, it is hoped to give additional perspective to the whole analysis. In the course of this exercise references are made to services and facilities available in foreign legislatures. It should be kept in mind that these 'comparative' comments derive from existing analyses and are not based on a systematic survey by us of foreign practice, which again is beyond the scope of this book.

9.1 THE PALACE OF WESTMINSTER

A fact of great importance in understanding the conditions under which Members work is that the setting for British parliamentary life has not been considered in a total way since the mid-nineteenth century. Even then, when the Palace of Westminster was rebuilt following the fire of 1834, it remained (as it does to this day) a royal palace. Although the Palace which was officially opened in 1852 was built primarily to provide a meeting place for the House of Commons and House of Lords, it has always incorporated elements, such as Westminster Hall, and has housed officials, such as members of the Lord Chancellor's Department, whose functions are not primarily parliamentary.

When the House of Commons chamber was destroyed by bombing in 1941, a Select Committee on House of Commons (Rebuilding) did indeed deliberate for two years. But as Crick has pointed out, the Committee's report was dominated by three things: restaurant facilities, lavatory accommodation and the design of the Commons chamber. In the end the old chamber was reconstructed essentially as it was before, and basic alterations of parliamentary facilities were not undertaken.[1] Crick has summarised the Committee's efforts as 'the one great opportunity – missed!'[2]

The fact is that no decision has been made in Britain to build a Brasilia, a Canberra or a District of Columbia, or, since the 1830s, to design and erect a building conceived to meet the needs of British parliamentarians, as was done, for example, in postwar Bonn. Drastic reordering of this kind has occasionally been advocated. Maxton proposed that Parliament should move to Hampstead. William Hamilton (Labour Member for Fife West) has said that he favours 'a new administrative city' in the North of England.[3] Wilfred Proudfoot (Conservative Member for Brighouse and Spenborough) has suggested: 'Use the present building for State occasions and let's have a modern working building.'[4] But such drastic recourses have never been seriously considered at Government level. Crick concedes:

[1] There has been remarkable continuity in the design of the House of Commons chamber. The Chapel of St Stephen, which served as the meeting place of the Commons from 1547 to 1834, was copied in essential respects in Barry's chamber, which came into use in 1852. Barry's chamber was copied, in turn, in the post-Second World War rebuilding.

[2] Bernard Crick, The Reform of Parliament, p 60, Weidenfeld and Nicolson (second edition, 1968).

[3] H.C. Deb., 1 August 1963, 682, c. 751.

[4] The Observer, p 13 (17 March 1963). A variation was put forward by the late Emrys Hughes (former Labour Member for Ayrshire South): 'One suggestion, which I am inclined to favour, is that Shell should be asked to remove [from its large modern building on the south bank of the Thames] to Glasgow ... or Newcastle ... The House of Commons could then move in, leaving the House of Lords where it is.' Parliament and Mumbo-Jumbo, p 140, Allen & Unwin (1966).

'. . . it would be really wild to argue that we should have a new Parliament building, built for use – as beautiful, convenient and as apt a blending of tradition and modernity as, for example, the Parliament House in Hanover or the Knesset Building in Jerusalem.'[1]

As has been suggested, services and facilities within the Palace have developed in an uneven, pragmatic way. A bit has been added here, and a bit there. This adaptive evolution, characteristic of the whole of British government, has accommodated a wide range of parliamentary contexts. As A. H. Hanson has noted:

'The adaptability of British parliamentary institutions is . . . astounding. That a deliberative body originating from the medieval royal council should have successively served the purposes of the fifteenth century feudal baronage, the sixteenth century monarchy, the seventeenth century "gentry", the eighteenth century aristocracy, the nineteenth century plutocracy and the "mass democracy" of our present age, is one of the world's political wonders.'[2]

As parliament has adapted itself, so, too, has its physical superstructure, in a gradual, sometimes halting way. The two processes are clearly interrelated. As Churchill said: 'We shape our buildings and afterwards our buildings shape us'.[3]

9.2   THE BICAMERAL FACTOR

An obvious constraint on the development of Commons services and facilities is that MPs must share their building with the House of Lords. This is a commitment which legislators are spared in unicameral parliaments, such as those in Israel, Denmark, Finland and New Zealand. At Westminster, as we have seen, the Clerk's Department, the Serjeant at Arms Department, the Library, the *Hansard* staff and other administrative personnel serving the Commons are kept scrupulously separate from counterpart establishments which serve the Lords.

[1] Crick, *The Reform of Parliament, op. cit.*, p 61.
[2] A. H. Hanson, 'The Purpose of Parliament', *Parliamentary Affairs*, **17** p 279 (Summer 1964).
[3] H.C. Deb., 28 October 1943, 393, c. 403.

Although there may be strong reasons for the separation, there is obviously an inefficient use of space and manpower in such duplicated services.[1] In 1967 a subcommittee of the Services Committee reported 'their strong view that joint Library and refreshment facilities with the House of Lords should be investigated'.[2]

Occasional disquiet has been expressed by MPs concerning the allocation of space. Tom Driberg (Labour Member for Barking) has said that the Lords should 'give up their excessive share of space in the Palace.'[3] In his standard work on back-bench MPs, Peter Richards notes that 'Many Members feel that [they] . . . have an unduly small share of the Palace in relation to the Lords and various officials'.[4] Emrys Hughes said:

'. . . at the one end of the Palace, across the frontier where the carpet becomes red instead of green, there will continue to be hundreds of rooms rarely used, indeed hardly used at all, while on the other side of the frontier the authorities have a perpetual headache in trying to find a few square feet for the people who want a little room in which to work.

'So the struggle between the haves and have-nots goes on in the Palace of Westminster.'[5]

In 1964 Tam Dalyell (Labour Member for West Lothian) attempted to determine how each part of the Palace was being utilised. After completing this 'incredibly difficult' task, he concluded that 140 rooms could immediately be taken over for the use of MPs and that many more rooms could be *converted* for MPs' use.[6] William Hamilton would 'like to see the House of

[1] For practical reasons there must be some common services. Patrick Cormack (Conservative Member for Cannock) has listed a number of them which are situated in the House of Lords part of the Palace. They include workshops, stores, the security control centre, facilities for staff from the Department of the Environment, accommodation for custodians, Ashworth's and 'half a dozen' rooms for the Houses of Parliament Sports and Social Club. H.C. Deb., 9 March 1973, 852, c. 740.

[2] 15th Report, Services Committee, 1966–67, H.C. 652, p x.

[3] Tom Driberg, 'The Picturesque Slum', *Sunday Times Magazine*, p 10 (6 June 1971).

[4] Peter G. Richards, *Honourable Members*, p 68, Faber (second edition, 1964).

[5] Hughes, *op. cit.*, p 139.

[6] Tam Dalyell, *The Architects' Journal* (19 August 1964). Quoted in Hughes, *op. cit.*, pp 135–6. Dalyell found that the electoral roll listed twenty-five persons as 'usually resident' in the Palace in 1961, an increase of six since 1951.

Lords put out completely, into the Palladium, so that the House of Commons could take over this building completely'.[1]

An additional factor which makes co-existence in the Palace more of an issue than in other national legislatures is the comparatively large membership – 635 – of the House of Commons.[2] If one considers only those national legislatures which play a significant role in the governing process, the Italian Chamber of Deputies alone rivals the Commons in terms of total membership.[3] The membership of the Commons has exceeded 600 since the beginning of the nineteenth century, but in recent decades an increasing number of Members have been working full-time at their parliamentary duties. This has meant increased demands on the facilities of the Palace of Westminster. Thus, so it is argued, the balance between MPs' and Peers' needs in the Palace has been changing in favour of MPs. However, it has also been argued that the Lords equally need more space.[4]

9.3 GENERAL APPRAISALS

One is hard-pressed to find wholly laudatory appraisals of the facilities available to Members. Various commentators have remarked on the excellence of the Palace as a West End Club, on the admirable setting it provided for Victorian MPs and for the architectural qualities of the building. There have also been more directly relevant arguments made on behalf of the Palace as a setting for a legislature. For example, Eric Taylor has commented:

[The Member] will probably find great enjoyment in his parliamentary life. What rooms are available to him in the

[1] H.C. Deb., 9 March 1973, 852, c. 844.

[2] The membership of the Commons increased from 630 to 635 at the last general election as a result of the redrawing of constituency boundaries. The House of Lords likewise has a very large membership in comparison with other second chambers, but this is a potential membership. Only a minority of Peers, although an important one, use the facilities of the Palace. As of March 1973 only about forty Peers, apart from Law Lords, had desks of their own in the Palace.

[3] There are 630 Members of the Italian Chamber of Deputies.

[4] It is undoubtedly true that since the creation of Life Peers an increasing number of Lords are working more diligently at their parliamentary duties. Further pressure in Lords' accommodation has resulted from the increased use of the Palace by the Lord Chancellor's Department.

Palace are extremely spacious and comfortable. The whole of the building has a dignity which modern erections, because of their economy and efficiency, are unable to achieve. Members felt this deeply when, in consequence of bombing, they were forced to move into the neighbouring Church House, an almost brand-new building, in 1940, 1941 and 1944.'[1]

Assuming that 'magic' is a useful environmental feature, this, too, has been commented on approvingly. '... the Palace of Westminster is full of magic still, a magic strong enough to grasp the imagination of everyone who works within its walls.'[2]

But such comments are often followed by qualifications. Taylor, for example, concedes that 'the average MP must still expect to lead a rather uncomfortable existence when attending upon his parliamentary duties'.[3] Richards has said that 'as a club the facilities may be satisfactory, yet for the central work-shop of a modern democracy they are absurd'.[4]

Many assessments, such as those which follow, are un-reservedly negative: 'It appears to be beyond argument that the conditions in which Members of Parliament work and the facilities accorded them drastically need improvement'.[5] 'The member of the British House of Commons is not given the staff, facilities and accommodation necessary to do the job as it should be done.'[6] 'The conditions under which we are expected to work are a public scandal.'[7] 'Despite recent improvements, MPs work in what is, by comparison with any modern town hall, a picturesque slum.'[8] Until adequate facilities for Members are provided, 'the public will continue to regard the working con-

[1] Eric Taylor, *The House of Commons at Work*, p 20, Penguin (eighth edition, 1971).

[2] Philip Marsden, *The Officers of the Commons 1363–1965*, p 16, Barrie and Rockliff (1966).

[3] Taylor, *op. cit.*, pp 19–20. One possible source of parliamentary discomfort received official recognition in 1972 when it was announced in the Commons that the complete eradication of mice from the palace was impossible. H.C. Deb., 18 July 1972, 841, c. 383–4.

[4] Richards, *Honourable Members, op. cit.*, p 68.

[5] Ronald Butt, *The Power of Parliament*, p 27 Constable (1967) p 27.

[6] Alfred Junz, 'Accommodation at Westminster', *Parliamentary Affairs*, **13**, p 108 (Winter 1959–60).

[7] Anthony Wedgwood Benn in the debate on procedure of 31 January 1958. H.C. Deb., 581, c. 688.

[8] Driberg, *op. cit.*, p 10.

ditions of Members as inefficient and absurd'.[1] 'The public . . . have a right to demand that their MPs should be given the normal facilities without which any managerial or professional man could not be expected to function.'[2] 'The British people, as well as their representatives, are paying a high price for the short-sighted parsimony that consigns the men and women who make the law of the land to working conditions that businessmen have long since recognised as false economy.'[3] 'Museum' is a frequently-employed metaphor.

But this brings us to the question of function. The primary facility is after all a palace. As tourists are aware, palaces are filled with corridors, this particular palace having two miles of corridors constituting 22 per cent of the building. As has often been suggested, corridors are not ideal places for dealing with constituents and secretaries. Similarly, the hundred staircases and eleven open courtyards lack utility from the point of view of Crick's 'managerial or professional man', who must work by artificial light at midday and meet 'strangers' in a Central Lobby which Richards has described as 'impersonal, comfortless and unfeeling'. If one considers other palaces used as legislatures – in France, Belgium and the Netherlands – one finds similar problems arising from a disharmony of functions.

The situation has been aggravated by the changing habits of Members. In the middle of the last century Members were in the building for shorter hours during fewer sitting days. Services and facilities tolerable then, it is contended, are no longer appropriate. According to Menhennet and Palmer, the Palace is 'a building designed in an age when the sphere of parliamentary and governmental activity was much smaller than it is now, when most of the legislators were "part-time", and when the urgency of public events was less pressing'.[4] There are dark suggestions that the executive approves of the lag. Mindful of its dominant position in the British political system, the Government, so it is argued, cannot be expected to be enthusiastic

[1] Andrew Hill and Anthony Whichelow, *What's Wrong with Parliament?*, p 85, Penguin (1964).

[2] Crick, *The Reform of Parliament*, *op. cit.*, p 67.

[3] John Morgan, 'Is This the Way to Run a Country?', *Daily Telegraph Magazine*, p 12 (13 May 1966).

[4] David Menhennet and John Palmer, *Parliament in Perspective*, p 97, Bodley Head (1967).

about enabling backbench MPs to become more effective adversaries by making parliamentary life 'efficient'. As Sir Hugh Linstead (former Conservative Member for Putney) has said, 'Neither the Executive ... nor the potential Executive ... is particularly anxious to see a large reinforcement of the facilities available to Backbenchers. ... The most we can hope for is a benevolent inertia'.[1]

9.4 ACCOMMODATION

A principal target for critics has been the specific arrangements relating to accommodation for Members and their secretaries. Not all comment is adverse, however. While indicating disquiet about arrangements in general, Richards sees at least one advantage in the present mode of work:

'... the absence of private rooms for ordinary Members may have a beneficial effect upon the parliamentary scene, for Members are forced into communal surroundings which serve to encourage the exchange of opinions and the moderation of tempers.'[2]

There is praise from various commentators for the bars, the Library, the Smoking Room and the Chess Room as facilities which promote friendship and proximity among Members who may not be proximate, politically or otherwise, in the House.

Anthony Fell (Conservative Member for Yarmouth) made this point during a debate in 1973 on the new parliamentary building:

'If the House seeks to widen the facilities to such an extent that every Member has his own office, his own research department, and everything else, the net result will be that hon. Members will spend no time in using the normal friendly fraternisation places of the House.'[3]

Suggesting that the process was already well underway, he noted that the once-crowded Smoking Room was nowadays almost

[1] H.C. Deb., 1 August 1963, 682, c. 755.
[2] Richards, *Honourable Members*, op. cit., p 64.
[3] H.C. Deb., 9 March 1973, 852, c. 838.

empty. 'This emptiness', he said, 'has coincided with the awarding of offices to Members all over the Palace'. In the same debate
John Wells (Conservative Member for Maidstone) remarked
that an advantage of working at a public desk in the Library is
that it enables Members to combine their work with 'gossiping
to those who pass . . . this is what this place is all about –
gossiping with those who pass'.[1]

But the onslaughts which have been directed at the existing
situation are legion. As one Member remarked:

'When I came here in 1950, I was given a key to a locker which
was no bigger than that which I had at school. That was the only
accommodation, the only amenity, I had in the building.'

But, he added, things have improved.

'I now have (in addition to my locker) a little desk . . . with
another seven Members in a room the size of the average dining
room in the average council house . . . we have to have artificial
light. . . . The room is ideal for a suicide.'[2]

Debates on accommodation and procedure are replete with
complaints by Members. They must dictate letters with 'twenty
other Members dictating letters at the same time in a crowded
room with typists'. When several Members are sharing an
office, 'it is virtually impossible to concentrate on research, on
speech-writing or on the telephone calls which one makes to
one's constituency'. Members cannot 'communicate freely with
each other'. Members lack 'proper research facilities'. Dimen-
sions of the much-maligned lockers are freely given, usually
with a reminder that 'it will not take the ordinary briefcase'.[3]
Members who do not have their own telephones have to 'make
the endless, senseless tramp around the corridors, waiting outside kiosks, with our papers'.

In advocating reform, Crick notes that 'Office accommodation

[1] H.C. Deb., 9 March 1973, 852, c. 807.
[2] Quoted in Hill and Whichelow, *op. cit.*, pp 84–5.
[3] Robert Cooke (Conservative Member for Bristol West) has said that when he
entered the House, 'I was obviously a very promising young Member because I
was given an upper, as opposed to a lower, cupboard – so that I could see into it,
I suppose'. H.C. Deb., 9 March 1973, 852, c. 783.

is not merely a convenience for the MP', but also a place where his secretary can deal with callers.

'Has no MP ever fully realized the disillusionment in the face of a constituent ... sending in the "Green Card" and then cooling his heels for thirty or forty minutes before he learns ... that his Member is not to be found – rather than being able to ring or call on a secretary for an appointment? ... he may be expected to state his business in a corner of a crowded lobby which has all the *confusion*, the noise and, indeed, the *décor* of the entrance to one of the London railway stations.'[1]

But the situation has been changing in important ways. As was noted in Chapter 3, when the new chamber opened in 1951, there were virtually no desks in the Palace allocated to specific back-bench Members. Since then, gradual efforts have been made to provide backbenchers with office and desk facilities, both in and near the Palace. Substantial conversions and new construction have produced more rooms in the Upper Committee Corridor, the Star Chamber Court, the Cloisters and the Oratory, and in a three-storey building which has been constructed on top of the Members' Tea Room. In March 1973 there were desks for about 500 Members within the Palace, including desks in the new building above the Tea Room. However, only 143 of these desks are in single rooms, and many of these are occupied by frontbenchers. There are of course additional desks for Members in buildings outside, but close to, the Palace. For Members' secretaries there are 210 typing desks available, in or near the Palace, eighty-three being within the Palace.[2] It is evident that the present situation represents a considerable advance over the position in 1951.

More striking than these piecemeal developments is the proposal to build a new parliamentary building across from the Palace in Bridge Street, in which every Member who wants a room of his own and is not accommodated in the Palace would get one, together with an adjacent working space for his secretary. Thirteen years have elapsed since the project was first

[1] Crick, *The Reform of Parliament*, op. cit., p 60.
[2] 1st Report, Services Committee, 1972–73, H.C. 196, pp 2–3. See also H.C. Deb., 9 March 1973, 852, cc. 739–844.

suggested by a Minister, but with a prize-winning design of the building selected, completion in the early 1980s is possible, now that Parliament has given the go-ahead. When this building materialises and the ideal of 'a room for every Member' is thereby accepted, a new era in the style of Parliamentary life will result.

In the new parliamentary building many of the complaints mentioned earlier will no longer be relevant or will be considerably diminished in relevance. But when this major scheme has been implemented, will the Mother of Parliaments still be deficient in its services and facilities compared with foreign legislatures? Some 'comparative' remarks one comes across suggest that this may be the case, that the British Parliament is incorrigibly deficient in a world of efficient legislatures. But what in fact is the position? Let us turn to a consideration of services and facilities at Westminster as they compare with corresponding arrangements in other national legislatures.

9.5 SERVICES AND FACILITIES IN CROSS-NATIONAL PERSPECTIVE

In undertaking this comparison it should be said at the outset that the material available on services and facilities in overseas legislatures is sparse, uneven and, in regard to some matters, non-existent. Therefore the following analysis will be far from comprehensive and in no sense definitive. Within these limitations the sequence of comparisons – after a few comments about comparisons with the American Congress – will follow the sequence in the previous chapters. It should also be said that we shall only be dealing with legislatures which play an important role in the governing process.

9.5.1 *The Deviant American Example*

A problem that bedevils efforts to place the Westminster situation in perspective is that comparisons are so often made to practices in the American Congress. The fact is that facilities available to American Senators and Representatives are so much more elaborate than those available to lawmakers anywhere else that the American case must be regarded as deviant and not a 'norm' against which British practice should be

measured. Each American Senator and Representative is provided with an air-conditioned suite of from two to five rooms
in one of five large office buildings joined to the Capitol by
underground railways. A Senator typically employs a staff of
about fourteeen professional and clerical assistants; if he is
from a large state he may employ as many as thirty people, and
allowances cover their salaries. A Representative gets an
allowance of approximately $50,000 a year enabling him to
engage a staff of up to twelve people. He also gets an allowance
for renting an office in his constituency and for travel by his
staff members, not to mention himself.[1]

The other services and facilities available to American
Congressmen are similarly untypical. For example, their
standing committees have very large staffs by the standards of
other legislatures. In 1971 the Senate Appropriations Committee
had a staff of thirty-nine; and the House Appropriations Committee, twenty-four. The entire committee staff in the House of
Representatives was recently found to total 770.[2] The resources
of the Library of Congress and its Congressional Research
Service (CRS) are legendary; in 1971 the latter's research staff
numbered 236; its support staff, 127. During 1971 the CRS
received more than 180,000 requests for research and reference
assistance from the offices of Senators and Representatives, of
which 75,000 were inquiries from constituents.[3] Every modern
office aid is employed in the Senate and House office buildings.
'An American Congressman', Crick tells us, 'collapsed with
shock on being shown the writing-rooms of the Library of the
Commons full of men writing letters in longhand: Members of
Parliament answering their constituency mail.'[4]

The question of role is again relevant. Consider, for example,
the case of former Senator Paul Douglas of Illinois. He was
once criticised by a constituent for harbouring a staff of twenty-
five whose total annual salary was $130,000. In reply, Douglas

[1] Allan Kornberg and Lloyd D. Musolf (editors), *Legislatures in Developmental Perspective*, p 113, Duke University Press (1970).
[2] Samuel C. Patterson, 'The Professional Staffs of Congressional Committees',
Administrative Science Quarterly, **15**, p 23, (March 1970).
[3] *Annual Report of the Congressional Research Service of the Library of Congress
for Fiscal Year 1971*, pp 13–14 and Appendix E, Washington (April 1972). The
Rules Committee of the House of Representatives has called for a trebling of the
CRS staff by 1975. *Ibid.*, p 43.
[4] Crick, *The Reform of Parliament, op. cit.*, p 58.

maintained that his staff was 'underpaid and overworked' in view of what a Senator, American style, has to put up with when representing a constituency with a population a fifth that of Britain.[1] Douglas said he received 500 letters and 100 telephone calls a day, was visited by 500 constituents each month, and was invited 300 times a month to speak and attend meetings; in the recent Congress, he added, he had to contend with 18,000 bills. He needed staff to help him sort all this out.[2] This scale of work in the context of the constitutional position of the American Congress is so alien to the reality of the working of British government that we are well advised to turn to more relevant parliaments to see how badly MPs are done by.

After descending from American luxury, Britain's position is difficult to place. In fairness we must assume at this juncture a Commons without the Bridge Street building, while keeping in mind that when it materialises Britain's standing in the facilities league table will be high. Even as things stand now, most national parliaments are worse off than the Commons in terms of staff and facilities. We are told in one of the few comparative studies of legislatures that in the 'new states' staff assistance for legislators is 'trivial and embarrassing when compared with that available in established parliaments' such as Britain's.[3]

9.5.2 Facilities

As far as the more established parliaments are concerned, the Boyle Committee has provided us with useful comparative data. During its inquiry into Members' pay the Committee investigated the amount of office accommodation in the legislatures of thirteen parliamentary democracies. In four cases – West Germany, Sweden, Canada and Australia – legislators clearly have better office facilities than British MPs do. In the first three, each Member has his own office. In five other countries – Finland, France, New Zealand, Norway and Denmark – the

---

[1] It is devastating, when viewed from outside the United States, to come upon comments by American political scientists on the inadequacies of Congressional services and facilities. James A. Robinson, for instance, has expressed regret that Congressmen do not have allowances for hiring consultants and convening conferences. James A. Robinson, 'Staffing the Legislature', in Kornberg and Musolf, op. cit., p 380.

[2] Junz, op. cit., pp 104–7.

[3] James A. Robinson, 'Staffing the Legislature', in Kornberg and Musolf, op. cit., p 366.

situation is similar to Britain's in varying degrees, i.e. offices are available, but there is sharing. It is significant that in three of these countries (Finland, France and New Zealand), as in Britain, schemes exist to provide a separate office for each Member. In the remaining countries cited by the Boyle Committee – Belgium, the Irish Republic, the Netherlands and Italy – the office situation appears to be worse than at Westminster. Except in Ireland, there are no offices for backbenchers in the parliaments of these countries. However, Italy is planning to make some available.[1]

It is interesting to find that Britain is in the middle of this ranking. Of course the survey omits many established parliaments, not least the amply serviced Japanese Diet, and so it is impossible to assess the Commons' position on a global basis. Japan in fact appears to be number 2 in the world league in parliamentary services and facilities. Each Member of the Diet is provided with a separate office and two secretaries.[2] In general, it can be concluded that the Commons is not a deficient case, but rather that it provides basic facilities to Members at a level which is common, even usual, in 'comparable' legislatures. Yet the Mother of Parliaments has been with us longer than the others, and therefore might be expected to be farther along than it is. Perhaps Harry Hanson provided an explanation when he said that there are dangers in being ancient; admiration for the long-established inhibits a willingness to change.[3]

9.5.3   Services

An impression that comes through in the chapters of this book is the general excellence of the various Commons services. One may quibble about the size of the Research Division of the Library or the number of Clerks available to man committees. There may be, and often is, an objection on grounds of quantity, but not on grounds of quality. It is in this latter area – competence in serving the Commons – that the staff may perhaps claim a certain pre-eminence internationally. The frequency with which officials of Commonwealth and foreign legislatures

[1] *Boyle Report*, Appendix E.
[2] Inter-Parliamentary Union (edited by Michel Ameller), *Parliaments*, p 73, Cassell (second edition, 1966).
[3] Hanson, *op. cit.*, p 279.

travel to Westminster to see how the Clerk's Department works or how *Hansard* is produced is a measure of the esteem in which the servants of the Commons are held. As Marsden has said, 'Whatever the complexion of the Government in office the House can be certain of receiving that completely impartial and professionally expert service for which its Officers enjoy a reputation second to none.'[1]

The quality of the Commons staff is often linked to its permanent and impartial character. In many legislatures, including the American Congress, there are varying amounts of staff turnover when party control changes, but this is not the case at Westminster. As Marsden has noted, 'The Staff which serve the Commons . . . are not answerable in any way to the Government of the day. Nor are they appointed by politicians or political organisations'.[2] In the Clerk's Department and the Library the recruitment of senior staff is through the Civil Service Commission. In the case of Clerks, applicants compete in the open examination for the Administration Group of the civil service, and graduate Library staff are chosen by open competitive interview. Once appointed, Clerks and senior Library staff are Officers of the House, to whom they owe exclusive loyalty. They are not civil servants and there is no interchange of civil servants between Whitehall and the House of Commons. Practices elsewhere are discussed in the study of fifty-five legislatures by the Inter Parliamentary Union:

'Many Parliaments employ staff directly from the civil service who remain subject to the ordinary regulations that apply to that service. In the Federal Republic of Germany for example the administration of Parliament is not considered to be autonomous. It is an integral part of the federal administration. . . . The position is similar in the Netherlands . . . Norway, Pakistan, the Philippines, Sweden, Somalia and Switzerland.'[3]

A further factor accounting for the prestige of the permanent staff at Westminster is the relatively long duration of its tradition of autonomy and impartiality, as compared with other

[1] Marsden, *op. cit.*. p 15.
[2] Marsden, *op. cit.*
[3] Inter-Parliamentary Union, *op. cit.*, p 90.

legislatures. Many current staffing practices in the Commons derive in general from recommendations made in 1833 by a Select Committee on the Establishment of the House of Commons and by successor committees in 1834, 1835 and 1836. One of the key reforms of this period was the introduction of fixed salaries for officials of the House, replacing a system of payment by the Treasury, by fees and by gratuities. Service in the House tended during part of the nineteenth century to be undertaken by persons having an independent income, but the autonomy and impartiality of the service was not generally compromised.[1]

The 1833 Committee noted the division of the staff of the Commons into two Departments – the Clerk's and the Serjeant at Arms' – and to this day responsibilities in the House have been divided between separate Departments. The Clerk is the senior permanent Officer of the House and has certain responsibilities outside his own Department, but in actuality the administration of the House is at present divided between five Departments. This arrangement can be contrasted with the position in many legislatures where a single official – a Secretary-General, Director-General or Greffier – is in overall charge.

It is difficult to compare the Department of the Clerk with a counterpart in other legislatures if only because the counterpart may be hard to identify. As was said earlier, the Department at Westminster has a senior establishment of forty-six and an overall complement of ninety-five. According to the IPU:

'In Switzerland . . . the Assembly's secretariat comprises a mere handful of staff, while in Brazil, Czechoslovakia, the Netherlands, New Zealand and Spain there are a mere twenty or thirty. Without counting junior employees the usual figure seems to be about one hundred though it is greatly exceeded in several countries such as the Federal Republic of Germany, France, Italy, Turkey . . . and the United States. In Japan each House employs a staff of more than one thousand.'[2]

It is almost impossible to draw conclusions from these figures

---

[1] For further historical information see Marsden, *op. cit.*, p 117*ff.*
[2] Inter-Parliamentary Union, *op. cit.*, pp 86–7.

because it is not clear how inclusive the duties of the secretariats are and whether they serve one or two Houses. The figures may also include party and personal, as well as official, staffs, if indeed any such distinction can be made.

There is also considerable disparity in the *functions* performed by Clerks in the Commons and their counterparts in overseas legislatures. For example an important part of the work of Clerks at Westminster consists in advising Members on the rules of order relating to Questions. The importance of this service in the Commons is evident from the fact that the cost to the Government of supplying answers to the thousands of Questions which Members ask each session is between £350,000 and £400,000.[1] In many important foreign legislatures, by contrast, there is no need to provide this service because there is no question time. Another area of disparity lies in the staffing of committees. In some legislatures, as at Westminster, committees are staffed by Clerks who also serve the House. In other legislatures committee staffs are an entirely separate establishment or, alternatively, such staff may come from the Library or each committee may engage its own staff privately.[2]

The remarkable editorial operation by which *Hansard* is produced was discussed in Chapter 4. Few such operations in overseas legislatures produce a report which, like the British *Hansard*, is both an accurate account of what actually was said on the floor and is available the following morning. Many legislatures provide only a summary report and permit extensive revision of speeches by Members. The latter practice delays publication and limits the authenticity of the report as a record of what was said in debate. An aspect of *Hansard* reporting at Westminster which, viewed internationally, is even more unusual than prompt, verbatim reporting of floor debates is the verbatim reporting of standing committees, normally with distribution the following morning.

One complication which the Editor of the Commons *Hansard* is mercifully spared is bilingualism. In Canada, Belgium, Switzerland and several other countries there is simultaneous or

[1] H.C. Deb., 9 August 1972, 842, c. 1724.

[2] For a comparison of British and American practice in staffing committees in particular, and the House of Commons and Congress in general, see Kenneth Bradshaw and David Pring, *Parliament and Congress*, pp 64–72, 244–7, Constable (1972).

consecutive translation of speeches, with a parallel recording of debates in the two official languages. Also alien to the Commons is the practice in some legislatures of permitting Members to 'extend' what they said on the floor either in the body of the official report or its appendices, and of including outside material, such as newspaper articles, in the appendices. All of these practices are permitted, for example, in the American *Congressional Record*, which also allows more extensive revision by Members of reporters' records of speeches than is permitted at Westminster.[1]

Turning to the House of Commons Library, it is notable that since 1960 the numbers of Library staff have virtually doubled, and, as was noted in Chapter 5, a variety of new services have been offered. But despite these advances, the Library establishment remains, in comparison with libraries in other legislatures of comparable importance, a fairly modest one. Its establishment of sixty-three in 1973 seems incongruously small in comparison with the 845 on the staff of the Diet Library in Tokyo, although this is also the Japanese national library; and the 120,000 books in the Commons Library is insignificant compared with the 2,500,000 books in the Diet Library. Another extreme example is the Library of Congress in Washington, which was mentioned earlier (see section 9.5.1). The Library of Congress, which is also a national library, had a budget in 1972 of $7,000,000.

One might expect to find more comparability in the old Commonwealth. Australia, as a case in point, has a Parliamentary Library which serves considerably fewer Members than at Westminster. Yet it had an establishment in 1971 of 108, which was nearly twice that of the Commons Library at that time.[2] On the other hand, the Library of the Canadian Parliament did not develop a research branch until as recently as 1965 when ten researchers were appointed.[3] The research branch at Ottawa now has a staff of thirty-three, of whom twenty-two are research officers.[4]

[1] Bradshaw and Pring, *op. cit.*, pp 131–2.
[2] The 1971 establishment of the Australian Parliamentary Library included twenty-three research specialists and seventeen graduate librarians. Its annual budget was $A812,000.
[3] Allan Kornberg, 'Parliament in Canadian Society', in Kornberg and Musolf, *op. cit.*, p 113.
[4] *Library of Parliament Annual Report 1971–72*, p 4.

But numbers aside, there is, to return to an earlier theme, the further factor of quality. In terms of its holdings of British and foreign official documents, and in terms of the relevance to the Member of its collection and services, the Commons Library is an excellent facility. It may indeed be said to have an important advantage over the giant, we-take-everything operation: a tight, highly pertinent collection can save searching and walking. At the same time, the reality of the situation is that the well-known territorial constraints of the Palace have set practical boundaries to the Library's operation. Crick intended it as high praise when he said that despite the handicaps of scale:

'The House has now . . . a Legislative Reference Service such as would grace an average size American State Legislature. I do not mean this ironically, for the comparison with the Legislative Reference Service of the Library of Congress . . . would be absurdly out of scale.'[1]

9.5.4 *Salaries, Allowances and Pensions*

The implementation of nearly all the recommendations of the Boyle Committee altered the financial position of Members of the House of Commons in an important way. Not only were Members' salaries substantially increased in 1972, even taking inflation into account, but their expenses and allowances were considerably extended. Moreover a fundamental distinction was drawn between the payment Members receive, and the expenses they incur, in carrying out their parliamentary duties. It can therefore be argued that the relationship between the Member and his parliamentary work has altered. A Member can no longer regard his job as an MP as only one of his occupations; he must now regard it as his dominant activity. As the *Boyle Report* says: 'By any reasonable standard . . . most Members must be considered as working on a full-time basis, and we consider that the level of remuneration should be assessed accordingly.[2]' Members are now paid as if they were full-time MPs. Thus in just over sixty years they have progressed from, in most cases, unpaid part-timers to, in most cases, professional legislators who get the rate for the job, severance pay and all.

[1] Bernard Crick, 'Whither Parliamentary Reform?', in A. H. Hanson and Bernard Crick (editors), *The Commons in Transition*, p 259, Fontana (1970).
[2] *Boyle Report*, para. 25.

But how – to continue our cross-national analysis – does the British MP compare with his counterpart in other countries? The Boyle Committee looked into this matter, and in its report the position relating to salaries, allowances and pensions in thirteen countries is examined in detail.[1] It is, of course, difficult to make comparisons because the position is fundamentally affected by differences in the cost of living from one country to another. Further difficulties arise because of variations in methods of remuneration. In New Zealand and West Germany, for example, all remuneration of Members is tax-free; in Belgium and France a proportion of Members' salaries is tax-free; in Denmark and the Irish Republic this concession applies only to allowances; while in the Netherlands and Norway all remuneration of Members is subject to tax. On the matter of allowances, Members in some countries receive an allowance that is intended to cover, or be a contribution towards, all or most of their expenses; in other cases they receive a variety of allowances to meet particular expenses. Moreover, while in some countries legislators receive an allowance to cover such items as travel, postal services and telephone services, in other countries they receive travel *concessions* and free or partially free postal and telephone services. Secretarial provisions illustrate the same tendency: they may be covered by a general allowance or a specific allowance or they may be paid for directly from public funds. Provision may be for a secretary for each Member, for a secretary shared by two or more Members, for a secretarial or typing pool, or, in a few cases, for secretaries supplied by the Member's party but paid for by the state. It is difficult enough in many countries to calculate the financial value to the Member of allowances and facilities, but infinitely more difficult to do so on a comparative basis involving so much variation.

The examples of Italy and West Germany illustrate the point very well. Taking the Italian case first: of the thirteen countries in which the Boyle Committee examined the remuneration of legislators,[2] those in Italy received the highest *gross* salary,

---

[1] *Boyle Report*, Appendix E.
[2] It should be noted that all thirteen countries had basically parliamentary rather than presidential-congressional systems, and that no comparison was attempted with, for example, the United States.

amounting to £8,443 per year. Moreover, only four-tenths of an Italian Deputy's gross remuneration, i.e. salary and allowances, is, after the deduction of social insurance contributions, subject to tax. Taken in isolation, however, this is misleading, since although Italian Deputies also receive a subsistence allowance and substantial travel concessions, they do not receive any secretarial assistance, nor do they have free postal or telephone services, nor do they at present have any office accommodation. On the other hand, Members of the West German Bundestag receive a gross salary of £4,080 which, together with their allowances, is tax free. They also receive a subsistence allowance, a secretarial allowance, substantial travel concessions, free telephone services and an office per Member.

In spite of such discrepancies, meaningful comparisons are possible, as the Boyle Committee suggests:

'If those countries in which the salaries are wholly tax-free are excluded, and the tax-free elements for expenses are deducted where appropriate, then the net pay before tax in the remaining countries falls into a band between £1,500 and £7,400, the average being £4,200, as compared with the British Member of Parliament's average net pay before tax [prior to 1972] of a little under £2,000.'[1]

This was of course the position before the raising of the British Member's salary to £4,500. It is now clear that in terms of net pay before tax British MPs are slightly above the average salary of legislators in the countries examined by the Boyle Committee. If the comparison is taken further by examining the allowances and facilities available to Members in the thirteen countries, it can be reasonably argued that those in Australia, Canada, France, New Zealand and West Germany are on the whole financially better off than British MPs, but that British MPs are on the whole financially better off than Members in Belgium, Denmark, Finland, the Irish Republic, Italy, the Netherlands, Norway and Sweden. Thus among legislators in the thirteen countries the British MP is clearly in the top half of the 'league' and could reasonably be placed third among his European counterparts.

[1] *Boyle Report*, para. 32.

It might be mentioned that in some countries the pay of legislators is linked to the salaries of civil servants. This is done, for example, in France and Japan. According to the IPU:

'This procedure ensures that the parliamentary salary remains satisfactory for members and also has the advantage of avoiding public debate when circumstances, especially a rise in the cost of living, make it necessary to adjust that salary.'[1]

As has been noted, such a linkage has always been rejected officially in Britain (see section 6.4). However, Hill and Whichelow, in their prescriptions for reforming Parliament, saw merit in the idea. They suggested a linkage between the salaries of MPs and Assistant Secretaries in Whitehall.[2]

As far as pensions are concerned, the British MP is now fairly well placed compared with his counterparts in the thirteen countries examined by the Boyle Committee. Only three of the thirteen have non-contributory schemes – Finland, the Netherlands and Sweden – and in general existing provisions for British MPs compare favourably with those in the other legislatures examined by the Committee. Moreover, as the IPU reported in its study of fifty-five legislatures, few countries outside Europe have any pension schemes at all for their legislators.[3]

Whilst noting that the financial position of British MPs now compares favourably with that of legislators in other parliamentary democracies, it should be stressed that this situation is of recent origin, dating from the 1960s in general and from 1972 in particular. At the same time, as in other aspects of services and facilities, these comparisons suggest that parallels with countries like the United States are misleading. This latter point was noted by Bradshaw and Pring when they attempted to compare the salaries of British MPs and American Senators and Representatives. After pointing out that in 1969 the salary of a Senator or Represenative was $42,500, or £17,700,[4] while the salary of a British MP in the same year was £3,250, they concluded that:

[1] Inter-Parliamentary Union, *op. cit.*, p 72.
[2] Hill and Whichelow, *op. cit.*, pp 86–7.
[3] Inter-Parliamentary Union, *op. cit.*, p 76.
[4] This translation of dollars to sterling takes into account the devaluation of the pound in 1967.

'... senators and congressmen are doing an essentially different job of work from that of their opposite numbers at Westminster. The difference ... is twofold. The first is a simple difference of scale [in terms of size of constituencies]. ... The second is a difference of function. An American member ... takes part in a range of inquiries and consultations with outside interests and staff of government departments which in Britain would be conducted within the executive.'[1]

Turning to staff allowances, they are far more generous in Congress than in any other legislature. A Senator from New York or California was entitled in 1969 to an allowance of $365,165 to use in employing a personal staff.[2]

9.5.5   Secretaries

The one aspect of the present study that required a survey of Members to obtain up-to-date information concerned secretaries and research assistants. Although neither is officially provided, a secretarial allowance is now available. An allowance of £500 was authorised in 1969. This was increased in 1972 to £1,000, of which £300 can be used for a research assistant. The present allowance can also be used towards 'general office expenses'.

Our survey showed that only a tiny minority of Members – 1·3 per cent – have no secretarial assistance at all. For the others, the amount of secretarial assistance has been increasing. The proportion of Members with full-time secretaries and with exclusive part-time secretaries – as opposed to shared secretaries – has been increasing and can be expected to increase more with the larger allowance. The change in the position since before the introduction of allowances is evident from the data in Chapter 7. The implications in terms of an increased need for secretarial facilities in and near the Palace are also evident.

As with office accommodation, the Boyle Committee looked into secretarial services in the legislatures of thirteen parliamentary democracies.[3] It appears that in three cases – Canada, Sweden and West Germany – Members are better provided for in the matter of secretarial assistance than British MPs are. It

[1] Bradshaw and Pring, *op. cit.*, p 122.
[2] Bradshaw and Pring, *op. cit.*, p 121.
[3] *Boyle Report*, Appendix E.

could also be argued that Australian Members are better off inasmuch as a constituency secretary is provided, as well as a secretarial pool in Parliament. Of the four, Swedish Members appear to be the best provided; they get a secretarial allowance and, in addition, have access to a typing pool and are provided further typing services by their parties.

In three cases – Belgium, Denmark and Finland – the position appears to be similar to Britain's, but this is a rough estimate. It assumes that in these countries the grants provided to political parties for the purpose of supplying their Members with secretaries produce a level of secretarial assistance comparable to that prevailing in the House of Commons. In the six remaining countries – France, the Irish Republic, Italy, the Netherlands, New Zealand and Norway – Members appear to be worse off than British MPs. In the Irish Republic, Italy and the Netherlands there is no provison at all for secretarial assistance. In France, New Zealand and Norway typing pools are provided.

Thus, as with accommodation, British MPs are found somewhere in the middle when the extent of their official secretarial provision is examined alongside comparable arrangements in overseas legislatures. It is significant, however, that the assessment is being made after 1969. Had it been made before the secretarial allowance was introduced at Westminster, British MPs would have been found underprivileged. At the same time, it should be kept in mind that such comparisons are based on *official* provision of secretarial support and do not take into account the secretarial assistance that Members may obtain in the absence of such support. As was shown in Table 7.2, the position among MPs two years before the introduction of the secretarial allowance was not markedly different from the position two years after its introduction. It is clear that the general financial capabilities of Members must be taken into account in assessments of this kind.

9.6 THE FUTURE

A decision to proceed with the new parliamentary building in Bridge Street 'in due course' has now been taken by Parliament, thus ending a period of considerable uncertainty inside and outside Westminster. That uncertainty had been heightened when an inconclusive debate took place in March 1973 on a motion by Patrick Cormack (Conservative Member for Cannock) 'That the proposed new Parliamentary Building be not proceeded with, and that alternative proposals for providing additional working accommodation, which would be available sooner and at a lower cost, be considered'.[1] The Government spokesman in the debate (Paul Channon, Minister for Housing and Construction) promised an early free vote to decide the matter. This vote took place in the House of Commons on 25 June 1973. The decision to proceed with the new building was taken by 292 votes to 68. The Spence-Webster design was accepted by 208 votes to 144.[2]

The possibilities inherent in the new parliamentary building were detailed in Chapter 3 and referred to in various connections throughout the book. It is clear that the facilities, and to a lesser extent the services, available to Members will change in important ways when each Member has a room of his own with adjacent space for his secretary, and various services can expand 'across the street'.

The fact that changes on this scale are presently envisaged by the Government and by Members on both sides of the House is evidence of the quickened pace of recent developments relating to services and facilities at Westminster. This quickening is perhaps symbolised by the decision to go ahead with the new parliamentary building and the approval of nearly all the recommendations of the Boyle Committee. Yet, as has been suggested, recent developments, like those in the past, have been piecemeal and not without their opponents.

The nature of the opposition to these developments is illustrated by the following recent comments by MPs: 'There is no doubt that by providing a lot of rooms where hon. Members can hide themselves away, something has been lost of the quality of parliamentary life'.[3] '. . . the parliamentary system is undergoing a radical change. Backbenchers are shutting themselves up and doing useless paper work for most of the time.'[4] 'The moment that we move over there [to the new parliamentary building], it will not be long before push-button voting and total

[1] H.C. Deb., 9 March 1973, 852, c. 739. [2] Ibid., 858, cc. 1270–6.
[3] Ibid., 9 March 1973, 852, c. 781. [4] Ibid., cc. 809–10.

disappearance become the order of the day.'[1] Bradshaw and Pring sum up the general point of view implicit in these remarks:

'The traditional approach has been that essential business is dispatched not in an office but in the debating chamber. An office, and still more an office block separated from the Palace, has been regarded with suspicion as tending to withdraw members from the debating chamber; and an individual telephonic link with the outside world has been resisted lest the public should press too closely and directly upon members of Parliament.'[2]

But Bradshaw and Pring add: 'Since World War II this approach has been changing'. As evidence of this change, one might consider a comment made by Crick, writing in 1967: 'Clearly a Member should be able to draw on public funds, or be reimbursed from them, for those essentials he needs to do his job properly: secretary, office, postage, telephone and travel'.[3] Just a few years after these words were written, improvements in each of these areas had been made or authorised. It seems clear that the recent and projected changes are a logical consequence of altered patterns of behaviour on the part of Members. Members are devoting more of their time to parliamentary activities and, as a consequence, they require more secretarial, research and other parliamentary resources. Services and facilities have changed, and will continue to change, to meet this demand.

[1] H.C. Deb., 9 March 1973, 852, c. 808.
[2] Bradshaw and Pring, *op. cit.*, pp 122–3.
[3] Crick, *The Reform of Parliament, op. cit.*, pp 66–7.

APPENDIX A

SALARIES, ALLOWANCES AND PENSIONS OF MINISTERS AND OTHER PAID OFFICE-HOLDERS

The discussion of salaries, allowances and pensions in Chapter 6 was devoted almost entirely to the backbench (and Opposition front-bench) Member. This Appendix examines salaries, allowances and pensions as they relate to Members who receive payments in addition to their parliamentary salaries. In this category are Ministers; the Speaker; the Chairman, Deputy Chairman and Second Deputy Chairman of Ways and Means; the Leader of the Opposition; and three Opposition Whips.

A.1 SALARIES AND ALLOWANCES

A.1.1 *Ministers*

Ministers of the Crown have long received some form of remuneration, although before 1831 this consisted in the case of several Ministers wholly or partly of gratuities and fees.[1] Since 1831–32 all Ministers have been paid annual salaries. Since 1972 these have ranged from £20,000 for the Prime Minister and Lord Chancellor to £4,000 for Government Whips in the House of Commons.[2] When MPs hold ministerial office, they continue to perform parliamentary duties as constituency representatives, but it was not until 1946 that any account was taken of this in assessing Ministers' remuneration. Only in exceptional (and often temporary) cases are persons appointed to ministerial office who are neither members of the House of Commons nor the House of Lords.[3]

---

[1] A similar situation applied to various permanent Officers and staff of the House of Commons before 1834. See Philip Marsden, *The Officers of the Commons 1363–1965*, pp 63–6, 84–7 and 118–68, Barrie and Rockliff (1966).

[2] For details of the history of Ministers' remuneration see the *Lawrence Report*, paras 87–116, and the *Boyle Report*, paras 75–80.

[3] Under the *Ministers of the Crown Act 1964* a maximum of ninety-one MPs may hold ministerial office.

In 1946 a Select Committee on Members' Expenses recommended that Ministers with salaries of less than £5,000 who were also MPs should receive a tax-free allowance of £500 per annum to meet their parliamentary expenses.[1] This proposal was accepted by the Government and implemented by the *Ministerial Salaries Act 1946*. The position remained unchanged until 1957, when the sessional allowance paid to MPs (but not to Ministers and other office-holders) was replaced by a salary increase of £750, which was regarded as an appropriate amount to cover necessary parliamentary expenses. From that date all Ministers who were also MPs (including the Prime Minister) were paid a parliamentary allowance of £750. In 1964 this was increased to £1,250, following the recommendations of the Lawrence Committee, and in 1972 to £3,000 as a result of the *Boyle Report*.

Ministers who are Members of the House of Commons are also entitled to the secretarial allowance, as introduced in 1969 and amended in 1972, and to the other allowances, services and facilities provided to MPs. However, Ministers and other office-holders who are provided with an official residence[2] do not receive the London supplement of £175 per annum, but all Ministers and other office-holders with a provincial constituency are permitted to claim up to £750 per annum towards the cost of living away from their London home.

Obviously, Ministers make less use than backbench Members of a number of the services and facilities available to Members. For example, since Ministers may not introduce Private Members' Bills nor ask parliamentary Questions, they make very little use, in their capacity as individual Members, of the services

---

[1] H.C. 93–1, 1945–46, p vii.

[2] The Prime Minister, the Lord Chancellor, the Chancellor of the Exchequer and the Secretary of State for Foreign and Commonwealth Affairs have official residences in London; the Speaker has a residence in the Palace of Westminster; and the Secretary of State for Scotland has a residence in Edinburgh. In addition there are three residences in Admiralty House in London which are allocated to Ministers by the Prime Minister. Chequers, Dorneywood and Chevening House, which are used by the Prime Minister, the Foreign Secretary and the Lord Chancellor respectively, are maintained by trust funds and are not classed as official residences. The use of Chevening House is not permanently linked with the post of Lord Chancellor; the Prime Minister may nominate any member of his Cabinet as resident. See H. C. Deb., 25 July 1972, 841, cc. *285–6* written answers; and *The Times* (13 July 1973).

provided by the Public Bill Office and the Table Office. As constituency representatives, however, they may have occasion to use the services of the Library. It is important to bear in mind that Ministers draw a sharp distinction between their duties as holders of ministerial office and their duties as constituency representatives. Thus, whilst a Minister may enjoy some advantage in being able to approach a ministerial colleague informally about a constituency matter,[1] he will normally employ a secretary to deal with his constituency correspondence and use the telephone and postal facilities in the Palace as if he were a backbench Member. Similarly, in their capacity as constituency representatives Ministers may claim expenses against income tax. In 1969–70 Ministers were allowed an average of £1,183 for expenses[2] against their parliamentary salaries of £1,250.

A.1.2 *The Speaker and Other Presiding Officers*

The Speaker, the Chairman of Ways and Means, and the Deputy Chairman and Second Deputy Chairman of Ways and Means are paid salaries as Officers of the House of Commons,[3] but since 1957 they have also received parliamentary salaries in their capacity as Members of Parliament. As with Ministers, they are also entitled to the other allowances, services and facilities provided to MPs. Similarly, they may claim expenses for income tax purposes in respect of their parliamentary duties against their parliamentary salaries.

The Speaker is at present paid a salary of £13,000, of which £4,000 is regarded as a flat-rate deduction for expenses against income tax in his capacity as Speaker.[4] The Chairman of Ways and Means is paid a salary of £6,750 and the two Deputy

---

[1] This avenue is not, of course, closed to backbench MPs, many of whom prefer to deal with constituency matters through informal contact with Ministers. Moreover, there is no doubt that Ministers and civil servants make every effort to avoid giving or appearing to give special treatment to problems arising in Ministers' constituencies.

[2] This was before the deduction of the secretarial allowance; the amount after deduction was £971. *Boyle Report*, Appendix D, Table 2.

[3] The Speaker's salary is paid out of the Consolidated Fund; those of the Chairman of Ways and Means and the two Deputy Chairmen are borne on the House of Commons Vote.

[4] Between 1834 and 1964 the Speaker was paid £5,000, including the flat-rate deduction of £4,000, plus parliamentary salary after 1957. In 1964 his salary was raised to £8,500, again including the flat-rate deduction of £4,000.

Chairmen are each paid salaries of £5,500.[1] In addition to these salaries for Officers of the House, each of the four receives a parliamentary salary of £3,000.

A.1.3 The Leader of the Opposition and Opposition Whips

The Leader of the Opposition has been paid a salary from the Consolidated Fund since 1937 and now receives a salary of £9,500.[2] The Opposition Chief Whip has been paid a salary since 1965 and two other Opposition Whips have been paid salaries since April 1972. The Opposition Chief Whip receives £7,500[3] and the two Whips £4,000. In the case of all four Opposition office-holders they also receive a parliamentary salary of £3,000 in their capacity as MPs and are entitled to the other allowances, services and facilities available to MPs.[4]

Although the Leader of the Opposition and the Opposition Whips are not, of course, subject to the same constraints as Ministers, there are some customary constraints on them. They do not normally introduce Private Members' Bills; the Leader of the Opposition normally questions Ministers by means of Private Notice Questions; and the Whips do not normally participate in debates. Nonetheless, in general they are likely to make greater use of the services and facilities provided for MPs than do Ministers and the four presiding officers.

A.2 PENSIONS[5]

A.2.1 The Prime Minister and the Speaker

Regular provision for the payment of a pension to former holders of the office of Prime Minister was first made in the *Ministers of the Crown Act 1937*, when the pension was fixed at £2,000 per annum. This remained the position until 1965 when

---

[1] The Chairman of Ways and Means was paid £3,250 and the Deputy Chairman £2,500 before 1964, plus £750 parliamentary salary in each case. In 1965 this was increased to £4,875 and £3,750 respectively, plus £1,250 parliamentary salary. The Second Deputy Chairman was first appointed in 1971.

[2] The Leader of the Opposition was paid a salary of £2,000 in 1937. This was raised to £3,000 (plus £750 parliamentary salary) in 1957 and to £4,500 (plus £1,250 parliamentary salary) in 1965.

[3] £3,750 (plus £1,250 parliamentary salary) between 1965 and 1972.

[4] In the House of Lords the Leader of the Opposition and the Opposition Chief Whip receive salaries of £3,500 and £2,500 respectively.

[5] See the *Parliamentary and Other Pensions Act 1972*.

the pension was increased to £4,000.[1] Following the *Boyle Report*, the pension was increased to £7,500 for any Prime Minister who ceased to hold office after April 1972.

Between 1832 and 1972 it was customary for Parliament to pass a special act on the retirement of a Speaker, awarding him a pension. The last such act was *Mr Speaker King's Retirement Act 1971*, which awarded Lord Maybray-King (formerly Dr Horace King, Speaker from 1965 to 1971) a pension of £5,000. In 1972 the Speaker's pension was fixed at £6,500 for any holder of the office who retired after April 1972.

In the event of the death of a serving Prime Minister or Speaker, or of former holders of these offices, pensions are paid to their dependants. This applies only to those who cease to hold office after April 1972, except where special acts were passed in the case of widows of former Speakers.

When the Parliamentary Contributory Pension Fund was first introduced, provision was made for the refunding of the contributions of Members who became Prime Minister, Speaker or Lord Chancellor, on their taking office. Under the revised scheme the trustees of the Fund pay a sum representing the value of the accrued pension rights of the Member who takes office as Prime Minister, Speaker or Lord Chancellor into the Consolidated Fund, and the aggregate of his personal contributions is refunded with interest to the contributor (or his estate) on his ceasing to hold office. The Prime Minister, the Speaker and the Lord Chancellor may not participate in the supplemental pension scheme for Ministers and other paid office-holders described below.

A.2.2 *Ministers and Other Paid Office-Holders*
Until 1972 no special provision was made for pensions for Ministers and other paid office-holders (except for the Prime Minister, Speaker and Lord Chancellor), although they were entitled to pensions as Members of Parliament under the *Ministerial Salaries and Members' Pensions Act 1965*. Under the revised scheme, as recommended by the Boyle Committee,

---

[1] The Lawrence Committee had recommended £6,000, but as part of its general reduction of the ministerial salaries recommended by the Committee the Government reduced the recommended levels of pensions for the Prime Minister, Speaker and Lord Chancellor.

Ministers and other paid office-holders automatically participate in the Parliamentary Contributory Pension Fund by having a sum equal to 5 per cent of a Members' salary, i.e. £4,500, deducted from their parliamentary salaries. In addition they *may* participate in a supplemental pension scheme by contributing 5 per cent of the amount by which the total of their official and parliamentary salaries exceeds the level of a Member's ordinary salary. Apart from this, the pensions of Ministers and other paid office-holders are subject to the same conditions as those for ordinary Members.

APPENDIX B

ARRANGEMENTS RELATING TO SECRETARIES AND RESEARCH ASSISTANTS

B.1 DETAILS CONCERNING SECRETARIAL ARRANGEMENTS

The analysis in Chapter 7 concerning secretarial arrangements was based on replies to a questionnaire which was sent to all MPs, with certain exceptions, in July 1971. The questionnaire was not sent to Ministers, the Speaker, the Chairman of Ways and Means, the Leader of the Opposition and the Opposition Chief Whip (total: 74). At the time of the survey there were three vacant seats in the House. Thus the questionnaire went to 553 backbench and front-bench Opposition Members. The response rate was 69·8 per cent.

Table B1 *Response to Questionnaire*

Party	Questionnaires sent	Respondents	Response rate, %
Conservative	258	191	74·0
Labour	284	188	66·2
Liberal	6	6	100·0
Other	5	1	20·0
TOTAL	553	386	69·8

B.2 ROWNTREE POLITICAL FELLOWSHIP SCHEME

The Joseph Rowntree Social Service Trust has established a scheme to provide research or personal assistants to senior member of the Conservative, Labour and Liberal parties. Apart from providing personal assistance to particular individuals, these political fellowships are also intended to give young, aspiring politicians the opportunity of acquiring first-hand experience of national politics and parliamentary life.

It was originally intended that each party should have two

assistants, but the Conservative Party has so far declined to participate in the scheme, so that appointments have been confined to the Labour and Liberal parties, although the Trust has made an award *directly* to a prospective Conservative candidate. Each party decides which of its senior members will have a personal assistant and the posts are publicly advertised. A shortlist of applicants is then interviewed by representatives of the Trust and the party concerned. Appointments are normally made for a period of three years.

In 1973 there were ten assistants. Five were attached to the Labour Party, four to the Liberal Party and one to the Chairman of Pressure for Economic and Social Toryism (PEST), who, as mentioned above, is also a prospective Conservative candidate. The Labour Party had five instead of four assistants because it decided to allot one assistant to the Deputy Leader and an appointment had already been made before Roy Jenkins resigned the deputy leadership. This appointment was continued and an additional assistant was appointed to serve Edward Short, Jenkins' successor as Deputy Leader. The other Labour assistants were attached to Denis Healey, Shadow Chancellor of the Exchequer; Anthony Crosland, Shadow Minister of the Environment; and the Shadow Cabinet team dealing with Northern Ireland. It is open to the Party to attach its assistants to other Shadow Ministers as circumstances alter, e.g. a change in parliamentary duties.

The Liberal Party allocated one of its assistants to David Steel, the Party Whip; one to John Pardoe (Member for Cornwall North); one to Russell Johnston (Member for Inverness); and one to Desmond Banks, a senior Liberal outside Parliament. Mr Banks' assistant was one of two attached to individuals who are not Members of Parliament, the other being the assistant assigned to the Chairman of PEST.

Table B2 *Secretarial arrangements of Members of Parliament*

Secretarial arrangement	Party								Date of entry						Total	
	Conservative		Labour		Liberal	Other			Pre-1964		1964–70		1970–			
	%	MPs	%	MPs	MPs	MPs			%	MPs	%	MPs	%	MPs	%	MPs
No secretarial help	1·0	2	1·6	3	–	–			1·7	3	1·0	1	0·9	1	1·3	5
Uses Ashworth's Agency only	4·7	9	4·8	9	–	–			7·4	13	1·9	2	2·8	3	4·7	18
Shares a secretary with three or more MPs	1·6	3	3·7	7	–	–			2·9	5	2·8	3	1·9	2	2·6	10
Shares a secretary with two other MPs	9·4	18	16·5	31	–	–			14·3	25	12·4	13	10·4	11	12·7	49
Shares a secretary with one other MP	24·1	46	13·3	25	–	–			13·1	23	20·9	22	24·5	26	18·4	71
One secretary working exclusively for the MP *part-time*	23·6	45	44·1	83	1	1			30·8	54	33·3	35	38·7	41	33·7	130
One secretary working exclusively for the MP *full-time*	29·3	56	10·6	20	4	–			21·7	38	22·9	24	17·0	18	20·7	80
Two or more part-time secretaries working exclusively for the MP	1·6	3	3·7	7	–	–			2·3	4	2·8	3	2·8	3	2·6	10
Two or more full-time secretaries	2·6	5	1·6	3	1	–			4·0	7	1·9	2	–	–	2·3	9
Combination of full-time and part-time secretarial assistance	2·1	4	–	–	–	–			1·7	3	–	–	0·9	1	1·0	4
TOTAL	100·0	191	99·9	188	6	1			99·9	175	99·9	105	99·9	106	100·0	386

Note – Where a Member employed two or more secretaries *part-time*, this was included in the overall total of those having full-time secretarial assistance.

Table B3 *Secretary's place of work*

	Party						Date of entry						Total	
	Conservative		Labour		Liberal	Other	Pre-1964		1964–70		1970–			
	%	MPs	%	MPs	MPs	MPs	%	MPs	%	MPs	%	MPs	%	MPs
Works in the Palace or nearby parliamentary accommodation	62·7	111	52·6	92	5	–	61·1	96	52·5	53	58·4	59	58·0	208
Works elsewhere	36·2	64	46·8	82	1	1	38·9	61	44·5	45	41·6	42	41·2	148
Both	1·1	2	0·6	1	–	–	–	–	3·0	3	–	–	0·8	3
TOTAL	100·0	177	100·0	175	6	1	100·0	157	100·0	101	100·0	101	100·0	359
No answer		3		1	–	–		2		1		1		4
Respondents employing secretaries		180		176	6	1		159		102		102		363

Table B4 *Use of services provided by Ashworth's*

| | Party | | | | | | | Date of entry | | | | | | Total | |
| | Conservative | | Labour | | Liberal | Other | | Pre-1964 | | 1964–70 | | 1970– | | | |
	%	MPs	%	MPs	MPs	MPs		%	MPs	%	MPs	%	MPs	%	MPs
Rely on Asworth's entirely	4·7	9	4·8	9	–	–		7·4	13	1·9	2	2·8	3	4·7	18
Use Ashworth's to supplement other assistance*	12·6	24	8·0	15	–	–		12·6	22	8·6	9	7·5	8	10·1	39
Use an agency other than Ashworth's*	1·0	2	3·2	6	–	–		3·4	6	1·9	2	–	–	2·1	8
No response	81·7	156	84·0	158	6	1		76·6	134	87·6	92	89·6	95	83·1	321
TOTAL	100·0	191	100·0	188	6	1		100·0	175	100·0	105	99·9	106	100·0	386

* These were 'write-in' responses, i.e. respondents were *not* specifically asked whether they used Ashworth's (or some other agency) to supplement other secretarial assistance, but were asked whether they relied *entirely* on the services of Ashworth's. The number of respondents who use Ashworth's for supplementary assistance may therefore be underestimated.

Table B5 *Additional secretarial assistance*

Type of assistance	Party						Date of entry						Total	
	Conservative		Labour		Liberal	Other	Pre-1964		1964-70		1970–			
	%	MPs	%	MPs	MPs	MPs	%	MPs	%	MPs	%	MPs	%	MPs
Assistance in constituency or at home	5·2	10	6·9	13	–	–	7·4	13	3·8	4	5·7	6	5·9	23
Assistance from wife or other relative	3·7	7	8·0	15	–	–	8·0	14	4·8	5	2·8	3	5·7	22
Assistance from business or trade union	6·8	13	2·7	5	–	–	4·0	7	4·8	5	5·7	6	4·7	18
No response	84·3	161	82·4	155	6	1	80·6	141	86·6	91	85·8	91	83·7	323
TOTAL	100·0	191	100·0	188	6	1	100·0	175	100·0	105	100·0	106	100·0	386

Note – This Table is based on 'write-in' responses, i.e. respondents were asked what additional secretarial assistance, if any, they had. The number of respondents who have such additional assistance may therefore be underestimated.

Table B6 *Use of research assistants*

	Party									Date of entry						Total	
	Conservative		Labour		Liberal	Other		Pre-1964		1964–70		1970–				Total	
	%	MPs	%	MPs	MPs	MPs		%	MPs	%	MPs	%	MPs			%	MPs
Full-time research assistant	8·9	17	4·8	9	2	–		8·6	15	4·8	5	7·5	8			7·2	28
Occasional/part-time research assistant	2·1	4	2·1	4	–	1		1·1	2	3·8	4	1·9	2			2·1	8
No research assistant	89·0	170	93·1	175	4	1		90·3	158	91·4	96	90·6	96			90·7	350
TOTAL	100·0	191	100·0	188	6	1		100·0	175	100·0	105	100·0	106			100·0	386
Respondents employing research assistants		21		13	2	–			17		9		10				36

Table B7 *Research assistants' places of work*

	Party						Date of entry						Total	
	Conservative		Labour		Liberal	Other	Pre-1964		1964–70		1970–			
	%	MPs	%	MPs	MPs	MPs	%	MPs	%	MPs	%	MPs	%	MPs
Works in the Palace or nearby parliamentary accommodation	38·1	8	41·6	5	2	–	56·2	9	11·1	1	50·0	5	42·9	15
Works elsewhere	61·9	13	58·4	7	–	–	43·8	7	88·9	8	50·0	5	57·1	20
Both	–	–	–	–	–	–	–	–	–	–	–	–	–	–
TOTAL	100·0	21	100·0	12	2	–	100·0	16	100·0	9	100·0	9	100·0	35
No answer	–	–	–	1	–	–	–	1	–	–	–	–	–	1

BIBLIOGRAPHY

The following bibliography is selective, particularly with regard to debates and questions in Parliament. There are frequent references in the text to the *Official Report* of debates (H.C. Deb.), but since these are mainly references to short, isolated statements, it is felt that such references are best restricted, for the most part, to the footnotes.

BOOKS

L. A. Abraham and S. C. Hawtrey, *Parliamentary Dictionary*, Butterworths (1970). (Third edition edited by S. C. Hawtrey and H. M. Barclay.)

Anthony Barker and Michael Rush, *The Member of Parliament and His Information*, Allen & Unwin (1970).

Maurice Bond, *Guide to the Records of Parliament*, HMSO (1971).

Kenneth Bradshaw and David Pring, *Parliament and Congress*, Constable (1972).

Peter A. Bromhead, *Private Members' Bills in the British Parliament*, Routledge and Kegan Paul (1956).

Ronald Butt, *The Power of Parliament*, Constable (1967).

D. N. Chester and N. Bowring, *Questions in Parliament*, Clarendon Press (1962).

Sir Barnett Cocks, *The European Parliament*, HMSO (1973).

David Coombes, *The Member of Parliament and the Administration*, Allen & Unwin (1966).

Bernard Crick, *The Reform of Parliament*, Weidenfeld and Nicolson (second edition, 1970).

Sir Bryan Fell, *The Houses of Parliament: An Illustrated Guide to the Palace of Westminster*, revised by K. R. Mackenzie, Eyre and Spottiswoode (twelfth edition, 1972).

S. E. Finer, H. B. Berrington and D. J. Bartholomew, *Backbench Opinion in the House of Commons, 1955–59*, Pergamon (1961).

Strathearn Gordon, 'The Library of the House of Commons', in R. Irwin and R. Staveley (editors), *The Libraries of London*, Library Association, pp 90–98 (second edition, 1961).

A. H. Hanson and Bernard Crick (editors), *The Commons in Transition*, Fontana (1970).

Andrew Hill and Anthony Whichelow, *What's Wrong with Parliament?*, Penguin (1964).

Inter-Parliamentary Union (edited by Michel Ameller), *Parliaments*, Cassell (second edition, 1966).

Allan Kornberg and Lloyd D. Musolf (editors), *Legislatures in Developmental Perspective*, Duke University Press (1970).

Philip Laundy, *The Office of Speaker*, Cassell (1964).

William Law, *Our Hansard*, Pitman (1950).

Philip Marsden, *The Officers of the Commons 1363–1965*, Barrie and Rockliff (1966).

Sir Thomas Erskine May, *Treatise on the Law, Privileges, Proceedings and Usage of Parliament*, Butterworth (eighteenth edition, 1971). (Editor of eighteenth edition: Sir Barnett Cocks, Clerk of the House of Commons.)

David Menhennet, *The Journal of the House of Commons: a Bibliographical and Historical Guide*, HMSO (1971).

Alfred Morris, *The Growth of Parliamentary Scrutiny by Committee*, Pergamon (1970).

Peter G. Richards, *The Backbenchers*, Faber (1972).

Peter G. Richards, *Honourable Members*, Faber (second edition, 1964).

Peter G. Richards, *Parliament and Conscience*, Allen & Unwin (1970).

Malcolm Shaw, *Assistants for Members of Parliament*, Institute for Social Research (October 1964).

Malcolm Shaw, *Proposals for Research Assistance for Members of Parliament: An Interim Report*, Institute for Social Research (June 1964).

Eric Taylor, *The House of Commons at Work*, Penguin (eighth edition, 1971).

J. C. Trewin and E. M. King, *Printer to the House: The Story of Hansard*, Methuen (1952).

B. C. Vickery and H. East, *Computer Support for Parliamentary Information Service*, Aslib Research Department (1971). (Restricted circulation.)

Norman Wilding and Philip Laundy, *An Encyclopaedia of Parliament*, Cassell (fourth edition, 1971).

Orlo C. Williams, *The Clerical Organization of the House of Commons, 1661–1850*, Clarendon Press (1954).

ARTICLES

Sir Barnett Cocks, 'Parliament Goes Abroad', *The Parliamentarian*, **52**, pp 8–13 (January 1971).

J. A. Cross, 'Reviewing the Pay of MPs', *ibid.*, **47**, pp 273–6 (October 1966).

Sir Edward Fellowes, 'Parliament and the Executive: Financial Control of the House of Commons', *Journal of the Parliaments of the Commonwealth*, **43**, pp 223–31 (July 1962).

Mark Franklin, 'Computers and the Modern Member of Parliament', *The Parliamentarian*, **54**, pp 80–5 (April 1973).

J. L. Hall, John Palmer and John Poole, 'An Experimental Current Awareness Service in the Social Sciences', *Journal of Documentation*, **26**, pp 1–21 (March 1970).

Vincent Hamson, 'The Production of Hansard', *Parliamentary Affairs*, **8**, pp 254–60 (Spring 1955).

David Holland, 'Parliamentary Libraries: Indexing of Material', *The Parliamentarian*, **50**, pp 28–32 (January 1969).

Alfred Junz, 'Accommodation at Westminster', *Parliamentary Affairs*, **13**, pp 100–13 (Winter 1959–60).

Geoffrey F. Lock, 'Statistics for Politicians', *Statistical News*, pp 9–12 (February 1971).

David Menhennet, 'The Library of the House of Commons', *Political Quarterly*, **36** (3), pp 323–32 (July–September 1965).

David Menhennet and John Poole, 'Information Services of the Commons Library', *New Scientist*, **35**, pp 499–502 (7 September 1967).

'New Parliamentary Building: Westminster', *The Parliamentarian*, **53**, pp 122–3 (April 1972). (With two photographs of the model in its setting.)

Martin Partington, 'Parliamentary Committees: Recent Developments', *Parliamentary Affairs*, **23**, pp 366–79 (Autumn 1970).

PARLIAMENTARY PAPERS (EXCLUDING REPORTS FROM THE SERVICES COMMITTEE)

1st and 2nd Reports, Select Committee on Library (House of Commons), 1945–46, H.C. 35 and H.C. 99–I.

Reports from the Select Committee on House of Commons Accommodation, 1952–53 (H.C. 309) and 1953–54 (H.C. 184). (Chairman: Richard Stokes.)

Report of the Committee on the Remuneration of Ministers and Members of Parliament, Cmnd 2516, November 1964. (Chairman: Sir Geoffrey Lawrence). Referred to in the text as the *Lawrence Report*.

5th Special Report, Estimates Committee, 1964–65, H.C. 161, *Temporary Technical or Scientific Assistance for Sub-committees*.

6th Special Report, Estimates Committee, 1964–65, H.C. 162, *Sittings of Sub-committees Overseas*.

Report from the Select Committee on the Palace of Westminster, 1964–65, H.C. 285.

2nd Special Report, Expenditure Committee, 1970–71, H.C. 436. (The question of supporting staff is discussed in paras 24–32.)

Review Body on Top Salaries, First Report, *Ministers of the Crown and Members of Parliament*, Cmnd 4836, December 1971. (Chairman: Lord Boyle of Handsworth). Referred to in the text as the *Boyle Report*.

Supply Estimates 1972–73, for the year ending 31st March 1973, Class I, Government and Finance, 1971–72, H.C. 159–I.

Supply Estimates 1973–74, for the year ending 31st March 1974, Class I, Government and Finance, 1972–73, H.C. 114–I.

1st Report, Select Committee on European Community Secondary Legislation, 1972–73, H.C. 143.

SELECT COMMITTEE ON HOUSE OF COMMONS (SERVICES)

Since it was first set up in 1965, this select committee has produced a series of important reports on the services and accommodation available to the

House of Commons. A selection only is given here; all those listed below are quoted in the text and are particularly relevant to the present study.

1st Report, Services Committee, 1965–66, H.C. 70, *Specialist Assistance for Select Committees and Expenses of Select Committees Travelling Abroad.*

3rd Report, Services Committee, 1965–66, H.C. 107, *Extension of Free Postage Facilities for Members.*

9th Report, Services Committee, 1966–67, H.C. 376, *House of Commons Telephone Services.*

15th Report, Services Committee, 1966–67, H.C. 652, *New Parliamentary Buildings.*

5th Report, Services Committee, 1967–68, H.C. 232, *Foreign Travel by Select Committees.*

6th Report, Services Committee, 1967–68, H.C. 289, *Telephone Services in the Palace of Westminster.*

3rd Report, Services Committee, 1968–69, H.C. 295, *Accommodation in the New Parliamentary Building.*

5th Report, Services Committee, 1968–69, H.C. 366, *Accounts of Refreshment Department for 1968.*

6th Report, Services Committee, 1968–69, H.C. 374, *Services and Facilities for Members.*

1st Report, Services Committee, 1970–71, H.C. 152, *Additional Accommodation for Members.*

2nd Report, Services Committee, 1970–71, H.C. 169, *Use of 'Official Paid' Envelopes.*

6th Report, Services Committee, 1970–71, H.C. 431, *New Palace Yard Underground Car Park.*

3rd Report, Services Committee, 1971–72, H.C. 163, *Accounts of Refreshment Department for 1970–71.*

4th Report, Services Committee, 1971–72, H.C. 263, *New Palace Yard Underground Car Park.*

5th Report, Services Committee, 1971–72, H.C. 342, *New Parliamentary Building.*

1st Report, Services Committee, 1972–73, H.C. 196, *Additional Parliamentary Accommodation.*

2nd Report, Services Committee, 1972–73, H.C. 217, *Accounts of Refreshment Department for 1971–72.*

4th Report, Services Committee, 1972–73, H.C. 265, *Temporary Parliamentary Accommodation.*

RECENT DEBATES IN THE HOUSE OF COMMONS

Debate on the Report of the Select Committee on the Palace of Westminster, opened by Herbert Bowden, H.C. Deb., 2 November 1965, 718, cc. 878–957.

Second Reading of the Ministerial and Other Salaries Bill and Debate on Motions relating to Parliamentary Remuneration and Parliamentary

Expenses, opened by William Whitelaw, H.C. Deb., 20 December 1971, 828, cc. 1129–1252.

Second Reading of Parliamentary and Other Pensions Bill, opened by Robert Carr, H.C. Deb., 22 May 1972, 837, cc. 1153–85.

Adjournment debate on the New Parliamentary Building, opened by Sydney Chapman, H.C. Deb., 9 August 1972, 842, cc. 1830–40.

Adjournment debate on Whitehall and Parliament Square, opened by Robert Cooke, H.C. Deb., 20 November 1972, 846, cc. 1047–58.

Debate on the Proposed New Parliamentary Building, opened by Patrick Cormack, H.C. Deb., 9 March 1973, 852, cc. 739–844.

Debate on the Proposed New Parliamentary Building, opened by James Prior, H.C. Deb., 25 June 1973, cc. 1206–76.

INDEX

Abbey Gardens, accommodation in 27, 78, 207.

Accommodation, Members' 37, 72–3, 75–82, 94–9, 198, 249–52.

Accountant, House of Commons 31, 38, 39.

Accountant, Deputy 39.

Accounting Officer for the House of Commons Vote 30, 39.

Acts of Parliament: House of Commons Members' Fund Act 1939 181; House of Commons Members' Fund Act, 1948 182; House of Commons Offices Acts, 1812–49 29, 30, 32, 37n; Ministerial and Other Salaries Act, 1972 193; Ministerial Salaries Act, 1946 269; Ministerial Salaries and Members' Pensions Act, 1965 183, 185n, 272; Ministers of the Crown Act, 1937 166, 271; Ministers of the Crown Act, 1964 268n; Parliamentary and Other Pensions Act, 1972 183–5, 271n; Parliamentary Papers Act, 1840 115.

Administration Department: accommodation for 76n; Establishments Section 37, 38, 39; organisation of 37–9, 58; staff of 37, 38–9.

Admission Order Office 36, 37, 74, 88–90.

Agriculture, Select Committee on 216, 231.

Allowances, Members, *see* Expenses and allowances, Members'.

Almon, John 114n.

Ameller, Michel 255n.

Amery, Rt Hon. Julian, MP 97.

Amery, Rt Hon. Leo, MP 127.

'Annie's Bar' 239.

Arding and Hobbs Ltd 93.

Aslib 157, 158.

Ashworth and Company 82, 199, 200, 201–3, 206, 245n.

Atcherley, Harold 192.

Baldwin, Rt Hon. Stanley 166.

Banks, Desmond 275.

Barber to the House of Commons 93–4.

Barker, Anthony 9, 22n, 132n, 133n, 134n, 159, 202n, 206, 209n, 210n, 223n.

Barrow's *Mirror of Parliament* 114n, 146.

Barry, Sir Charles 27, 143, 240n, 243n.

Barry, E. M. 240n.

Bartholomew, D. J. 69n.

Bear, L. W. 131.

Beeching, Lord 192.

Benn, Rt Hon. A. W. MP 247n.

Berrington, H. B. 69n.

Blackburn, Michael 216.

Black Rod 92.

Blandford, Lord 163.

Bond, M. F. 138n.

Bowring, N. 52n.

Boyd-Carpenter, Rt Hon. John 214, 219.